# THE

# TRAIL

# OF MISGIVINGS

## A SCOURGING JOURNEY

ii

# THE TRAIL

# OF MISGIVINGS

## A SCOURGING JOURNEY

### DANIEL F. JEROME

Ed & Barbara,
this is just an
attempt to preserve the
educational history
of the Reg.

Dan

North American Heritage Press

# THE TRAIL OF MISGIVINGS
## A Scourging Journey

## Copyright © MMVI
## by
## Daniel F. Jerome

For permissions, or for serialization, condensation, or for adaptations, write the author at: PO Box 1177, Belcourt, ND 58316

Library of Congress Control Number: 2006936697

International Standard Book Number: 0-942323-41-6

## North American Heritage Press
A DIVISION OF
CREATIVE MEDIA, INC.
Minot, North Dakota

Printed in the United States of America

# Preface

The purpose of this book is to present the development of the formal education of the Ojibwa people known legally as the Turtle Mountain Band of Chippewa Indians. The words *formal education* are used so as not to imply that the Ojibwa were uneducated before the white man's arrival in their world. The educational system that exists today where buildings are erected and a standard curriculum established for the schools within the state is prescribed will be referred to as formal education. All cultures and societies of Man taught their children to cope with their environment in which they lived, as did the Ojibwa of the Turtle Mountain.

To grasp the progress of the education of the Turtle Mountain Indian people, it is necessary to study the historical development and the economic and social forces that influenced the lives of the Ojibwa people for the past 350 years.

# Contents

# Acknowledgements

My son asked, "I understand you were writing a book?" I responded, "That was fifteen years ago." "Let's get started," he said. Ten months later, we have the finished product. His photography, probing, editing, and formatting have made this book a reality. I am especially grateful for the opportunity to walk this journey with him.

Special thanks should be given to Betty Poitra at the Turtle Mountain Agency Education office whom I called on regularly. I am likewise grateful to Ronald Poitra and Gaylene Belgarde who gave of their time and information and to Dr. Larry Belgarde and Cheryl Marion Kulas who shared their theses as sources of references.

Dwane Getzlaff, Rolette Country School Superintendent, was very cooperative in assisting with the documents used for research in the Rolette County Records office.

I must acknowledge Sandy Thomas, Bev Witt, Debbie Albert and Sue Ellen Tayal for proof reading the script.

Kathe Peltier Zaste, assisted with the formatting of photos and text that made the publishing possible.

The administration and staff of the area schools who contributed information to this writing have been very supportive.

Special thanks to all those people who helped compile the list of principals and reservation principals who have served the Turtle Mountain Community School system.

My wife, always positive in everything I do, gave much encouragement and help organizing the writing, and calming me down when frustration was at its peak. She deserves special recognition for her confidence in me.

# The Trail of Misgivings

# Chapter 1

## Turtle Mountain People

Oral history relates that the Plains Ojibwa also referred to as Chippewa, of the Turtle Mountain Band came from the Big Waters of the Great Lakes region or perhaps even farther east. Their paths can be traced to Woodland Ojibwa tribes still living in Michigan, Wisconsin, Minnesota and Ontario. Some local elders can place their parents' births to eastern Dakota Territory and that of their grandparents still aback the path from whence they came. Once on the plains, Ojibwa lifestyle was transformed. They became more dependent on the buffalo for food, clothing, tools, shelter and a source of income. Through this journey westward, two distinct groups of people – full-blood and half-breed – made up the Ojibwa as they adapted to the plains. The half-breed had some European ancestry and their number greatly exceeded that of their full-blood cousins on the reservation.

The separation of the Plains Ojibwa from the mother tribe took place perhaps in the period of 1780 to 1800 according to James Howard.[1] Joseph Howard believed that the half-breed were in Sault Ste. Marie in 1654 and "'made a rendezvous' at Mackinac before 1670." Howard further suggested that these first half-breed

---

[1] James H. Howard, "The Plains-Ojibwa Or Bungi: Hunters and Warriors of the Northern Prairies with special reference to the Turtle Mountain Band," *Museum News, South Dakota Museum*, University of the South Dakota, Vermilion, S. D., Volume 24, Nos. 11 & 12, November, December 1963, p. 9.

were descendants from the Huron and Algonquin women and the men of Champlain's Company. As this new breed of men traveled westward, they married women of the Cree and Chippewa. The French, Scotch and English followed, and they too took wives among the Cree and Chippewa tribes.[2] Patrick Gourneau in his history of the band alludes to this particular ancestral mix: ". . . a little bit of Cree, a little bit of Ottawa; and also a little bit of Assiniboin and Sioux."[3] He does not take into account the Huron, Algonquin, Scotch, French, English, etc.

Other distinctions between these two included the language, the art and music, the religion, and, in general, the way of life. The Chippewa language was spoken by the full-blood while the half-breed spoke a jargon of Cree, French, Chippewa, and English. The drums, the rattles and the singing voices were used to accompany the full-blood ceremonies and powwows while the half-breed generally participated in the Catholic liturgies and used the fiddle/violin for their entertainment.

This new nation of people, " . . . were the best boatmen, best guides, hunters, trappers and traders." Other tribes accepted them as relatives and friends. Coupled with their skills, their familiarity of the area, and their knowledge of the Indian and European languages, they were the most likely people to be the trade intermediaries of the civilizations of the red man and the white man.[4]

As more settlers crowded the eastern shores, more whites rushed into Indian country, creating a rippling effect that caused the tribes to move farther west. In 1825, the Chippewa and the Sioux agreed on the Treaty of Prairie du Chien. This was an important pact for the Chippewa as the United States accepted the boundaries established by the treaty. It was a clear declaration of

---

[2] Joseph Kinsey Howard, *Strange Empire: A Narrative of the Northwest*, p. 39.
[3] Patrick Gourneau, *History of the Turtle Band of Chippewa Indians*, Ninth Edition, May 1993, p. 5.
[4] Joseph Howard, p. 40.

Chippewa ownership of the land described by the boundaries. But by the 1860's, a number of white settlers were coming to the area, and the Pembina and the Red Lake Chippewa decided it was in their best interest to cede land of the Red River area to the United States. They reasoned that they would be compensated for land that the whites already settled, and they thought it would guarantee the tribes land on which the white man could not settle.[5]

Various terms were used to describe the admixture of Cree, Ojibwa, half-breed and other races. Most of the names conveyed prejudice and disgrace. As time went on, the terms "half-breed" and "breed" no longer described the integration and intermarriages that occurred for generations. The changing continues today as the newer generations mix with people of other races. Certainly, the new race is seldom exactly one-half of any one race for long. With the constant intermarriages among the half-breed, the Indian and the white, the offspring would be less or greater than one-half. Therefore, the term of "Métis" the French word for *mixed blood* or *crossbred* tends to identify this group of people more accurately. Encountering the Métis of the Turtle Mountain today, the word "Mechif" (which is a distortion of the word "Métis") may also be heard instead of Métis.

Acculturation of the Turtle Mountain people included mixing the languages of Cree, French, and English. The Turtle Mountain people designated the language as "Cree." Today the "Cree" name for the language has almost completely given way to the word "Mechif." There are a few people today who understand and can speak the Mechif language. French and Cree influences are obviously present in the language. A French speaker would understand much of what is said in Mechif but would find much of the French language archaic. A Métis would find it difficult to understand much of modern French. Woodland Ojibwa speakers find little in common with the language as used in the Turtle

---

[5] Management Concepts Incorporated, *Turtle Mountain Band of Chippewa Indians: Historical Overview and Tribal Government*, p. 1 – 4.

3

Mountain.  The Plains Cree of Montana understand most dialogues in "Mechif" or "Cree" if the speaker uses "Cree" liberally.  The unique "Cree" dialect has speakers in southern Saskatchewan and several reserves in Manitoba.

## Their Means of Existence

The Métis conducted two buffalo hunts annually that became a lucrative business.  The hunts took place in the summer and fall, and were both exciting and dangerous, ". . . but a great business involving many thousands of dollars and netting men far more on the average and probably in volume than the gold rushes of the same period provided."[6]  Joseph Howard stated that the efforts of the 1840 fall buffalo hunt rewarded the hunters 1,200 pounds of sterling, which was greater than all the farmers in the area received for that season.[7]

The Métis buffalo hunts of the period were well-organized expeditions.  After the gathering of hundreds of Métis families at Pembina or St. Joseph (now Walhalla, North Dakota), ten captains were elected by the men of the hunt.  A governor or chief was then selected from the ten.  Each captain had ten men under his command, and these men were responsible for enforcing the rules of the camp.[8]

This method of hunting the buffalo in a large organized group began in 1820 and continued until it became unprofitable due to the decrease in the number of buffalo.  The hunts reached their peak during the 1840's.  The excitement and tension of the coming hunt prompted: "About June 1, the 'Plains mania' seized the Red River Métis. . . .  Meanwhile the Anglo-Saxon farmers watched primly, deplored 'casting off the habits of industry to go to the prairies,' blind to the fact that in the week of preparation for this

---

[6] James Michael Reardon, P.A., *George Anthony Belcourt: Pioneer Catholic Missionary of the Northwest, 1803-1874*, pp. 136-137.

[7] Joseph Howard, pp. 305-306.

[8] Joseph Howard, p. 302.

Figure 1-1: *The Métis* by the late Albert Lee Ferris.

mass movement and two months on the Plains the Métis did more work than the farmers did in a year, and braved more hardship than the farmers did in a lifetime."[9]

The summer hunt of 1840 was perhaps the largest of these Métis buffalo hunts. This huge undertaking numbered "620 hunters, 650 women and 360 children." The expedition lasted two months and necessitated 1,210 carts and an equal number of draft animals, either oxen or horses, to draw the carts plus 403 horses to be used for the hunt.[10] While on these hunts, they did not forget about the education of their children as a priest usually accompanied the families on the hunt. Mass was said daily and classes were held for the children.[11]

Reardon's account of the buffalo hunt mentions that a hunter, riding next to a herd of stampeding buffalo, could down as many

---

[9] Joseph Howard, p. 300.
[10] Joseph Howard, p. 301.
[11] "Buffalo Hunts Annual Events In Old Days," *Turtle Mountain Star*, June 23, 1938 Edition, Reprint 1988, p. 43.

as three or four buffalo within a distance of 50 rods (275 yards) with a muzzle-loading musket. Reardon explained that only the first load was rammed into the breech. For the other loads, it was primed only with powder and ball. The rider had bullets in his mouth with the powder horn at his side. After the first shot was fired, the powder was poured down the muzzle followed by the bullet. The saliva enabled the bullet to stick to the powder at the breech, and the rifle was ready to fire the next shot.[12]

According to David P. Delorme, "While the buffalo hunt was the principal source of their cash income, the majority of the Métis also engaged in limited agriculture, trading, trapping, and trucking. During the middle and latter part of the nineteenth century – until the advent of the railroad into the area – their transport operations to various destinations, characterized by long processions of horse and pony-drawn carts, assumed the proportions of big business. Trains of five hundred or more carts were not uncommon."[13]

Buffalo meat was the most significant source of food for the Métis; however, other wild game was also plentiful in the area. The lakes and streams produced fish in abundance.[14] An assortment of wild berries, puckans (nuts), plums and les navoo (wild turnips) were also available.

In addition to the natural food sources, another staple was galette; unleavened bread made from flour, lard, salt, baking powder and water. This was the preferred bread because it was filling, and kept for a long period of time. Galette is still made and eaten today by the people of the Turtle Mountain Reservation, but not as frequently as it once was. At large gatherings, such as funerals, weddings and other celebrations where food is served, you will find galette.

---

[12] Reardon, p. 69.

[13] David P. Delorme, *History of the Turtle Mountain Band of Chippewa Indians, North Dakota History,* Vol. 22, No. 3, July, 1955, p. 128.

[14] John Hesketh, *History of the Turtle Mountain Chippewa*, Collections of the State Historical Society (Grand Forks, North Dakota, 1923), V, p. 88.

James Howard describes a traditional New Year's meal of the Plains Ojibwa and the Métis. His comments about the food served was ". . . *galettes* (bannocks), *boulettes* (meat balls, made with chopped onions), and a stew with the unappetizing name *boueau* meaning 'slop' or 'filth.' This stew was formerly made of buffalo pemmican and potatoes, and probably got its name from the fact that careless cooks often left some buffalo hair in the pot."[15] Howard defined the term *boueau* correctly, but he failed to hear the French or Métis pronunciation in the term bouillon meaning broth.

Joseph Howard made the same error in his description of the New Year's meal. *Boueau* pronounced *boo you* and bouillon is pronounced *bwee you* in the Mechif language.[16] Speaking with others Métis who have a good command of the Mechif language, they use the term *bwee you* or as the French would say *bwee on*, which means broth by its use. A recipe in the St. Ann's Centennial Cook Book on page 23 has it spelled *Li boo yawn* describing a kind of soup.[17] At the beginning of the New Year 2006, some of the younger people were asking what the terms *boulettes* and *bangs* meant. *Boulettes* is French for meatballs and *bangs* is a corruption of the French word *beignet* meaning fritters.

## Attire and Pastime

The Métis attire was a combined style of the Indian and the white man with more color and individuality put into them. Joseph Howard describes Métis clothing of the 1800's as follows:[18]

> The Métis Plains hunter was partial to buckskin shirts with bright beaded designs usually in the floral figures of the Cree, and black woolen trousers bound below the knee with beaded garters or ornamented leggings of wool or buckskin. The "Assomption sash" . . . was bound around his waist or looped over one shoulder; tobacco pouch, powder bag and other articles were tied to the sash or stuffed under it. His headgear originally was a handmade pillbox cap of wool

---

[15] James Howard, Volume 25, Nos. 11 & 12, November, December, 1964, p. 20.
[16] Joseph Howard, p. 335.
[17] St Ann's Parish 1985 Centennial Cook Book, p. 23.

bordered with an ornamental design in beads or porcupine quills; later he adopted a bright feather cockade or beaded band. He was invariably shod in moccasins. The standard garb for women was a loose dress of rough black woolen stuff and head scarf of black silk, varied on special occasions by the addition of colorful embroidered shawls or aprons. They wore 'squaw boots' moccasins with attached tops of soft buckskin, usually intricately beaded, men and women wore out several sets of footwear on every hunt and much of the wives' time was spent making moccasins.

Figure 1-2: Métis family and Red River carts showing their dress in the late 1800's. Courtesy of State Historical Society of North Dakota.

A picture of seven Jerome brothers in Figure 1-3 illustrates the attire of the Plains Objiwa in the early 1900's. Shown here they are dressed much like the white settlers of the time. Note that some are wearing moccasins and the Assomption sash.

There are excellent paintings done by the late Albert Lee Ferris, a member of the Turtle Mountain Band that illustrate the clothing worn by the Métis. One of his works is titled *The Métis* (Figure 1-1) depicting hunters on a buffalo hunt. Another painting *Turtle Mountain Morning* is a winter scene with a hunter dressed

---

[18] Joseph Howard, p. 301.

Figure 1-3: Seven Jerome brothers in the year 1905. From left to right are Louie, Eli, Andrew, David, Jerome, Daniel and Joseph. At their brother Andrea's home near the mouth of Two River where it flows into Red River. Their brother Roger is not in picture as well as their six sisters.

in a Hudson Bay coat. Ferris had always been meticulous in his paintings. In his own statement regarding this, ". . . My job as a Government illustrator requires that all the artwork that I do be thoroughly researched so it is technically and anatomically correct. I carry this requirement over to my paintings. I am illustrating the past as it was lived and told to me. I paint fact, not fiction. I paint life not pretty pictures. I thank God for the gift I was given, and being able to share it with you . . .."[19]

One of the Métis' favorite pastimes was dancing to the tunes of fiddle or violin music. The most popular dances were the quadrilles (square dances), jigs and reels. Actually, the Métis jig

---

[19] Albert Lee Ferris, brochure on art, undated.

step, which includes an Ojibwa traditional dance step making it unique in itself, was blended into the square dances. The language of the callers was a mixture of the distorted French and English words as they directed the dancers with "allemande left." Bruce Sealy stated the caller mixed the French with English as he called his directions to the dancers "a la main left" instead of using the French words *a la main gauche.* The words were further altered to "allemande left."[20] Today neither the callers nor the dancers of the Turtle Mountain have any idea what the word "allemande" means. The dancers, however, have no problem responding to the caller.

The elders well remember the days of the "bush" dance. These dances usually took place at someone's home and involved family and friends and "peters" (the uninvited). The youngsters were housed for the night at the homes of relatives. All the furniture, except the kitchen stove, was removed from the house. Makeshift benches were placed around the room. Upon the arrival of the fiddler and guitar players, the dance began. A lunch of sandwiches and coffee was served at midnight, after which the dance continued till three or four o'clock in the morning.

## Métis Revolts

Alvin M. Josephy, Jr. speculates that the two Canadian Métis revolts were the results of ". . . their French Catholic attitudes of defiance to Protestant officialdom." He came closer to the reason for the revolts when he wrote, ". . . a cause that promised the establishment of a separate, independent half-breed and Indian state in central Canada to be called Assiniboia."[21] According to G. F. G. Stanley, the revolts did not come about because of the differences between Catholic and Protestant beliefs. Stanley seems to think that the problems were of a cultural nature – ". . . clash between primitive and civilized peoples. In all parts of the world,

---

[20] Bruce Sealey, *One plus One Equals one, The other Natives the-les Métis,* Vol. I – Tome -Premier 1700 –1885, p. 8.

[21] Alvin M. Josephy, Jr., *The Indian Heritage of America,* (NY: Alfred A. Knoph, 1969), pp. 342-343.

in South Africa, New Zealand and North America, the penetration of white settlement into territories inhabited by native people has led to friction and war; Canadian expansion into the North-West led to similar results."[22]   When someone's way of life is threatened, there will be conflict especially when it involves loss of land on which livelihood depends.   In reality, the revolts came about because of the destruction of their life style due to the intrusion of the white man.   However, it was inevitable that the tribe's way of life would change with the depletion of the buffalo herds coupled with their own business of transportation challenged by the railroads.

The Métis first set up the Métis Province of Manitoba in 1870.   Although they successfully obtained provincial status, this success was short lived. They elected their leader Louis Riel to the

Canadian Parliament as a representative of the Province of Manitoba.   He was exiled and not allowed back into Ottawa, and therefore, did not take his seat.[23] "Persecuted and discriminated against, many of those Métis who had taken the most active part in the events of 1869-1870, sold their rights in the land grant in Manitoba and fled to the valley of the Saskatchewan, where, for a few years, they were able to reconstruct the traditional Métis society."[24] Many of the Métis settled in the Turtle Mountain area after the

Figure 1-4: Louis Riel, a Canadian Métis leader (1844-1885). Courtesy of St. Ann's Centennial Book.

[22] G. F. G. Stanley, *The other Native the les Métis,* Louis Riel: Patriot or Rebel? Vol. I – Tome- Premier 1700 – 1885, pp. 177-178.
[23] Joseph Howard, pp. 242-246.
[24] G.F.G Stanley, *Confederation 1870 – A Metis Achievement, The Other Natives the – les Metis,* Vol. 1 – Tome Premier 1700 – 1885,p. 85.

conflict with the Canadian Government.

A second attempt to protect the rights of the Métis came in 1885 – more often called the Riel Rebellion. The outcome of this venture is well known. In short, the Métis army was defeated at Batoche, Saskatchewan, and Riel was tried for treason and hanged.[25] It is interesting to note that an American soldier, Lt. Arthur L. Howard, in the Connecticut National Guard Unit, introduced the Gatling machine gun in the fight against the Métis. Two Gatling guns were aboard the *Northcote*. The *Northcote* towed two barges and carried two hundred men with supplies and ammunition.[26] The Métis put the *Northcote* temporarily out of commission. It did not play a significant role in the battle at Batoche. Ashore at Batoche the Canadian troops had another Gatling gun, which was used to their advantage. With the Métis being significantly outnumbered, the battle of Batoche was over in four days.[27]

On May 15, 1885, Riel surrendered to the British General Middleton; Gabriel Dumont, appointed "adjutant-general" of the rebellion, escaped to the United States.[28] The rumblings of the rebellion subsided, but struggles continued.

Riel was charged with high treason on July 6, 1885, for leading the revolt against the Crown. His trial was set to convene on July 20, in Regina, Manitoba, Canada. If convicted, under the British Crown Law, the penalty would be death.[29]

Howard stated that "the circumstances of Louis Riel's trial were immoral. Whether the trial itself was also illegal has been debated ever since it was held." Riel had a jury of six people instead of twelve as required for the type of crime charged. All six

---

[25] Joseph Howard, pp. 556-561.
[26] Joseph Howard, pp. 451-454.
[27] Joseph Howard, pp. 422-477.
[28] G.F.G. Stanley, *Louis Riel; Patriot or Rebel*, *The Other Natives the-les Metis*, Vol. 1 – Tome Premier 1700–1885, pp. 196, 199.
[29] Joseph Howard, p. 507.

were of "Protestants of Anglo-Saxon stock." None of the jurists were familiar with the French language. Though Riel was bilingual, using English placed him at a disadvantage. He pleaded not guilty to the crime. No safe conduct was given to any of Riel's witnesses, therefore, they did not appear because they could have been tried for the same crime as Riel. Gabriel Dumont wrote a letter (through his attorney) and claimed that he alone was in charge of "the rebel's military operation that the *exovidat,* not Riel, had voted to launch the rebellion. . . ." ("The term *'Exovede'* puzzled all recipients of Reil's communications for months – until, after his arrest, he explained it himself. He had taken it from Latin, he said: *ex*, from; *ovede*, flock. It was intended to designate him as 'one of the flock,' as were all members of the council, which he called the *'Exovidat'*. . . .")[30]

The Crown rested its case July 29, 1885. It took only two days to hear eighteen witnesses. The defense presented its case in less than a day using only five witnesses. To the jury Riel stated, "Gentlemen of the jury, my reputation, my liberty, my life are at your discretion. . . . I do respect you, although you are only half a jury; but your number of six does not prevent you from being just and conscientious, does not prevent me from giving you my confidence. . . ."[31]

At two o'clock in the afternoon of August 1, 1885, the jury retired and the court recessed. The jury returned one hour and twenty minutes later with a guilty verdict. After the verdict, Riel was again allowed to speak, ". . . the smile that comes to my face is not an act of my will so much as it comes naturally from the satisfaction that I experienced seeing one of my difficulties disappearing. Should I be executed – at least if I were being to be executed – I would not be executed as an insane man. It would be a great consolation for my mother, for my wife, for my children,

---

[30] Joseph Howard, pp. 385, 508-512.
[31] Joseph Howard, pp. 512-533.

for my brothers, for my relatives, even for my protectors, for my countrymen. . . ."[32]

September 18, 1885, Riel was sentenced to hang. His sentence was carried out that day.[33]

According to Indian and Northern Affairs Canada, (www. Ainc–inac.Gc.ca), one hundred seven years later in 1992, the Parliament of Canada and the Legislative Assembly of Manitoba formally recognized Riel and the Métis as founders of Manitoba and Riel's contribution to the development of the Canadian Confederation. The Canadian Government also issued a notice of Reconciliation to the Indian people of Canada in March 1998.

---

[32] Joseph Howard, pp. 538-539.
[33] Joseph Howard, p. 543.

# Chapter 2

## Establishment of the Turtle Mountain Reservation

The Turtle Mountain Reservation proper is a six-by-twelve-mile rectangular-shaped tract of land located in north central North Dakota about seven and one-half miles south of the Canadian border. Much of the area can be described as wooded to the north and hilly prairies to the south with many small lakes and sloughs throughout the region. There is one fishing lake (Fish Lake/Belcourt Lake) entirely within the boundaries of the reservation. Gordon Lake and Jarvis Lake, two other fishing lakes in the vicinity of the reservation, are both partially bordered by tribal land. Most of the trees in the area are poplar, oak, aspen, ash and birch. Wild nuts and fruit trees are also abundant in the area. The reservation is comprised of two townships. The Couture Township encompasses the eastern half of the reservation, and the Ingebretson Township the western half.

According to Reardon, the name of the Turtle Mountain came from how and where one viewed the hills. When the hills are approached from a certain direction, the hills have a likeness to turtle backs.[34] Pat Gourneau, a long-time resident of the Turtle

---

[34] Reardon, p. 135.

Mountain and a former tribal chairman of the Turtle Mountain Band of Chippewa Indians, writes:[35]

> The naming of Turtle Mountain goes back a long time, versions from white men and Indians. To mention only three Chippeway versions, it indicates that it was the early Chippeway migrants from the woodlands of the east who named it Turtle Mountain. None of the three versions carry the name Turtle Mountains. As far back as my memory goes, I have not ever heard a full blood term the hills as Turtle Mountains, and the same applies to the "Mechifs." The Chippeway name is "Mekinauk Wudjiw" (Turtle Mountain). If it was Turtle Mountains it would be "Mekinauk Wudjiw wum" (plural). The "Mechifs" referred to the hills as "La Montagne Torchue." "La Montagne Torchue" is French meaning Turtle Mountain.

> One version, and very likely the first one, is that when the Chippeways first approached the wooded hills from a distance west from straight north, the high butte which juts out high above other hills a few miles northeast of the International Peace Garden, on the Canadian side, reminded them of a turtle because of its shape, like the back of a turtle. For that reason they named it Turtle Mountain. The second version when the hills were approached from the south, the distant view was like seeing a turtle with the head being in the west and the tail in the east. The third version is that a famous Indian hunter named Mekinauk (Turtle) walked the full length of the hills from west to east in one day. To honor him for the feat, the whole hill range area was named as his mountain by a Ceremony performed on an east side Indian camp, close to where the Rolla View Ski Slope is now located, Rolla, North Dakota.

Since the name "Turtle Mountain" has been misused for so long, it has become common practice to use the plural or the singular interchangeably to designate the area. The singular form will be used in this document.

When the U.S. and British Governments agreed that the 49th parallel would be the boundary between the two countries in 1818, the Indian and Métis peoples did not recognize this line and moved freely across the borders of the two countries. However, with the creation of the Turtle Mountain Reservation in 1882, the

---

[35] Gourneau, pp. 19-20.

governments of each country not wanting to be responsible for the inhabitants of the other country, had to work toward resolving the border crossing problem. In an effort to resolve this, "Canadian Mounted Police killed all the buffalo found near the line to keep the U.S. Indians from crossing into Canada and voce-versa [vice versa]."[36]

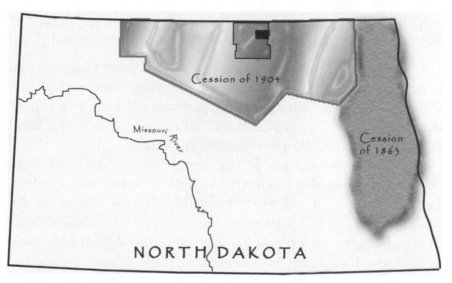

Figure 2-1: Cession map of Ojibwa lands by treaty. TM Reservation in 1882, then reduced to black area only in 1884. Courtesy of Kathe Peltier Zaste.

Since the reservation was occupied mostly by Métis – both from Canada and the United States, coupled with the fact that the reservation was created for the full-bloods, the nationality and enrollment issue was compounded.[37] With the reservation being only two townships and the three groups of people living within or in the vicinity, one could readily see the problem – too many Indians and not enough land base.

---

[36] James H. Howard, Reprints In Anthropology Vol. 7. Pp. 23-24

[37] Stanley N. Murray, *The Turtle Mountain Chippewa, 1882 – 1905, North Dakota History, Journal of the Northern Plains Volume* 51, Winter 1984, No. 1, pp. 14-37.

# The Trail of Misgivings

The treaty [Old Crossing Treaty of 1863] was negotiated among three parties – Pembina Chippewa, Red Lake Chippewa, and the United States. The land along the Red River was ceded for rations and annuity payments which were to last for twenty-five years. The treaty was signed in 1864. "Yet even while the ink was drying white settlers were moving into unceded, Pembina land. Those whites began insisting that the Indians be moved out of their homeland altogether and be relocated. They began pressuring the Secretary of the Interior and the U.S. Congress for more land."[38]

As a result of the pressure on the Secretary and Congress, the U.S. made an attempt to move the Pembina Band out of the Dakotas. In 1873, Congress even appropriated funds to purchase land on the White Earth Reservation to induce the Pembina Band to move. The Federal Government withheld the annuities to the Pembina bands in an effort to force them to move. The bands were already experiencing poverty coupled with the Federal Government's action of withholding their money. Some of the group succumbed to the pressure and moved while others refused to move defying the Federal Government. The defiant ones were those "who today call themselves the Turtle Mountain Band is most clearly, directly traced to this stubborn and persevering group of Indians who, in the 1870's, refused to give up their homeland."[39]

The Turtle Mountain Indians were not opposed to the idea of reservation living. They had seen "the handwriting on the wall" that they could not win a battle with the federal troops. They requested that the Federal Government set aside a reservation for them in the Turtle Mountain. The Federal Government recognized the legal rights of the Turtle Mountain Band to the land on which they hunted and roamed. Despite the law, the Federal Government

---

[38] *Historical Overview and Tribal Government*, p. 1 – 5.
[39] *Historical Overview and Tribal Government*, p. 1 – 5.

opened the land to white settlers. By 1880, foreigners flowed in filling the land with unfriendly, land-hungry whites.[40]

President Chester A. Arthur answered the need to establish a reservation for the Turtle Mountain Band by the first Executive Order on December 21, 1882. Its territorial boundaries carved out twenty townships in the western part of what is now Rolette County. A second Executive Order reduced the reservation to two townships on March 29, 1884.[41] Later, on June 3, 1884, a third Executive Order changed the two townships to Ingebretson and Couture. The whites, still not satisfied, wanted the band moved to Fort Berthold. White settlers also flowed into the two townships. Meanwhile, McCumber was attempting to finagle the band to move, and relinquish the remaining two townships. In response to McCumber's slyness, Chief Little Shell, a member of the band responded, "We are unlearned and cannot read or write, and we ask the Commission not to deceive us, but to inform us truly whether or not this land has even been ceded to the Government. . . . The Government, powerful as it is, should be ashamed to arbitrarily take the lands from them, who are defenseless to protect it. . . . Some going so far as to declare they would never leave it, and if it was God's will that they and their children should perish by hunger, they would die in the country the Great Spirit had given them."[42]

As mentioned above, the first Executive Order of December 21, 1882, established a tract of land roughly 24 by 32 miles as the

---

[40] *Historical Overview and Tribal Government*, p. 1 – 5.

[41] Executive Order, March 29, 1884
    The *St. Ann's Centennial Book* and Charley White Weasel's Book are in error. They both have the description as TN 162 N, Range 70 W and TN 163 N, 71 W. The second Executive Order clearly describes it correctly TN 162 N, Range 71 W, TN 163 N, Range 71 W. Hesketh found the same error, and said "Royce in his report of Indian treaties in the Report of the Bureau of Ethnology misquotes this treaty and gives . . . the wrong description." See *Appendix A*.

[42] *Historical Overview and Tribal Government*, p. 1 – 8.

# The Trail of Misgivings

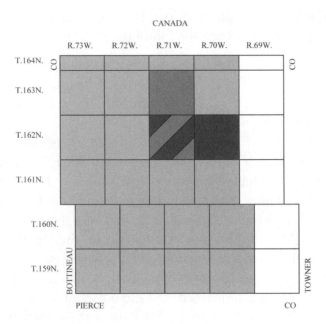

Figure 2-2: Turtle Mountain Reservation maps as determined by the Executive Orders of 1882 and 1884, Chester A. Arthur, President. Above, the shaded townships of Rolette County, North Dakota, are from the 1882 order that made the reservation 20 townships in size, the dark gray and black are from the second and third orders of 1884, respectively.

reservation, which included much of the present day Rolette County. In fact, upon examination of the Executive Order, the tract included 20 of the 25 townships in the western part of the county. Theoretically, a township is a six-by-six tract of land. The townships that border the international boundary are oversized townships and extend about an additional one and one-half or so miles north to the boundary. In Rolette County, these townships consist of Willow Lake, Holmes, Hutchinson, Baxter, and Fairview. The first Executive Order included all of the above townships except Fairview.

A misleading count of the people living on the reservation resulted in a second Executive Order, March 29, 1884, which reduced the size of the reservation to two townships. The two townships, according to the Executive Order, were described as township 162, north, range 71 west and township 163 north, range 71 west, which were the Ingebretson and Hutchinson townships. The exchange did not include a tract of land the size of the extended Hutchinson Township, but rather it was minus the mile-plus wide strip at the US/Canadian boundary. It is interesting to note that the land comprising the reservation is almost absent of good farmland. According to David P. Delorme, when the officials recognized the lack of farmland in the creation of the reservation, they prompted a follow-up Executive Order.[43] This third Executive Order exchanged the southern six-by-six mile tract of Hutchinson Township for the Couture Township. The description of the reservation is now township 162 north, range 70 west and township 162 north, 71 west. This increase in farmland was minimal. Stanley N. Murray stated, "Not only was the best farm land in the reserve restored to the public domain, but even after the exchange of one remaining township for one with more open land, only 13,000 of 46,080 acres in the reduced reserve were suitable for normal farm operations."[44]

Some Indian people of the reservation made improvements on the land on which they "squatted" and were promised government funds and legal assistance in filing for the land; however, they defiantly refused to file claims for land that the tribe had not ceded to the Federal Government. According to them, the land was still legally theirs. The white man, on the other hand, scurried about looking for land that had not been claimed and filed a claim regardless of whether the land was occupied or not.[45] Without a legally filed claim, the Indians lost their holdings. The native people were right in one respect by not filing – they were the rightful owners, and to file a claim would admit that the Federal Government had the right to restore the land to public domain.

---

[43] Delorme, p. 132.
[44] Stanley N. Murray, *The Turtle Mountain Chippewa – 1882-1905*, p. 23.
[45] Stanley N. Murray, p. 24.

Since the government had made and had broken many treaties with the tribe, the Indians should have anticipated the outcome.

The reduction of the size of the reservation by the second Executive Order, according to Gourneau, resulted from using an incorrect count of the Turtle Mountain Band. Cyrus Beede, government representative, who conducted the survey counted only the number of full-bloods on the reservation and ignored the hundreds of Métis in the area. The McCumber Commission's count only a few years later in 1892 counted 283 full-bloods and 1476 Métis for a total number of 1759 Indians. This survey also rejected 522 people, who could have possibly been eligible for the tribal rolls.[46]

The Federal authorities still hoped to reject the Métis from the count, but Miske Piness (Red Thunder), a respected Cree leader, according to Gourneau gave the following argument: "It is not the fault of the half-breeds ('Mechifs') if they are not regarded as Indian nor white people. It was the fault of the white man by taking Indian women as wives and raising families with them. Although most of these first white men stayed with their families until they passed on in death, the white man now wants to throw away what was produced by raising families with Indian women. We, the full-bloods, will not throw them way. We pity them because of what the Government white man is trying to do. So, we will gladly accept them as our own people."[47]

With these developments and the limited land base, the people of the reservation reluctantly settled in. They were able to survive because there were plenty of fish in the lakes and streams, and the fur-bearing animals including the buffalo were in abundance. However, the last organized buffalo hunt was perhaps in the year 1882, according to Joanne Pelletier.[48] With the buffalo gone, the

---

[46] Gourneau, p. 14.
[47] Gourneau, p. 14.
[48] Joanne Pelletier, *The Buffalo Hunt,* (Regina: Gabriel Dumont Institute of Native Studies and Applied Research, 1985), p. 17.

Métis experienced many more hardships, especially during the extreme cold winters. Father Genin, a Catholic priest, who was prompted to write to the editor of the *Duluth Journal* in 1888, aptly documented the severe conditions of the people: [49]

> It is now too late that I may have time to look for the official report I had to make in June, 1888, about the deplorable state of affairs and the intolerable suffering of the Turtle Mountain Indians, and send it to you . . . . In the winter of 1887 and 1888 there were counted 151 persons, big and small who died there of starvation. I buried a number of them myself, taking three, the mother and two grown children, out of one single family. The Sisters of Mercy, who support there a large number of orphans and destitute boys and girls, deprived their house of all they could in order to help me carry pork, flour, sugar, tea, bread, etc., to all those we could reach. There were lots of young mothers who, after giving birth to their children, had to wait patiently for a meal until their husbands would return home from the hunt with a gopher or two, nothing else being found. I state facts, remember, I do not put up stories.
>
> You will ask: Why did not the lazy creatures provide themselves with provisions by cultivating the land? Why did not they? In the first place they had no seed of any kind; and where the United States government was made to believe so many bushels of wheat, corn and potatoes had been distributed. If you had been there you might have found that so many things never reached the unfortunate; or, if any at all was obtained, it was only by a few favorites, while the others were rebuked and sent to do for themselves. . . .

In 1993, Charles (Gourneau) White Weasel worked with the North Dakota State officials to commemorate these people who died of starvation in the winter of 1887-1888. Today a historical marker is erected in front of the old campus of the Turtle Mountain College, Belcourt, North Dakota as a memorial for the 151 people who died.

Manifest Destiny was still in the hearts of the American people, and their hunger for land did not stop with the 1840's and

---

[49] Delorme, David P. p. 134. Linda W. Slaughter, *Leaves from Northwestern History*, (Bismarck: Collections of the State Historical Society of North Dakota, 1906), Vol I, p. 289.

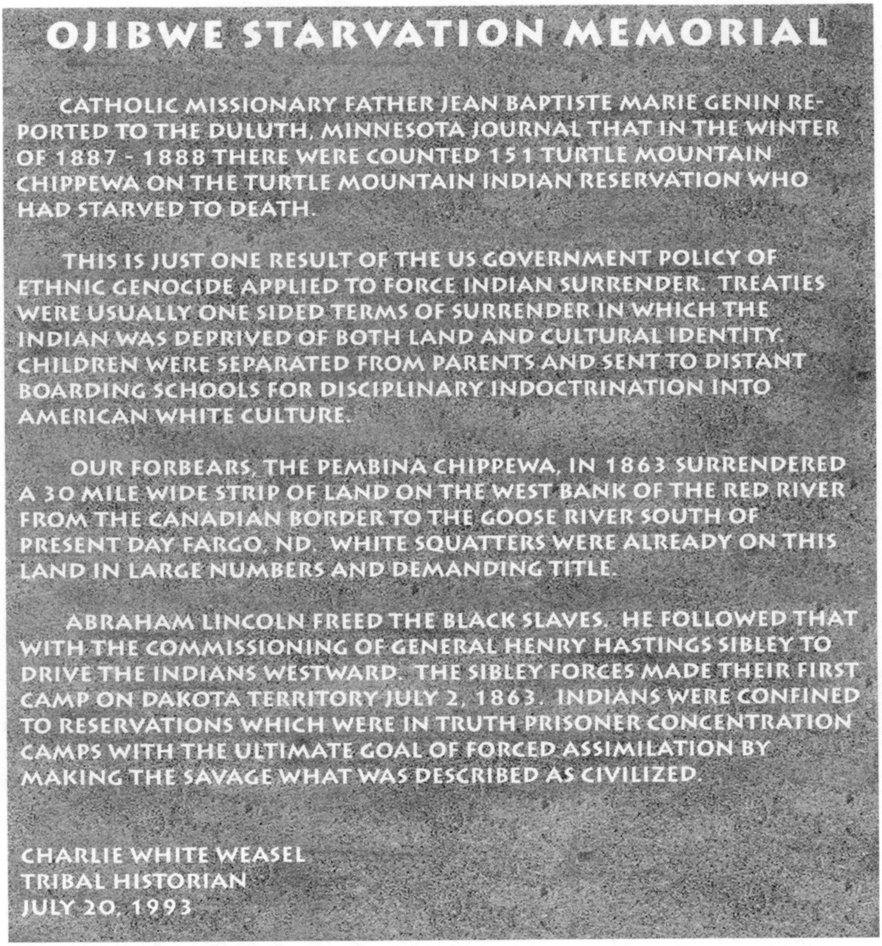

## OJIBWE STARVATION MEMORIAL

CATHOLIC MISSIONARY FATHER JEAN BAPTISTE MARIE GENIN REPORTED TO THE DULUTH, MINNESOTA JOURNAL THAT IN THE WINTER OF 1887 - 1888 THERE WERE COUNTED 151 TURTLE MOUNTAIN CHIPPEWA ON THE TURTLE MOUNTAIN INDIAN RESERVATION WHO HAD STARVED TO DEATH.

THIS IS JUST ONE RESULT OF THE US GOVERNMENT POLICY OF ETHNIC GENOCIDE APPLIED TO FORCE INDIAN SURRENDER. TREATIES WERE USUALLY ONE SIDED TERMS OF SURRENDER IN WHICH THE INDIAN WAS DEPRIVED OF BOTH LAND AND CULTURAL IDENTITY. CHILDREN WERE SEPARATED FROM PARENTS AND SENT TO DISTANT BOARDING SCHOOLS FOR DISCIPLINARY INDOCTRINATION INTO AMERICAN WHITE CULTURE.

OUR FORBEARS, THE PEMBINA CHIPPEWA, IN 1863 SURRENDERED A 30 MILE WIDE STRIP OF LAND ON THE WEST BANK OF THE RED RIVER FROM THE CANADIAN BORDER TO THE GOOSE RIVER SOUTH OF PRESENT DAY FARGO, ND. WHITE SQUATTERS WERE ALREADY ON THIS LAND IN LARGE NUMBERS AND DEMANDING TITLE.

ABRAHAM LINCOLN FREED THE BLACK SLAVES. HE FOLLOWED THAT WITH THE COMMISSIONING OF GENERAL HENRY HASTINGS SIBLEY TO DRIVE THE INDIANS WESTWARD. THE SIBLEY FORCES MADE THEIR FIRST CAMP ON DAKOTA TERRITORY JULY 2, 1863. INDIANS WERE CONFINED TO RESERVATIONS WHICH WERE IN TRUTH PRISONER CONCENTRATION CAMPS WITH THE ULTIMATE GOAL OF FORCED ASSIMILATION BY MAKING THE SAVAGE WHAT WAS DESCRIBED AS CIVILIZED.

CHARLIE WHITE WEASEL
TRIBAL HISTORIAN
JULY 20, 1993

Figure 2-3: Starvation Memorial Monument located within the area of the old Turtle Mountain Community College campus on Main Street in Belcourt.

1850's, but continued into the late 1800's and the early 1900's. As the white settlers poured in, the hunting and trapping diminished. Transportation changed with the coming of the railways, and agriculture became the major industry of North Dakota, which gained statehood in 1889. The Plains Ojibwa were left to shift for themselves in an area of two townships with inadequate tillable land to farm. Their traditional lands were reduced from nearly 10,000,000 acres in North Dakota to 46,080 acres – or a mere two townships. In search for food and furs, they did not respect the United States-Canadian border, and crossed the imaginary line freely to hunt and trap as they pleased. The once proud people of the Plains saw their economy crumble to a state of starvation by 1887.

In 1881, Helen Hunt Jackson wrote an investigative book titled, *A Century of Dishonor.* She relates some of the true stories of the west, which makes the reader uncomfortable. Stories such as the Sand Creek massacre revealed how a band of Cheyenne was invited to camp near the fort for their protection. The band was later moved about 40 miles away with the guarantee of safe conduct. Meanwhile, a separate incident happened for which the Cheyenne were blamed. The soldiers wrongfully attacked the Cheyenne camp in retaliation. A Congressional investigation concluded: "It scarcely had its parallel in the records of Indian barbarity. Fleeing women, holding up their hands and praying for mercy, were shot down; infants were killed and scalped in derision; men were tortured and mutilated. . . . A war ensued which cost the government $30,000,000 and carried conflagration and death into the border settlements."[50] In her book, Jackson gave ". . . a historical account of governmental injustice in treating and cheating the Indian."[51]

Bishop H. B. Whipple of Minnesota wrote the introduction for Jackson's book: "The American people have accepted as truth the teaching that the Indians were degraded, brutal race of savages, who it was the will of God should perish at the approach of civilization. If they do not say with our Puritan fathers that these are the Hittites who are to be driven out before the saints of the Lord, they do accept the teaching that manifest destiny will drive

---

[50] Harold E. Fey and D'Arcy McNickle, *Indians and Other Americans, Two ways of Life Meet*, Harper and Brothers Publishers, New York, pp. 35-36.
[51] Thomas A. Bailey, *The American Pageant, A History of The Republic,* D.C. Heath and Company, Boston, 1956, p. 569.

the Indians from the earth. The inexorable has no tears or pity at the cries of anguish of the doomed race."[52]

The Dawes Act of 1887 was the Federal Government's response to the public's outcry of injustice in the treatment of the Indian tribes. The provisions of the Act were to sever the legal entity of the tribe by ending the tribal ownership of the land, and in turn allot 160-acre tracts to individual family heads. "But lest designing whites be tempted to get the Indians drunk and trick them into signing away their birthright for a song, the holdings were made inalienable for twenty-five years."[53] Senator Teller of Colorado was against the Act describing it as "a bill to despoil the Indians of their lands and to make them vagabonds on the face of the earth."[54]

Meanwhile, on the House side, they were considering similar legislation:[55]

> However much we may differ with the humanitarians who are riding this hobby, we are certain that they will agree with us in the proposition that it does not make a farmer out of an Indian to give him a quarter section of land. There are hundreds of thousands of white men, rich with the experiences of centuries of Anglo-Saxon civilization, who cannot be transformed into cultivators of the land by any such gift. . . . The real aim of this bill is to get at the Indian lands and open them up to settlement. The provisions for the apparent benefit of the Indian are but the pretext to get at his lands and occupy them. . . . If this were done in the name of greed, it would be bad enough; but to do it in the name of humanity, and under the cloak of an ardent desire to promote the Indian's welfare by making him like ourselves, whether he will or not, is infinitely worse.

---

[52] Fey and McNickle, p. 35.

[53] Bailey, pp. 569-570.

[54] Fey and McNickle, pp. 72-73.
   Senator Teller's remarks and related debates are found in the *Congressional Record*, 46th Cong., 3rd Sess., Vol. XI, June 20, 1881.

[55] Fey and McNickle, p. 73.
   The minority committee report is in House Report No. 1576, 46th Cong., 2nd Sess., May 28, 1880.

The McCumber Agreement of 1892 better known as the "ten cent treaty" compelled the Indian people of the Turtle Mountain to give nearly ten million acres of North Dakota land to the United States for a sum of $1,000,000. The U.S. Legislature approved this Agreement in 1904 with amendments.[56] According to Gregory Camp, a revision to the Act shortened the trust period of twenty-five years to when the Bureau of Indian Affairs determined that the individual was competent.[57]

Because of the small land base of the Turtle Mountain Reservation, many of the people were given allotments off the reservation. The lands allotted to people were great distances from the Turtle Mountain ranging from Devils Lake, North Dakota to the middle of Montana. According to Murray, ". . . about fifteen families filed upon land in the area known as Graham's Island (a peninsula of Devils Lake, just west of Spirit Lake Sioux Reservation), three hundred ninety families located at Trenton, just west [southwest] of Williston, North Dakota. One hundred forty-nine individuals took up land in Montana . . . and fifty adult males were allowed to remain on public land that had been part of the larger, original Turtle Mountain Reservation."[58]

Camp stated that Cato Sells, the Commissioner of Indian Affairs, made "A Declaration of Policy" whereby a fee patent was issued automatically to those people who were one half or less Indian. "Mixed bloods unaware of the ramification of land ownership suddenly found themselves owners of land. Many of these people had not asked for the fee patent, but had it thrust upon them. Defending his policy, Sells declared the dawn of a new era,

---

[56] Delorme, p. 133.

[57] Gregory Camp, *North Dakota History, The Dispossessed: The Ojibwa and Metís of Northwest North Dakota,* Journal of the Northern Plains, Vol. 69, Nos. 2, 3, & 4 – 2002, p. 66.

[58] Stanley N. Murray, p. 32.

one which the Indian would no longer be treated as half-wards and half-citizens. In short, the beginning of the Indian problem."[59]

Camp further states, ". . . the disastrous effect of the Declaration of Policy was even more bitter. It was reported that between 90 percent and 95 percent of those mixed-bloods that obtained fee patents for their lands sold them within a year. Moreover, the amount received for the land was at times below market value. McQuigg (Turtle Mountain Superintendent) immediately saw the problems the Declaration of Policy caused, and reported that the loss of land was acute. Encouragement to mortgage their lands for items like automobiles meant a short-lived windfall for the Indians. Mortgage foreclosure became a tragically common occurrence for the Turtle Mountain People, and doomed any hopes in the land as a long-term solution."[60]

Perhaps it would have been better for the Bureau of Indian Affairs if all Indians had gained a fee patent and sold their lands. The hundreds of heirs to a single allotment today only complicate the many problems for the Bureau in its record keeping. Each year the land is divided into smaller and smaller pieces as the heirs to these tracts continue to grow.

In the early 1900's, seasonal farm work became the way of life for many of the Turtle Mountain people. Personal testimony recalls a mother who related how she was often hired as a cook on a farm, and that many young men worked as farm hands. Her husband talked about working as a farm hand during the harvest season and being paid by the day. The farmers took advantage of the day wage by extending the workday to fourteen and fifteen hours. As a youngster, he talked about going to bed without eating the evening meal because of being so tired.

---

[59] Gregory Camp, *The Turtle Mountain Chippewa and Metís,* 1797-1935, (Albuquerque: The University of New Mexico, 1987) p. 188.
[60] Camp, *Turtle Mountain Chippewa*, pp. 180-181.

Conditions deteriorated even more for the people of the reservation in the latter part of the 1920's. Those returning to the reservation after parting with their allotments swelled the reservation population. The annual cost of relief from Rolette County funds grew from $2,644.25 to $17,304.02 in the period 1916 to 1926.[61]

The following pictures illustrate how work on school buildings and road construction furnished some employment for the people of the reservation prior to the Roosevelt administration. It was not until Roosevelt became President in 1933 that employment conditions began to improve. Reservation people had the opportunity to work close to home as they participated in these work programs. Those people who still had possession of their land allotments on the reservation or nearby were assisted with gardening projects. Many of the people who had horses worked on the new roads being built for the bus routes. Others made concrete

Figure 2-4: Fresno Scrapers were dragged behind teams of horses to remove earth and grade the road.

---

[61] Camp, *Turtle Mountain Chippewa*, p. 185.

culverts for the roads or worked as labor hands, but even with seasonal work, poverty still existed. Thus was life on the reservation.

Figure 2-5: Horses along with modern machinery were used in the construction of roads.

Figure 2-6: The Roosevelt years brought about numerous amounts of tree planting projects. Joseph P. Gourneau is in the forefront; others are unknown.

Figure 2-7: Old school construction, which began in 1929 now being considered as a possible historical monument.

Figure 2-8: Typical log and mud house of *tawn kayawsh*. Courtesy of Sandy Belgarde Thomas.

# Chapter 3

## The People and the Reservation Today

Today, the number of full-bloods has dwindled, perhaps to less than twenty families, while the Métis population has increased significantly. Physical traits and characteristics of this latter group vary from definite darker skin, hair and eyes to light tones with no semblance of "Indian features." Some Métis consider themselves Ojibwa rather than Métis, still others have chosen a more traditional way of life. There are those who completely shy away from the Indian culture, while some walk with comfort and dignity between the two worlds that are intertwined in their lives. The Plains Ojibwa religion and traditional way of life is practiced by those who study, participate and adhere to the commitment that it entails while a few cling to remnants of Woodland *Midewiwin* or both. In recent years, more Métis than full-bloods have taken part in Sun Dances, sweat lodges, and pipe ceremonies to express their prayers and devotions to the Great Spirit. It should also be emphasized that there are some that live and practice the traditional lifestyle, in addition to their Christian beliefs and practices. Many Métis have great devotion to Roman Catholic teachings.

Pow-wow participants and spectators are made up of Métis and full-bloods. Though the languages in both cultures are being lost, schools have made an effort to preserve them, and schools incorporate both cultural aspects into their curriculum. The Turtle

Mountain Community College is currently teaching the Ojibwa language.

Other cultural aspects of Turtle Mountain people are being lost. For example, the traditional meal on New Year's Day may still be served, but the tradition of younger brothers and sisters visiting older family members has diminished. At one time, families might have most of their relatives visit in the course of the week. Today, fewer families tend to show up and visiting seems to be is limited to the first of January. The New Year greeting *"la bonne annee"* may continue for several days. Modern transportation no doubt has played a role for seeing more people in the course of the day or meeting relatives at various businesses, but the visit to the home is curtailed. The New Year celebration in the days of horse and sleigh would extend the time period longer if the people wished to see all their relatives.

Some still like to dance to fiddle music, and there are a number of musicians who play the fiddle, but rock, country, and other modern music of the radio and television are the tunes of the times. Bush dances are a thing of the past. Both the Ojibwa and Métis have dance groups that are helping to preserve these aspects of the culture. There are traditional drum groups that participate in various ceremonies. These groups exhibit at ceremonies and celebrations.

## Land

The tribe had purchased additional acreage under a special appropriation land-purchasing program authorized by the Act of 1940.[62] The bulk of the land purchased off the reservation is in nearby Hillside, Holmes, Hutchinson, and Baxter townships. But this Act did not come without problems.

---

[62] *Turtle Mountain Band of Chippewa Indians, Historical Overview and Tribal Government* Falls Church, VA and Albuquerque, NM. Management Concepts Incorporated. April 1980, p. 1 – 9.

# The Trail of Misgivings

The 1990 Turtle Mountain Reservation profile states that there are 25,022.68 acres of individual trust land on the reservation and another 8,412.12 acres within Rolette County. (Trust land is held and managed by the Federal Government.) Another 7,109.62 acres of individual trust land is located in western North Dakota in and around the town of Trenton. There are 1,800 enrolled Indian people in the Trenton area that make up a political subdivision of the Turtle Mountain Tribe. The Tribal Trust land in Rolette County is 36,265.21 acres of which 8,643.33 are on the reservation. The Federal Government owns 159.18 acres on the reservation and 30 acres off the reservation. There are 126,585.18 acres of Trust land held by individuals in Montana.

Much of the land on the Turtle Mountain Reservation is non-taxable land. The Federal Government owns some of the land; a portion of the land is held in trust by the Federal Government for the tribe and for individual Indian landowners. There is also other non-taxable land such as owned by St. Ann's Church in Belcourt. The 1993 school records indicate the remainder of the land held by owners who pay taxes has a taxable valuation amounting to $278,870. This amount is so insignificant it would not generate enough money to operate the kindergarten grades at the Turtle Mountain Community School. So both the State and the Federal Governments are depended upon for funding education on the reservation.

The State of North Dakota cannot impose taxes on trust land, or income tax on tribal members who live on the reservation. Even items like washers and dryers, or a vehicle purchased off the reservation, if delivered to the reservation, the band member is exempted from State taxes. The Federal Government also cannot impose tax on the trust land nor the income that is generated from the land. The Tribe, however, has the right to impose a sales tax on the people who purchase local goods.

The Turtle Mountain Band is commonly described as a sovereign nation owing to the fact it does possess some special tax privileges. But it is not unlimited in its powers, because the tribe surely is not independent.

A government must have both internal and external sovereignty in order to be a truly sovereign nation. Even though the tribe has internal sovereignty where it governs its people within the reservation making and enforcing laws, they lack the ability of external sovereignty where they can deal with other governments independently. The Federal Government removed the external sovereignty of the tribe whereby the tribe can deal only with them.[63]

The Cherokee won a major case in 1831–32 when the state of Georgia tried to claim Cherokee land and place the Indian under state control. The federal court recognized the tribe as a "state." Therefore, "Georgia had no right to impose their laws on the Cherokee." Chief Justice Marshall also "found that tribes, after conquest and through treaty, had agreed to be under the protection of the United States." The drawback of the Marshall decision was that the tribe lost its external sovereignty by accepting U.S. protection. It also gave legislative power over tribes.[64]

## Tribal Government

The Turtle Mountain Band of Chippewa is governed by an elected nine-member tribal council that consists of a tribal chairperson and two representatives elected from each of the four districts in Rolette County. Council members serve a two-year term. Elections are held every two years and coincide with the federal, state and county elections. Enrolled members of the Band, eighteen years and older, elect the chairperson and the councilpersons at-large. The chairperson has veto power, which is subject to over-ride by six members of the Council. This Council has the responsibility, among other things, for education moneys contracted with the Federal Government for Turtle Mountain

---

[63] *Historical Overview and Tribal Government*, p. 2 – 2.
[64] *Historical Overview and Tribal Government*, p. 2 – 5.

Figure 3-1: Turtle Mountain Reservation Tribal Council 2004–06. Back row (L to R): C. Timmy Davis (District 4), Willie Grant (District 2), Elmer Davis Jr. (District 3), Jim Baker (District 1), David "Sandy" Morin (District 3), Ron Trottier (District 2),; seated (L to R): Janice Azure (District 4), Chairman Ken W. Davis, Troy DeCoteau (District 1).

Community High School, Ojibwa Indian School and Head Start. The present Tribal Council members are: Chairman Ken W. Davis; council members: District I - Jim Baker and Troy "Big D" Decoteau; District II – Will Grant and Ron Trottier; District III – David "Sandy" Morin and Elmer Davis, Jr.; District IV – Janice LaFountain Azure and Tim Davis. Separate from this Legislative Body is the Judicial Board.

## People

In the Act of 1940, Congress defined the membership for the Chippewa Band. Thus, Congress usurped the powers of the Band to establish its membership. The flawed 1940 census was used as a basis to establish membership rolls for the Band. All the errors of the census are now "frozen into law and fact."[65] "Pilate answered, 'What I have written I have written.'"[66]

According to Debbie Gourneau Marion, Enrollment Officer, Bureau of Indian Affairs, there are presently 28,681 enrolled Indians on the Tribal roster. Of the total, 12,014 of the enrolled members live within the service area of the Bureau of Indian Affairs or within Rolette County. The remaining 16,677 people reside in every state in the Union, including the countries of Canada and West Germany.

Bob Smith, Steve Myer and others, while having coffee at the local mall, were attempting to name tribal people living in each State of the Union. Others were questioned as they came into the restaurant. Soon names were found of people living in each State plus the countries of Canada and West Germany – not including our men and women serving in the military.

The enrolled members of Turtle Mountain Band can be found in most professions. You will find doctors, pharmacists, lawyers, judges, school administrators, university/college professors, computer experts, counselors, religious, teachers, artists, entrepreneurs, nurses, law enforcement officers, newspaper editors and writers, musicians, brick layers, carpenters, electricians, plumbers, welders, contractors, foresters, engineers, photographers, traditional crafters and more working in just about all the fields of employment including show business.

## The Community

The community of Belcourt is within the boundaries of the Turtle Mountain Reservation. The 2000 census places the population at 2,440 people. There are five educational institutions: Turtle Mountain Community School (K-12), Ojibwa Indian School

---

[65] *Historical Overview and Tribal Government*, p. 1 – 10.
[66] The Jerusalem Bible: The Gospel of John 19:22.

Figure 3-2: St. Ann's Church serving the largest congregation in the area.

(K-8), St. Ann's Native American School (K-6), Head Start (preschool) and Turtle Mountain Community College.

There are three churches in the area. St. Ann's Catholic Church is the largest in the community. There is a Turtle

Figure 3-3: Gift of Hope Outreach Center.

Mountain Worship Center on the east side of town and to the west near the Knights of Columbus building is the Baptist Church, Gift of Hope Outreach Center.

Belcourt has several avenues for sharing the news and getting out information. The community has a radio station and two weekly news publications: *The Turtle Mountain Times* and *The Turtle Mountain Morning News.* The *Times'* first issue was published October 27, 1992. The *Morning News* was established in December of 1998. The KEYA radio station was established in 1974 and on air in 1975.

The Bureau of Indian Affairs Agency and BIA/Tribal Law Enforcement Agency are in a central area of town. Besides Law Enforcement and Administration, the BIA functions are Education, Employment Assistance (Job Placement Training), Employment, Facility Management, Finance, Land Operations, Probation and Parole, Probation and Pretrial, Property and Acquisition Management, Reality, Roads, and Social Services.

Nearby is the Public Health Service Clinic/Hospital that

Figure 3-5: Turtle Mountain Agency Building.

Figure 3-6: Dialysis Center.

provides health services for the Indian people. The hospital has a 29-bed capacity with a comprehensive health care clinic that is able to handle obstetrics, pediatrics, dialysis, and various kinds of surgeries. They have both air and ground ambulance services.

Figure 3-7: Fitness Center.

Figure 3-8: Quentin Burdick Memorial Hospital.

The clinic provides dental care and has a full-time optometrist and audiologist. There is also a fully staffed Mental Health Department.

The Turtle Mountain Retirement Home provides efficiency apartments for elders of the community. The older sections, which were built in two phases, have eighty rooms and presently house eighty-seven elderly people. With the completion of a new building, there will be an additional twenty rental apartments for the elderly. This building will be completed the summer of 2006. The older structure has a central dining area, and the caretakers provide tenants a hot meal daily Monday through Friday. Four recreation settings and three laundry facilities are in this section. There are also laundry and recreation areas in the new section. Each of the recreation rooms has a television set and tables for playing cards, checkers, and other games. A weekly mini bingo is scheduled for the entertainment of the residents. Tenants have an exercise program Monday, Wednesday, and Friday with many participating. Catholic Mass is scheduled each Friday. Transportation services are also available.

Figure 3-9: Turtle Mountain Retirement Home.

In the heart of town there is the mall that contains Jollie's Super Market, the county's largest grocery store, Scalp-um barbershop, Jollie's One Der Land dollar store, Karen's Restaurant, the United States Post Office, and Dacotah Branch

Figure 3-10: Jollie's Supermarket.

Figure 3-11: Mini Casino and Sheen Wah Restaurant.

Bank. At the beginning of each month, vendors display their merchandise throughout the hallways.

Across from the mall is another building owned and operated by the Tribe. It houses the mini casino that has 67 slot machines,

Figure 3-12: Belcourt Oil.

two keno machines, plus two black jack tables. Adjoining the mini casino is the Sheen Wah Chinese restaurant. In the former bowling area is Puds On and Off Sale and Laducer's Technologies.

Brunelle's Belcourt Oil Company is a distributor of LP gas, fuel oil and gasoline products. It has several trucks that deliver supplies to the local businesses and to individual customers. The business has a three-stall garage attached to the office. Other services include oil changes, tire repairs, and tire sales.

Figure 3-13: LaDots, picture taken in July of 2006.

LaDots is a conglomerate operation of a gas station and convenience store that includes a food service counter with soft drinks. In another section of the structure, it has a liquor license to operate a bar and off-sale. To the back of the building is an adjoining area that is rented for large gatherings such as wedding receptions and other festivities. To the northeast about 50 feet is LaDots Laundromat and Rainbow Automatic Car Wash.

The Utter Stop is a combined gas station and convenience store. The Lilley-Dionne Post #262 Headquarters shares the

Figure 3-14: The Utter Stop gasoline station and mini mart.

building. This land is owned by the Legionnaires, and its lease is their only means of generating money. To the south of the building, which is still Legion property, there is a Taco John in the construction stage near completion.

Figure 3-15: 1-Stop Market gas station and mini mart.

# The Trail of Misgivings

Speedy Stop and 1-Stop Market are other gasoline stations. Speedy Stop has a mini convenience store. 1-Stop operates a grocery store and is the only business not fully owned and operated by Indian people of the community.

Figure 3-16: Sky Dancer Casino.

Figure 3-17: Sky Dancer Hotel.

Sky Dancer Hotel and Casino is owned and operated by the tribe. It is located less than five miles west of Belcourt on Highways 5 and 281. The complex has 97 guestrooms, swimming pool, restaurant, meeting rooms, and is licensed to serve liquor.

Figure 3-18: Bingo Palace in the Sprung building.

The gaming area includes over 300 slot machines, six blackjack tables, a couple of poker tables.

The Turtle Mountain Bingo Palace, located in the Sprung structure, is about four miles west of Belcourt on Highways 5 and 281, and seats 500 people. In addition to holding bingo, the tribal council holds their open meetings here. Attached to the Sprung building is the Tribal Council Headquarters.

Other community services and businesses include Public Utilities, Laducer's Sanitation, an apartment complex, building supplier, construction, electrical companies, bars, restaurants, auto parts store, St. Ann's Bed and Breakfast, daycare services, Schindler's DVD and Cable TV, Ripley's Photography, thrift stores, and hair salons. There is a fitness center that is tribally

Figure 3-19: Tribal Headquarters.

operated.  There are other privately owned Indian businesses in the Dunseith, Rolla, and Rolette communities as well.

Four non-profit organizations are active in the community: Knights of Columbus, Catholic Daughters, Lilley-Dionne

Figure 3-20: Knights of Columbus.

American Legion Post #262, and Veterans of Foreign Wars (VFW), which is a Rolette County organization.

Figure 3-21: St. Ann's Centennial Monument.

# Chapter 4

# Early Education of the Turtle Mountain Indian People

As early as 1802, an Act of Congress authorized an annual appropriation of $15,000 for the purpose of civilizing the Indian tribes. Then seventeen years later, on March 3, 1819, a second Act established a permanent annual sum of $10,000 for the same purpose. The Act stipulated, "The President may, in every case where he shall judge improvement in the habits and conditions of such Indians practical, and that the means of instruction can be introduced with their own consent, employ capable persons of good moral character to instruct them in the mode of agriculture suited to their situation; and for teaching their children in reading, writing, and arithmetic. . . ."[67]

"This act remains the basic authorization for the educational activities carried out by the government in behalf of the Indian people." The annual appropriation of the Act of 1819 was distributed among the various religious organizations to be used for the purposes of educating the Indian peoples.[68]

Contrary to the idea of the separation of church and state attitude, the Federal Government and the church were closely

---

[67] Harold E. Fey and D'Arcy McNickle, p. 108.
[68] Harold E. Fey and D'Arcy McNickle, p. 108.

aligned in the early education of the American aborigines. The treaties made with the Indian people were primarily for the purpose of obtaining more land from the tribes. The treaties generally contained a provision for education. Their primary objective was to Christianize the Indian as well as civilize them.

After the treaty making between the United States and the tribes was ended in 1871, the making of agreements continued with congressional approval.[69]

It is important to recognize some of the early men and women who contributed much to the education of the Ojibwa and Métis peoples before the education system of the Turtle Mountain Reservation is discussed. These were Father George Anthony Belcourt, Father J. F. Malo (both Catholic priests), Reverend Wellington Salt of the Episcopal Church, and the Sisters of Mercy.

The community of Belcourt is named after Father Belcourt, who was born April 22, 1803, in the Province of Quebec, Canada, near the village of Bais-du-Febvre. Father Belcourt was ordained March 10, 1827.[70] No specific documentation could be found as to when he first came to the Turtle Mountain, but the *St. Ann's Centennial Book 1885 – 1985* places him in the area in the 1830's.

Father Belcourt was at odds with the Hudson Bay Company for expressing his political views and his constant siding with the Métis. This prompted Governor Simpson to write a letter dated March 3, 1848, to Father Belcourt, which says in part, ". . . the assurance you have given me that, in the event of your return to the country, you will confine yourself to the legitimate object of your mission, in no way meddling or interfering with the policies of the country. . . . Father Belcourt's differences with the Hudson Bay Company prompted his move to the Pembina area."[71]

---

[69]Felix S. Cohen, *Handbook of Federal Indian Law with Reference Table and Index*, United States Government Printing Office, Washington, 4th 1945.
[70] Reardon, pp. 3, 6.
[71] Reardon, pp. 88-89.

# The Trail of Misgivings

In the winter of 1850, Father Belcourt traveled to Mandan country. On his return trip, he was caught in a violent winter storm that nearly ended in disaster. He and his guides found protection from the storm at the foothills of the Turtle Mountain. They dug into a snow bank and waited until the storm passed. After the weather cleared, they found themselves at the foot of a high ridge. Father Belcourt named the butte, Butte St. Paul, in honor of St. Paul whose feast day fell on January 25, the day they survived the storm. They also erected a wooden cross as a monument on the top of the butte.[72] Nature or fire destroyed this monument, but others replaced it. Presently, there is a cairn of stone about ten to twelve feet high including a cross at the top. A bronze plaque on the south side of the monument has the inscription:

Figure 4-1: Inscription on Butte Saint Paul monument, found approximately 8 miles west and 5 miles north of Dunseith, ND.

## Early Educators

Murray points out that Father Belcourt's first established school for the Turtle Mountain people was at the community of St.

---

[72] Reardon, pp. 120, 121.

Joseph (now Walhala, N.D.) in 1848.[73]  That is perhaps a correct date as Reardon indicates that Father Belcourt went to Washington on behalf of the Indian people in 1854.    During    his    visit, Washington officials asked him to submit a brief in the Indians' behalf.    Within his brief, point number 6, is quoted as follows: "Six years ago I founded three schools   in   Pembina,   French, English,   and   Indian.    I   suffer privations to meet the expense each year.  Last year for the first time I received five hundred dollars.  Can I expect a continuation of this subsidy?    I   would   ask   further assistance for the building of a school, the old one being too small.

Figure 4-2: Father George Belcourt for whom the town of Belcourt is named (1803-1874). Courtesy of St. Ann's Centennial.

I have consecrated my life and soul to the welfare to these poor people, and hence I make free to address you candidly."[74]

This brief was written in 1854, and if you subtract six years you get 1848 that makes the date in Murray's paper correct; however, it is Pembina not St. Joseph at which Father Belcourt established a school for the Turtle Mountain people.  It was later in 1850 that he moved to St. Joseph, and at that time opened a new mission.  According to Reardon, the move was prompted by the constant threat of flooding in the Pembina area along the lowlands of the Red River.[75]

Father Belcourt added a postscript to his brief three days later. He asked for a regular stipend from the Federal Government so as

---

[73] Robert Murray, *History of Education in the Turtle Mountain Indian Reservation of North Dakota.* August 1953,  p. 22.

[74] Reardon, pp. 140-143.

[75] Reardon, p. 122.

to continue his educational work. He thought he could offer an education to the people if he could obtain regular yearly funding from the government. To emphasize the benefits the Indian people would receive, he outlined his school program for them as follows:[76]

1. Four hours a day of French for Indians and half breeds who want to learn the language. The number is from 30 to 38 all the year.

2. Four hours a day of English for those who wish to learn it. 20 to 25 all the year.

3. Indian for those who wish to be taught in their own language, 25 to 30 all year, a total of ninety-three children.

A small number of men come to the English school in the evening. Instruction in religion every day in the year for 80 to 100, two hours a day in different localities. The school program consists of reading, writing, arithmetic, algebra, mathematics, grammar, designing, embroidery (for girls) domestic economy and music. I have devoted my patrimony to the building a permanent school, but it is too small. It should be enlarged and improved but I have no money.

I believe the government knows what I am trying to do for the Indians and half breeds and I hope it will consider it a duty to help me in these undertakings.

There was no standard curriculum, and each teacher set up his/her own program to accommodate the students with whom they worked. The courses in mathematics were somewhat advanced to include a course in algebra. Note Father Belcourt was determined to educate the people with or without federal funding.

In 1882, Father J. F. Malo opened the first school in the area now known as Rolette County. Father Malo was one of the pioneer missionaries who came to this area from Manitoba. He built and operated this school north of St. John at the Mission of St. Claude. The school was constructed with logs and had a dirt roof. The students, in grades one through four, seated themselves

---

[76] Reardon, pp. 142-143.

on wooden benches and read from the old Harpers readers.[77] Hesketh stated that 40 students attended the school at the mission. He pointed out that, "The aim of the school is to give the Indians an English education and to teach them the industries most useful to them afterward."[78]

Figure 4-3: Father John Malo (died in 1904 at the age of 75) was buried in the St. Ann's old cemetery. Courtesy of St. Ann's Centennial.

According to Yvonne (Putch) Marion Frederick, Father Malo took two young boys to St. Joseph's School in Rensselaer, Indiana in 1889. One of these young boys was Putch's grandfather, Louis Marion, who planned to study for the priesthood.

Reverend Wellington Salt was born August 11, 1860, in Ontario, Canada, of Ojibwa ancestry. He received his high school education in Ontario, and attended college for a time. In 1887, he went to work in the lumber camps of northern Minnesota. While in Minnesota, he received an invitation to come to Fargo by Bishop Walker of the Episcopal Church. During the meeting of the two men, the Bishop requested Reverend Salt to go to the Turtle Mountain area to help the Indian people. He agreed, and in May of 1888, he arrived in Belcourt. In 1890, he took a position with the government teaching in one of the day schools on the Turtle Mountain Reservation. With the exception of a two-year period, he remained in the area the rest of his life. During his two-year absence (1900–1902) he was transferred to the Pine Ridge

---

[77] *Turtle Mountain Star,* 50th Anniversary Edition, June 23, 1938, p. 8.

[78] John Hesketh, North Dakota Historical collections Vol. V. pp. 85-154, *History of the Turtle Mountain Chippewa,* pp. 115-117.

Figure 4-4: Reverend Wellington Salt, Episcopal Minister (1860-1920). Courtesy of St. Ann's Centennial.

Reservation in South Dakota where he assumed the duties of principal of the boarding school.[79]

Reverend Salt built a mission north of Dunseith and worked with the Indian people there. Two years later he taught in one of the early log schools that the government had built in 1895. The schools were very inefficient, and new buildings were built ten years later. In 1905, the Reverend moved to a newer school structure where the Agency grounds in Belcourt are presently located.[80] According to older people living in the area, they say that the Belcourt Day School was located where Highway 5 is presently and due south of the Agency Office grounds.

When the responsibility of education changed from Federal to State jurisdiction in 1916, Reverend Salt remained as a Federal Government employee, and was assigned to the federal school north of Dunseith.[81] According the www.genealogy.com web site, he died in 1920.[82] Note that all of the men who were responsible for much of the early education of the Turtle Mountain Indian people were Canadian born and educated.

The Sisters of Mercy had a financial setback with the school and convent they founded in Yankton, South Dakota, in the 1880's. A disagreement with the bishop compounded their

---

[79] John Hesketh, pp. 115-116, *Prairie Past and Mountain Memories a History of Dunseith, N.Dak. 1882 –1982,* p. 298.

[80] *The New Earth*, Fargo Diocese's publication, June 1982, p. 16.

[81] *The New Earth*, 1984/rev. 2003.

situation. The bishop put an end to their work there. Two of the nuns, Mother Genevieve Sheridan and Sister M. Angela McCarthy then came to Belcourt in 1884, and the others returned to the Mother House in Omaha, Nebraska.[83]

Upon their arrival in 1884, the Sisters of Mercy continued with their plan to establish schools for the Indian children. They erected a 24-by-24-foot log-mud structure. It was a three-story building with a full basement. The students who attended walked to school. This was the first school in the Belcourt area, and it quickly grew

Figure 4-5: The Sisters of Mercy mission school was located in Belcourt to the west of hospital road in the vicinity of what is now St. Ann's. Picture is taken from the picture collection of the State Historical Society of North Dakota.

too small for the number of students. The nuns turned to Mother Katherine Drexel [canonized 10/1/2000] of Philadelphia for help.

---

[82] Genealogy.com. Rev. Wellington Salt, (April 2006)

[83] Sisters of Mercy of the Americas, Omaha Regional Community, *Our History: North Dakota*, p. l. (http://www.mercyoma.org/north_datkota.htm).

Mother Drexel responded with funds that enabled the nuns to erect a large school building and living quarters for the sisters. The structure was also suited to care for boarding students, thus converting the day school to also a boarding school. The school with grades one through eight had an enrollment of about 300 students. The funding for the operation of the school was mainly derived from the Sisters of Mercy; however, contributions from the local people were made in kind. They donated hides and furs that were sold in Canada. The Federal Government also met their obligation by furnishing rations for the student meals.[84]

The Sisters of Mercy school was in operation twenty-two years before it burned down in 1907. The Sisters then left Belcourt and moved to Devils Lake where the community already had opened a hospital.[85] The children were not completely left without a school since there were four newly built government schools in the area in 1905.

In 1887, St. Anthony's Day School was opened in Alcide/Laureat and was administered by Diocesan priests. It was closed in 1890 and reopened again from 1894 to 1897.[86]

## Off-Reservation Mission Schools

The local government school facilities were inadequate to handle all the students who wished to pursue an education. This resulted in the parents taking the responsibility for their children's education, and sending them to off-reservation mission schools. In search for reasons, former students were asked the question why they attended these mission boarding schools. Their responses were that it was the proper thing to do as a good Catholic, and it relieved their parents of some financial responsibilities in winter months. (Those contacted were people who attended mission high schools in the 1950's.) Another reason given was that they

---

[84] Robert Murray, p. 26.

[85] *The New Earth*, June 1982, p. 16.

[86] Fargo Diosease's publication 1984/rev. 2003.

Figure 4-6: A typical schoolhouse of the early 1900's. Picture taken circa 1930's shows its use for a Mass celebrated by Fr. Hildebrand.

followed their friends. Many children went to far away boarding schools because of broken homes, or they were orphaned, or for some other hardship reason.

It was nearly thirty years before a Catholic missionary built another school in the Belcourt area. Even so, missionaries continued to educate the Turtle Mountain people in academic and religious instructions by encouraging them to attend mission boarding schools. Many of the students from the Turtle Mountain found themselves in mission schools miles away from home.

The mission school at Seven Dolors at Fort Totten, North Dakota housed students from the Belcourt area in the late 1890's. According to Sister Anthony Davis, an Oblate of the Blessed Sacrament, and an elder member of the Turtle Mountain Band, Seven Dolors Mission School was destroyed by fire around 1925 while she was in attendance as a third grader. Those students attended the government school at Fort Totten while the mission school was being rebuilt. In the fall of 1928, the mission re-opened its doors under the name of Little Flower School at St. Michael near Fort Totten.

The Benedictines were responsible for a number of mission sites. Their Immaculate Conception Mission was an Indian school at Stephan, South Dakota that many students from the Belcourt area attended. According to the Stephan web site, the school was established in 1886. They were funded by the Bureau of Catholic Indian Missions for the construction of an 18-by-30 foot building. They also received financial help from Katherine Drexel. The school was located on the Crow Creek Reservation in South Dakota. The Benedictine's St. Paul's Indian Mission (Marty, SD) and Priests of the Sacred Heart's St. Joseph's Indian Mission (Chamberlain, SD) were two other mission schools that provided education for the children of the Turtle Mountain community area.

Enrollment at these schools continued to increase. Murray reports that in 1925 there were 17 students attending Little Flower Mission at St. Michael, and 9 were enrolled at Marty, South Dakota. In 1930, there were 95 students attending all four mission schools at Stephan, Marty, St. Michael and Chamberlain. In the 1952-53 school term that total climbed to 194 students for the four mission schools. The individual school attendance was 50 students for Stephan, 32 students for Chamberlain, St. Michael had 56 children for its enrollment, and Marty had a total enrollment of 56 pupils all from the Turtle Mountain area.[87]

It is not surprising that many families wished to send their children to mission boarding schools because the people in the area were pre-dominantly Catholic and these were Catholic schools.

Stories of the unduly firm, strict and harsh disciplines and practices in the early days, at these mission boarding schools, cast dark shadows. (The federal boarding schools practices are no exception). Mrs. Stella Delorme Garcia attended Marty Mission

---

[87] Robert Murray, pp. 29, 33.

as a high school student from 1935 – 1938. She describes her boarding school experience as "tough." She witnessed the younger children being physically punished, and this caused her much anguish.[88]

Nearly twenty years later, conditions seemed to have improved for the older students, but there are boarding school horror stories as late as the 1970's. Some former students when questioned about their experiences at boarding school just shake their heads in dismay and refuse to comment. Patti Jeanotte Belgarde and many others who were recently interviewed speak highly of their mission boarding school experiences as high school students.

The inside cover and the following page of Patti Belgarde's copy of Marty Indian Mission 1956-yearbook – *Smoke Signals,* have a summer aerial photo of St. Paul Indian Mission. There is a striking view of the majestic church with a high steeple and a cross on the top that dominates the attractive boarding school campus. Turtle Mountain students appear in every class picture. Names such as Jeanotte, Dauphinais, Azure, Frederick, Baker and others appear throughout the book identifying Turtle Mountain students. The student enrollment was 121 high school students and 282 for the elementary grades for a total student population of 403. Slightly over ten percent of the student count came from the Turtle Mountain area.

## School Districts Established

Dunseith School District #1 was formed June 23, 1885. Twenty-one more school districts in Rolette County were established before 1900. The Mylo School District #26 was formed November 8, 1907. Nine years later, however, the last two school districts to be established in the county were Couture School District #27 and Ingebretson #28. These two latecomers were established within the Turtle Mountain Reservation July 18,

---

[88] Personal Interview with Mrs. Garcia. June 2006.

1916.[89]   The boundaries of these two districts coincide with the boundaries of the Reservation proper dividing the six-by-twelve-mile tract of land in two sections with Couture School District in the eastern half and Ingebretson School District in the western half.

Even though the districts were both established on the same date, the Couture School District elected its board of directors in 1917.  Three people were chosen as directors to serve on the board. They were S. T. Ladoucer, Joseph L. Ladoucer, and John R. Wilkie.  One year later in 1918 the Ingebretson District elected George A. Courteau, David Dauphinais and John Renault for the board of directors.[90]   Each district board consisted of three members elected at large from the eligible voters of the district with two members appointed by the board of directors.   The treasurer and the clerk were board-appointed non-voting members.

Murray states that the establishment of the two school districts came about because, ". . . it was felt by the people of the reservation and by the Rolette County authorities, that the Turtle Mountain people were ready to assume full responsibility for their own educational facilities."[91]   However, the tax base on the Turtle Mountain Reservation would not have been adequate to generate enough money to operate a school system, and the people would not have been so naïve as to believe they could run a school without money.   The government had contracted with early missionaries up to the time Congress no longer appropriated money for that purpose.  Therefore, it is highly unlikely that the local people made the first move.

Murray's source in the above paragraph is from the Turtle Mountain Superintendent's Annual Report, which in reality is the superintendent's opinion or his method of "washing his hands of it."  It is very likely that the superintendent encouraged the local

---

[89] *Turtle Mountain Star*, 50th Anniversary Edition, June 23, 1938, p. 8.
[90] Rolette County Records.
[91] Robert Murray, p. 37.

people to take the responsibility for the education of their own children, and the Federal Government, in turn, would transfer the existing buildings including the equipment and supplies to the districts. In addition, the government offered a tuition payment for each student attending the schools. Then and only then would the local people accept that responsibility.

Nevertheless, the aforementioned stipulations were in the contract that the districts made with the government. In addition, the child to be educated had to possess ¼ or more Indian blood. The tuition payments were paid on a quarterly basis. The payments were derived, ". . . by figuring the exact per pupil cost of education which was borne locally, or would have to be borne locally, if taxes were levied on the non-taxable lands."[92] The kicker for the Federal Government was they would pay the districts only for actual days the student attended. The Federal Government had problems keeping the students in school for various reasons (too far to walk, overcrowded buildings, lack of trust, etc.). A clause for the noon lunch was mentioned in the contract. The government would pay the food cost to any school offering a noon meal to the students. Not all schools offered a school lunch program even with this stipulation in the contract. A greater allowance was stipulated in the contract for the curriculum improvement – such as the hiring of qualified teachers, furnishing improved teaching supplies and improving the plant facilities.[93]

In an attempt to rectify the attendance problem, the Federal Government made it mandatory. They hoped that if they placed the local people in charge of the school, the poor attendance situation might change. If it did not, the blame would be on the local people. Payment for only the actual days the student attended school was a hindrance to the local boards during the transitional period of running the schools. It was difficult to get effective teachers to come to a remote area such as the Turtle Mountain.

---

[92] Robert Murray, p. 38.
[93] Robert Murray, pp. 38-39.

# The Trail of Misgivings

*The Turtle Mountain Star* mentioned that in 1898, the teacher's salary was $35 per month. A male teacher received about $5.40 more on the average than a female teacher. In 1937 the average teacher salary was $80.01 per month. The male teacher received $91.65 as average monthly salary while the female received an average of $72.49 monthly.[94] The average pay for teachers in the Turtle Mountain Reservation in 1919 was $80 per month for Couture School District and $70 per month for Ingebretson School District. Couture had a teacher with a college degree who received $90 per month. The other teachers, who were high school graduates, received $75 per month. All Ingebretson's teachers were people who at least had finished high school.[95]

The Rolette County Teacher's Report reveals that the school terms varied from 20 to 140 days. One might suspect that the children went only 20 days per year in some years, but that was not the case. A school may have started a term on March 31, and ended on July 1 and began another term July 5, and ended on December 12.[96]

On the next page is one of the day school's Daily Program and Classification reports of 1919 (Table 4-1). This report is from Ingebretson School #1. Its school term was for 20 days beginning July 1 and ending July 25. The teacher taught grades one through eight:[97]

In 1918, the Bureau created a Day School Inspector position to deal with and report on the district schools. This inspector assumed the duties of making contracts with the two districts. He monitored students attending non-reservation schools. He made regular visits to the Couture and Ingebretson Schools to determine whether the districts were fulfilling their contractual obligations. One of the problems that appeared as soon as the district schools

---

[94] 50th Anniversary Edition, *The Turtle Mountain Star*, June 23, 1838, p. 8.

[95] Rolette County Records, Teacher's Report, 1919.

[96] Rolette County Records, Teacher's Report, 1919.

[97] Rolette County Records, Teacher's Report, 1919.

## Table 4-1: Teacher's Report of 1919

| Time (begin) | Length (min.) | Subject | Grade | Pupils (by reference number) |
|---|---|---|---|---|
| 10:00 | 10 | **Opening Exercises** | | |
| 10:10 | 10 | Arithmetic | Primary A | 30, 34, 36, 33, 7, 18, 19, 21, 23, 24, 25 |
| 10:20 | 10 | Arithmetic | Primary B | 35, 39, 3, 5, 6, 10, 14, 22, 26, 31, 32 |
| 10:30 | 10 | Arithmetic | First | 17 |
| 10:40 | 10 | Arithmetic | Second | 3 |
| 10:50 | 10 | Arithmetic | Third | 4 |
| 11:00 | 10 | Arithmetic | Fifth | 2 |
| 11:10 | 20 | Arithmetic | Eight | 1, 20 |
| 11:30 | | **Recess** | | |
| 11:45 | 15 | Reading | Primary A | same as primary arith. |
| 12:00 | 10 | Reading | Primary B | same as primary arith. |
| 12:10 | 10 | Reading | First | 17, 13 |
| 12:20 | 10 | Reading | Second | 4 |
| 12:30 | 15 | Reading and Physiology | Fifth | 2 |
| 12:45 | 15 | Reading | Eight | 1, 20 |
| 1:00 | | **Noon Intermission** | | |
| 2:00 | 15 | Reading | Primary A | same as primary arith. |
| 2:15 | 10 | Reading | Primary B | same as primary arith. |
| 2:25 | 10 | Reading | First | 17, 13 |
| 2:35 | 10 | Reading | Second | 4 |
| 2:45 | 15 | Language | Third | 4 |
| 3:00 | 15 | Language | Fifth | 2 |
| 3:15 | 7 | History | Fifth | 2 |
| 3:22 | 8 | Grammar | Eight | 1, 20 |
| 3:30 | | **Recess** | | |
| 3:45 | 8 | Reading | Primary A | same as primary arith. |
| 3:53 | 8 | Reading | Primary B | same as primary arith. |
| 4:01 | 8 | Reading | First | 17 |
| 4:09 | 8 | Spelling | Third | 13, 4 |
| 4:17 | 8 | Geography | Fifth | 2 |
| 4:25 | 11 | Geography and Civics | Eight | 1, 20 |
| 4:36 | 8 | Spelling | Fifth | 2 |
| 4:42 | 8 | Spelling | Eight | 1, 20 |
| 4:50 | 10 | Oral Physiology & Writing | | |
| 5:00 | | **Dismissal** | | |

became operable was that there were students living within the districts not meeting the Bureau criteria of ¼ Indian and others who were not of Indian descent at all. These students had to be educated.[98] The districts were responsible for their education. One cannot imagine the State not paying some cost for these students.

## The Need for New School Buildings

In 1917, the Couture School District board assumed responsibility for the operation of one school the Federal Government turned over to them. In 1919, Couture was given a second school, and that same year the board built an additional third school at a cost of $860.67. In 1924, they constructed a fourth school at a cost of $677.66 to meet the demands of the increasing enrollment. Couture School District then had four schools in the district – two were one-room schools and two schools had two or more teachers. Belcourt school had two or more teachers.[99] It is possible that these buildings were actually add-ons to existing buildings. The cost is considerably less than what Ingebretson paid for its schools.

In 1926, one of the one-room schools must have closed as the Rolette County record shows that Couture listed three schools – one was a one-room school and two schools had two or more teachers. However, Couture identified five schools within its boundaries in the 1928 report. The County report indicates four schools were one-room structures and one school was designed for two or more teachers. (When and how these two other schools came about is not recorded and how the loss of a school that had two or more teachers is not explained.) In 1929, 1930 and 1931, Couture again listed three schools – two one-room schools and one school for two or more teachers.[100]

---

[98] Robert Murray, p. 40.
[99] Rolette County Records, Clerks' Annual Report for year ending June 30, 1919, 1922 and 1924.
[100] Rolette County Records, Clerk's Annual Reports for year ending June 30, 1926 and 1928 – 1931.

Ingebretson School District took charge of two schools in its district in 1919. That same year the board built a third school at the cost of $1,187.75. Ingebretson School District found it necessary to construct a fourth school in 1924 to meet the needs of its growing number of students. According to county records, a fifth school was built at a cost of $1,975 in 1925. However, the amount of four schools remained on the report, which could indicate a replacement school. Two of these schools were single classrooms, and the other two were two or more teachers schools. These four schools were in operation until the Bureau opened the Turtle Mountain Consolidated School in 1931.[101]

These new additions brought the total number to seven schools that served students on the reservation in 1925. There were then four schools in Ingebretson and three schools in Couture.

It must be "in the eye of the beholder" that others saw the need for additional space long before the Federal Government. Murray mentions in his thesis the need for more classrooms and more schools came after the districts' assumed responsibility. The need was there before the districts' takeover. The Sisters of Mercy School burned ten years before the government control of education had been transferred over to the districts. Their school housed 300 students, and the Bureau built four one-room school structures to assist the overflow of the mission school. Granted some children were sent off to boarding schools, but those four buildings were inadequate to accommodate the number of students in the area. Ingebretson built a school the same year of the takeover and continued to build until 1925. Couture built a school as it assumed the responsibility of its second school in 1919. The Rolette County Records do not indicate whether the districts were replacing schools that the Bureau turned over or schools that were built by the boards.

---

[101] Rolette County Records, Clerks Annual Reports for Ingebretson year ending June 30, 1919 – 1926, and 1928 - 1931.

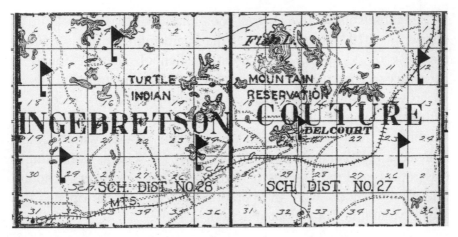

Figure 4-7: Map of reservation schools between 1905 and 1931.

Murray's Table II on his page 41, indicates the schools were re-numbered #1 through #3 in the Couture District and #1 through #4 in the Ingebretson District. Apparently, Ingebretson just numbered the newer two schools as #1 and #2, with the older schools retaining #3 and #4 as previously assigned. The additional school in Couture School District was located in the northeast part of Couture Township section twelve. This school was named School #3 for identification purposes. It was also called the Kanick School (see map on Figure 4-7). In the Ingebretson School District both schools were built in the northern part of the township. The first school, or School #1 was located in NE¼ Section nine of Ingebretson Township. School #2 was located in the NW¼ of Section eighteen. The previous numbers assigned to Gourneau and Roussin Schools must have remained the same.

# Chapter 5

## Early Government Schools on the Turtle Mountain Reservation

It is not surprising to learn that the first federal schools to appear on the reservation were log structures. These one-room log school buildings were built in 1895 in the more populated areas on the reservation where they were able to serve the most families.[102]

According to Murray, these schools were very inadequate – lacking equipment and proper teaching tools. They provided studies for grades one through three, and each classroom housed about twenty-five students. The students were over-aged, fourteen or fifteen years old, and their attendance was very irregular thus hampering their achievements.[103] There was never a single explanation why the attendance was so poor and the students were over-aged. It has already been said that it may have been because there were no educational facilities within walking distance from the student's home, or there were too few schools and those few were overcrowded, or the parents had a lack of trust in the Federal Government and questioned what good an education would do for their children.

---

[102] Robert Murray, p. 72.
[103] Robert Murray, p. 72.

# The Trail of Misgivings

Murray states that one of those log schools was built one and a half miles southeast of the old Roussin School. The Roussin landmark is no longer there. An old *Rolette County Atlas* marks the old Roussin School in the NE¼ of the SW¼, Section Twenty-nine of Ingebretson Township. One and a half miles southeast of Roussin School would place the log school in Section Thirty-three of Ingebretson.

The second log school was built in the community of Belcourt. Murray stated, ". . . where the present Agency is presently located." The Rolette County atlas identifies the Agency location to be in both Sections Twenty and Twenty-one of Couture Township. An old map of Couture Township places the school in Section Twenty. The map identifies other locations fairly accurately so the reference seems to be reliable. According to local elders they indicate that the school would be very close to Highway 5. There was no highway running through this area until 1942.

The third log school was located about two and a half miles southeast of Belcourt according to Murray. This school could be located in the northwest quarter of Section Twenty-six of Couture Township.[104]

The Federal Government abandoned these log schools after ten years, and rebuilt four larger schools in 1905 and 1906. These schools were constructed to alleviate the crowded conditions at the Belcourt Mission School operated by the Sisters of Mercy. The school buildings conformed to the common school design that the Federal Government built in other parts of Indian Country.[105]

Each building had one classroom and a kitchen for cooking the noon meal for the students. A section of the building was used

---

[104] Atlas Rolette County, North Dakota, Thomas O. Nelson Co. Fergus Falls Minnesota, 1959, p. 3.

[105] Turtle Mountain Star, p. 25.

as living quarters for the teacher. With each school, a barn was built to keep a team of horses and perhaps a cow.[106]

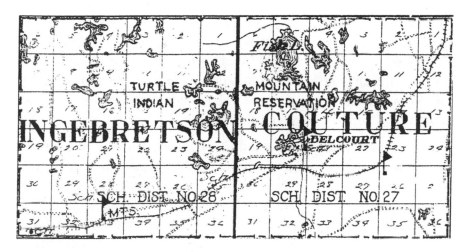

Figure 5-1: Log schools of 1885 to 1905.

A conversation with Mrs. Elise LaFromboise, age 90, and her son Richard "Jiggers" LaFromboise January 6, 2006, made it possible to locate the four schools mentioned above. The schools were built in populated areas within the reservation to accommodate as many students as possible within walking distance of the school. The Federal Government assigned numbers to each school for identification purposes. The people quickly re-named them associating the name with the land on which the school was built. School #1 was in the Belcourt community on federal land, located near where the log school was formerly built. School #2 was located in Couture Township in Section Twenty-six about three miles south and east of the Belcourt community. It was known as the Wilkie School. School #3 was about three miles west of Belcourt and in Ingebretson Township, Section 25. It was called the Gourneau School. School #4, known as Roussin School

---

[106] Robert Murray, p. 73.

was in Ingebretson Township, Section 29 as mentioned earlier. It was about six miles west and one mile south of Belcourt.

Grades one through six were taught in these schools. They were larger than the old log schools and accommodated about 30 students each. The government sought to hire a married male teacher so that the wife could be employed as a housekeeper and cook for the students. She would also have the duties of teaching cooking and sewing to the girls. The schools still had to contend with the problem of over-aged students.[107]

The teacher had extra community responsibilities in addition to his teaching duties. He was expected to be liaison officer for the Federal Government. These functions included the issuing of rations (commodities), settling disputes of law and order cases, raising a vegetable garden for the school noon lunches during the school year as well as setting an example for the families in the school area to follow. He served as a nurse administering first aid, and actually ran a small farm besides his duties as teacher. A team of horses was at his disposal for transportation, and for plowing and cultivating the land for the garden. He maintained one or two cows that produced the milk for the school lunch program. At the school there were different pieces of farm machinery on hand, and were made available to Indian people living in the area for their personal use.[108]

Each school served as a hub for community activities. Dances and card parties were held there along with other entertainment events such as the organization of ball teams and adult classes.[109]

---

[107] Robert Murray, pp. 73-74.
[108] Robert Murray, p. 74.
[109] Robert Murray, p. 74.

# Early Government Schools on the Turtle Mountain Reservation

## Curriculum

In 1909, Miss Estelle Reel, Director of Indian Schools, issued the course of study set forth for Indian schools throughout Indian Country: [110]

An outline course of study for the Indian schools is herewith submitted to you, and I trust it will receive your cordial and active support.

The course is designed to give teachers a definite idea of the work that should be done in the schools to advance the pupils as speedily as possible to usefulness and citizenship.

The aim of the course is to give the Indian child knowledge of the English language, and to equip him with the ability to become self-supporting as speedily as possible.

Methods of instruction and subjects of study have their limitations in value, and in view of the aims and purpose in educating the Indian, who is just starting on the road to civilization, such methods must be employed as will develop the various powers and capacities with which the child is endowed, and by systematic industrial training to give him the skill in various directions designed to be serviceable in meeting the demands of active life, making him a willing as well as an inquiring learner.

. . . . In this course, practical lessons in every branch are outlined. The child learns to speak the English language through doing the work that must be accomplished in any well regulated home, and at the same time is being trained in habits of industry, cleanliness and system. He learns to read by telling of his daily interests and work with the chalk on the blackboard. In dealing with barrels of fruit, bushels of wheat, yards of gingham, and quarts of milk; in keeping count of his poultry and in measuring his garden, he comes familiar with the numbers in such a practical way that he knows how to use them in daily life.

It should be the constant aim of the teacher to follow this course and do as much more in each grade as he or she has time to accomplish; but the chief end in view should be the attainment of practical knowledge by the pupil, and no teacher should feel restrained from asserting his or her individuality in bringing the pupils mind to a

---

[110] Robert Murray, pp. 75-76. Dept. of Interior, Course of Study for the Indian Schools, Washington Government Printing Office, 1901, pp. 5-9.

realization of the right way of living and in emphasizing the dignity and nobility of labor.

As far as possible, teach the children that cultivation of good habits, self-control, application, and responsiveness are recognized as being on a higher educational plane than a knowledge of definitions and unimportant dates; that the development of character is the only imperishable object for which we can work; that consequences follow action with unfailing certainty; and that "it is the purpose that inspires use and the motive that holds us to our task that limits the extent and value of our service. . . .

Murray stated the course of study that followed the introduction outlined the courses for older students, and the courses were vocational in nature. Courses such as agriculture, basketry, bakery, carpentry, harness making, printing, shoemaking, engineering, dairying and tailoring were emphasized. Many of these same types of courses were offered in the boarding schools.[111] Only a small area of the study guide was intended for the schools in this area at the time it was published. The Turtle Mountain schools had only grades one through six. Murray alluded to this fact, stating, "The lower grades, which included the ones then offered on the Turtle Mountain reservation were chiefly interested in the outline on reading, language, and sub-primary work; arithmetic, spelling, nature study, cooking, music and gardening were covered in the course."[112]

Much of the course of study that Murray described fit the well-acquainted course of study of the 1940's. Girls studied basketry, pottery, arts and crafts, and sewing in home economics. Boys attending the Turtle Mountain Community School took agriculture and carpentry classes from grades seven through twelve. Those subjects were mandatory for all male students. The Bureau of Indian Affairs still had the idea that all Indian men should be farmers. It must have slipped their minds that the

---

[111] Robert Murray, p. 77.
[112] Robert Murray, p. 77.

government had just stripped them of their land. Or perhaps they thought the white farmers needed skilled labor on their farms.

Figure 5-2: Vegetable garden.

The report of the Committee of One Hundred was released in 1924. One of the sections studied was on Indian Education. The committee report "recommended an increase in federal appropriations for the appointment of competent personnel, provision of adequate school facilities, increased Indian enrollment in public schools, and scholarships in high schools and colleges for Indian youngsters."[113]

The same year Haskell Institute was the only school where the Federal Government offered courses beyond the eighth grade. The report left the Bureau scrambling to make improvements. The government's response was to make an effort to increase Indian students in public schools and to tailor their curriculum after the state curriculum. All federal day schools on reservations offered

---

[113] Fey and McNickle, p. 112.
For comment on the recommendations of the Committee of One Hundred, see Downes, "A Crusade for Reform," Chapter X.

work through the sixth grade. Reservation federal boarding schools extended studies to the eighth grade while some off-reservation boarding schools extended work beyond the eighth grade. In 1929, there were only six government schools offering high school courses.[114]

## Off Reservation Federal Schools

In the early 1900's, there were people living north of Dunseith that neither the Federal Government nor the State Government would recognize as their educational responsibility. The tract of land that these people lived on was in the Dunseith School District. State law requires each district to educate the children in its jurisdiction. However, these people had land held in trust by the Federal Government; therefore, the district argued that these people were the responsibility of the Federal Government.

It is not known how long the disagreement went on. The Dunseith School District #1 was established June 23, 1885, before the allotment period. Ten years later the Federal Government began building schools on the reservation. Before that time, the Federal Government was dependent on mission or public schools to educate Indian children living on the reservation. Today it is clearly stated in both federal and state laws that each has the responsibility for the education of these people.

In 1912, the Federal Government finally gave in and made the move to build a school about two and a half miles north of Dunseith. Since the government had four other schools on the reservation this school became Day School #5 or the Dunseith Day School. This school was typical of the other schools on the reservation. It offered education for students in grades one through six. The number of students was limited to 30. There were many

---

[114] Fey and McNickle, p. 112.

more pupils who lived in the area and still did not have an opportunity for an education.[115]

The *North Dakota Blue Book* pays a tribute to the Federal Government for the advancement of Indian Education: ". . . wisdom of those holding his future, 'in trust' than to cite that in less than a quarter of a century the Indians have advanced from a stage of barbarian to a form of our own civilization and those responsible for his welfare had adopted methods entirely in keeping with this progress."[116] Today's elders do not consider their fathers and mothers as barbaric or inferior in anyway, but that is a notch above a savage.

The *Blue Book* also mentions schools in North Dakota for Indian children that were located in Bismarck, Fort Totten, Fort Berthold, Fort Yates, Belcourt and Wahpeton.[117] The Indian school at Bismarck opened about the year 1908. It closed its doors nine years later in 1917 when the Commissioner of Indian Affairs did not see the necessity of keeping the school in operation especially since it was not self-supporting. It reopened January 1, 1919. Besides the regular academics of the times – reading, writing and arithmetic – industrial and vocational work were taught to the pupils. The boys learned subjects relating to the raising and caring of farm animals. The girls were taught how to care for the home, which included cooking, sewing, and washing cloths.[118] The Bismarck Indian school was permanently closed in 1937.[119]

---

[115] Robert Murray, p. 80.

[116] *North Dakota Blue Book –1919*, Legislative Manual, Published under the Direction of Thomas Hall. Secretary of State, Bismarck Tribune Co. Printing and Binding, Bismarck, North Dakota, p. 331.

[117] *N.D. Blue Book*, p. 131.

[118] *N.D. Blue Book*, p. 232.

[119] David P. Gray and Gerald G. Newborg, *North Dakota a Pictorial History,* The Donning Company/Publishers Norfolk/Virginia Beach, 1988, p. 35.

# The Trail of Misgivings

The military post at Fort Totten was established in 1867. In 1882, a federal act authorized the use of any abandoned military facilities for the education of Indian children. The Fort was decommissioned in 1890. It was turned over to the local government officials. The industrial and mission schools were then consolidated. In 1890, however, the Federal Government abolished contract schools, and the Grey Nuns from St. Boniface in Winnipeg, Manitoba, Canada, who operated the school, then accepted positions as teachers.[120]

## Insights

Ferdinand and Emily LaFromboise Jerome attended school at Fort Totten. Ferdinand talked about his problem of not being able to speak the English language when he went to school in the late 1890's and early 1900's. The requirement at school was that the native tongue was not to be spoken. One could easily understand his dilemma. Emily's son, Joe, remembers her telling about how she and her younger sister, Rose, traveled in a wagon to get to the Fort. She mentioned that her sister was very young. Their graduating class pictured below indicated a sixth grade achievement. Most Federal Government boarding schools extended the course of study to include eight grades in 1923. The picture was taken in 1922. According to Rose's daughter-in-law, Theresa Brien, Rose completed her 7th and 8th grades at the Bismarck Indian School before attending Haskell, at Lawrence, Kansas.

Leon Poitra, an elder, talked about his early school days. Leon stated, "They shipped me off to Fort Totten on a bus of a kind in 1927." He said he spoke no English at the time and the Sioux he met spoke no English. He added, "In time he began learning a

---

[120] Cheryl Rose Marion Kulas, *The Impact of Indian Education courses on The Instruction of Teachers in North Dakota,* A Thesis Submitted to the Committee on American Indian Studies in Partial Fulfillment of the Requirements for the Degree of Master of Arts In The Graduate College, The University of Arizona, 1989, pp. 41-43.

little bit Sioux and English." (This story was related on December 30, 2000.)

Figure 5-3: 6th Grade graduation, Fort Totten, ND. From left to right standing (Mary Morin, unknown, Adele Grandboise, Rose LaFromboise), from left to right seated (Agnes Azure, Florestine Jacquemart, Emily LaFromboise).

On a different occasion, another elder, Pete Delorme, related the following story. "They put me on a train at Rolla with my older brother Bill and other students from the Turtle Mountain. When the train came to a stop at Devils Lake, they took me off the train, and sent me to Fort Totten while my brother Bill was left on the train to continue his journey to Wahpeton. I had tears in my eyes when my older brother Bill went on to Wahpeton." According to his daughter, Lillian Delorme Houle, the year was about 1912. He was about eight years old. She said, he stayed at Fort Totten until he finished the sixth grade. He must have cried many days and nights. How legal was it to take the children from their homes and send them to far away schools for years at a time?

# The Trail of Misgivings

Sandy Belgarde Thomas recalls her dad, Martin Belgarde, relating the ordeal he went through when his mother and two brothers died in a flu epidemic in 1917 or 1918. He was not allowed to come home from Fort Totten for their funerals. "Can you imagine the pain of coming home at the end of the school year with no mother and two of his brothers gone? He was 11 or 12 at the time."[121]

If parents were not cooperative with sending their children to school, the government representatives were allowed to withhold rations from the family according to a policy of the Federal Government since 1877. There were only four government day schools in the area when Pete was of school age. Those schools were inadequate to accommodate all the children. Therefore, boarding schools were the alternative and actually the preferred schools of the government at the time. The more distance from home the better. The child could not run away, and boarding schools separated all influences of the parents from the child. The people in charge had to be insensitive and cruel to make those decisions. The government employees surely committed an act of child abuse. To separate siblings was another count of child abuse. It must have been heartbreaking for both children and parents. "Barbaric" describes this treatment.

## Why Educate the Indian?

The question to be asked: Why educate the Indian? Was it for the purpose of civilizing the Indian? Or was there another reason? In the late 1700's, the Cherokee Nation decided to become civilized. With the aid of missionaries, and other help that was provided in their treaty with the United States, they set themselves up in farming and had an educational system. In exchange for the assistance the United States gave them, the Cherokee tribe ceded

---

[121] Note from Sandy Thomas, July 9, 2006.
*St. Ann's Centennial*, 1885-1985, p. 224, states the 1918-1919 flu epidemic caused the deaths of hundreds of people on the Turtle Mountain Reservation; whole families were wiped out.

land. In 1830, when the eastern frontier became crowded, and the white man needed more land, Congress passed the Indian Removal Act. The Cherokees went to court to be recognized as a self-governing society, won their case, yet were forcibly uprooted from their homes and were forced to relocate west of the Mississippi. President Jackson refused to recognize the court decision of Chief Justice John Marshall. The other four of the Five Civilized Tribes – the Choctaw, Creek, Seminole, and the Chickasaw tribes suffered the same fate.[122] The purpose of education now became clearer. Land was what the white man wanted, and they demanded more. The white man wanted to civilize the Indians because their lifestyle (hunting) in the plains occupied too much land; their scheme was education. Ship the children off to far away boarding schools. "Kill the Indian and save the man," was the motto of Colonel, later General, Pratt, who headed the Carlisle Indian School in Pennsylvania. Then give them a small piece of land and make them docile farmers. Thus was the "Trail of Tears" to education.

Most Indian children had to travel *the trail of misgivings – a scourging journey*. They were sent to boarding schools that were programmed to depersonalize and destroy the child's identity. However, the trail to education had become more tolerable and productive in recent years. Some students have had a favorable experience while attending a federal boarding school in the late 1940's and early 1950's and vouch for the improved educational standards, living conditions, and effective human relationships, yet retaining their tribal identity. However, there are other students who have haunting memories.

To date, only a few Turtle Mountain children still attend schools at Wahpeton, North Dakota, Flandreau and Pierre, South Dakota. This 2005–06 school term, Pierre has 31 students in grades one through eight from the Turtle Mountain Reservation.[123] Wahpeton Indian School student population is gradually

---

[122] Fey & McNickle, pp. 30-31, 93-94.
[123] Letter from Pierre Indian Learning Center dated 2/16/2006.

decreasing. During the 1972–73 school year, 190 Turtle Mountain students were enrolled there. By the 1985–86 school year, the number of Turtle Mountain students had dropped to 61. Flandreau Indian School had 36 students from the Turtle Mountain area in 1976–77 school year. In the 1981–82 school year, the Turtle Mountain enrollment at Flandreau dropped to 12; however, in the 1985-86 school year it jumped back to 38.[124]

In 1889, the Commissioner of Indian Affairs announced he would no longer contract with sectarian schools for the education of Indian children. His actions created some controversy, and the practice of funding continued for a time, but on a smaller scale. In 1897, Congress settled the issue by not appropriating funds for the operation of sectarian schools. The Supreme Court upheld the action by Congress in 1908. The Bureau of Indian Affairs enrolled Indian children in public schools as early as 1890. The Bureau reimbursed the school districts for whatever increases in cost the Indian students incurred.[125]

By the turn of the twentieth century, there were 307 government, mission, and private schools for Indian children with a total enrollment of 26,451, and yet only 246 students were in public schools. The total enrollment of Indian students increased significantly by 1926. In just twenty-six years, this enrollment stood at 69,892. The big increase was in the public school enrollment with a total of 37,730.[126] The government finally did have some success in getting many Indian students to attend public school, however, they were not concerned about the students' needs being met.

Stories of the horrors of boarding schools echo clearly from the past hinting that this same prejudice still exists today. The April 3, 2006, edition of the *Turtle Mountain Times* reports that the

---

[124] TM Agency Records.
[125] Fey & McNickle, p. 111.
[126] Fey & McNickle, p. 111.

American Civil Liberties Union (ACLU) recently filed a civil rights lawsuit on behalf of the Indian students against the Winner School District. The lawsuit alleges that the South Dakota district is forcing the Indian students to sign confessions for breaking minor rules. The signed confessions are used many times to convict the students in Juvenile Court according to ACLU. Jennifer Ring, the executive director of the Dakotas ACLU had this comment: "These experiences demonstrate the reasons why Native American children so often fail to reach graduation – hostility of peers, discrimination of school officials and knee-jerk police involvement." The lawsuit indicates that within the Winner School the Indian students were "more than three times more likely to be suspended and 10 times more likely to be referred to law officers than are white students." According to the *Times'* article forced confessions were obtained from the students by isolating the students in a room depriving them bathroom privileges and the right to call their parents.[127] To prejudge the outcome of this case would be a *misgiving*. [128]

## Bureau Setbacks

Three reports or surveys from different study groups bring the failure of Indian Education to light. The first study was conducted by the Committee of One Hundred in 1923. This committee concentrated on the needs of Indian education, even though their efforts covered other aspects of Indian affairs. The recommendations were to increase federal funding ". . . for the appointment of competent personnel, provision of adequate school facilities, increased Indian enrollment in public schools, and scholarships in high schools and colleges for Indian youngsters." The Bureau of Indian Affairs immediately began to enroll more students in public schools. The Bureau schools revised their

---

[127] *Turtle Mountain Times*, Belcourt N.D. April 3, 2006, p. 8B.

[128] In the 1970's, the Belcourt School Superintendent recalls coming to the rescue of a TMC Middle School student serving ten days in the Rolette County jail for stealing a 29 cent candy bar.

course of study to be modeled after the public schools and extended grades taught in day schools to grade six.[129]

The Meriam report of 1928 was the second setback for Indian Education in the Bureau. The survey harshly judged the concept of the boarding schools. More than 80 percent of Indian children who attended government schools were enrolled in boarding schools. The care for the children in these boarding schools was inadequate. The diet, the dormitories, the medical services were all substandard. The manual work that the students performed may have violated child labor laws. The Meriam survey did recognize that the boarding schools provided services to those students who did not live near a school, students without parents, and those students experiencing other hardships, such as coming from broken homes. The report also recommended that the schools should provide a course of study parallel to other state educational systems for a student who wished to further his/her education. The survey favored adult use of the day schools for various community activities. The report further recommended that "Indian day schools be increased in number and improved in quality." Attention was given to "overageness" of the children attending Bureau schools. It reflected the Bureau's inability to get the children in school at an early age, and once they were in school to keep them in attendance.[130] The above critiques did not exhaust the recommendations made by the Meriam report for education, but some of the important issues have been mentioned.

The National Advisory Committee on Education report of 1931 was the third critique of Indian Bureau schools. Under the direction of the President, the Secretary of Interior established this committee in 1929. They labeled the Indian education policy of the Federal Government a "tragic failure." The recommendations

---

[129] Fey & McNickle, p. 112.
For comment on the recommendations of the Committee of One Hundred, see Downes, "A Crusade for Reform," Chapter X.

[130] Fey & McNickle, pp. 68, 113-114.

of this Committee were similar to those in the Meriam report. Since some boarding schools could not be closed readily, the Bureau converted them into high schools as means of improvement. The Bureau increased the use of government day schools, and food and health care were improved. In 1938, the standards of Bureau teachers were raised requiring the teacher to have a four-year degree with eighteen hours of his/her program in education.[131]

---

[131] Fey & McNickle, pp. 114-117.

# Chapter 6

## St. Ann's and Ojibwa Indian Schools

Father Hildebrand Elliot, O.S.B., arrived in Belcourt June 1933 to assume the pastoral duties of the St. Ann's Indian Mission. Coming here from Marty Mission in South Dakota, he was determined to provide a Catholic education to the Indian children. That same year he appealed to the Benedictine convent at Ferdinand, Indiana, for Sisters to aid with religious instruction for the children. His request was rewarded with four nuns: Sisters Flavia Neu, Felicitas Halter, Vita Nirmeier, and Delphine Karessel. Miss Cora Daunhouer, a lay missionary, also arrived with the group of sisters. Sister Camilla Halter came in 1934. Father Hildebrand began building a church and school in 1934 and completed the work in late 1935. School opened Easter Monday of the following year. The enrollment was one hundred for the first school term.[132] On that first day after Mass, students marched down a short hallway from the east door of the church to the classrooms. The children were directed into classrooms apparently according to student height. There had to be at least two grades in each classroom as there were eight or nine grades and only four classrooms. The new church and school had a basement, and a centralized kitchen and dining facilities plus a large storage area

---

[132] *St. Ann Centennial, 1885 – 1985, One Hundred Years of Faith*, pp. 35-38.

Figure 6-1: Picture from the late 1930's of St. Ann's students with Fr. Hildebrand. Students from left to right are Tiny Brien, Dan Jerome, Jim Croteau and Morris Baker.

and root cellar. No tuition was charged to the students. The school was totally supported by the mission benefactors.

Eleven students graduated from St Ann's eighth grade June 20, 1937.[133] In 1939, Father Hildebrand began building again. This time the parish hall was erected. It had a basketball court larger than the local federal school that was built in 1931. The hall had a stage and a movie projector booth and contained a full basement that was used for different social activities.

In 1942, St. Ann's school was experiencing growing pains so another classroom was set up to keep up with the increasing enrollment. The influx in the number of students demanded more space at the elementary level, and the newly constructed Madonna Hall in 1948, built to be the high school, was used instead to help alleviate the overcrowded conditions. Despite his efforts, Father Hildebrand's plan for a high school was never realized.[134]

---

[133] *St. Ann Centennial 1885 – 1985*, p. 38.
[134] *St. Ann Centennial 1885 – 1985*, p. 46.

# The Trail of Misgivings

St. Ann's had an enrollment of about 300 students in the 1952–53 school term and operated four buses.[135] With this enrollment and only eight classrooms, the teachers had to have exceedingly large classes – 37 to 38 students per class. A larger gymnasium was built in 1966 complete with bleachers and a large playing court for basketball and other games and activities. It had a stage to the west of the gym with a full basement that contained a cafeteria and extra rooms.

Figure 6-2: Left -- St. Ann's old mission school then and now. Right – Ojibwa Indian School. Center – OIS administration building and gym.

They were on a summer schedule, which had its advantages and disadvantages. There were savings on the cost of fuel. Roads were not always open in the winter. At times walk-in students had a cold walk to school. On the other hand, in the heat of the summer months without air conditioning, keeping students on task could be quite difficult. This trend continued for 26 years through

---

[135] Robert Murray, p. 31.

the 1961–62 school term. The following year they changed over to the winter schedule.[136]

Beginning in 1936, students at St. Ann's were taught by the Sisters of St. Benedict. Sister Judith Emge was Principal of St. Ann's Indian Mission School from 1968 through the transition period, then continued as Principal of Ojibwa Indian School until her retirement in 1992.

## Transition

In 1970, Abbot Alan Berndt of Blue Cloud Abbey notified various reservations in the Dakotas that they would transfer the operations of their missions and schools at Marty and Stephan, South Dakota, and St. Ann's at Belcourt, North Dakota, to the local Indian people. An era of more than half a century of Indian Catholic boarding and day schools by the Blue Cloud Benedictines had come to an end. A St. Ann's transitional School Board was appointed and established in 1970 for the purpose of determining the fate of the St. Ann's Mission School. The newly formed board had to contend with the issue of how to finance the school that was being handed over to them during the transition period. According to the Centennial Book writers, the board members appointed were Roy LaFontaine (President), John Monette, Alvin McLeod, Sister Judith Emge and Fr. Theophane Gonnelly with Patti Belgarde serving as Secretary for the board.

At this same time the Turtle Mountain Community School was scrambling for more space to house its swelling student population. Since St. Ann's had buildings that could be renovated into classrooms, the Bureau of Indian Affairs and the Couture School District #27 cooperated in renovating several buildings at St. Ann's. Part of the "bundle" building was converted into two classrooms; the parish hall was made into four classrooms; and a seventh classroom was built in the basement of the new gymnasium. All of the first grade classes of the Turtle Mountain

---

[136] *St. Ann Centennial, 1885 – 1985*, p. 51.

Community Elementary School were moved into the renovated rooms. The Couture School District remodeled the dining area of St. Ann's and took charge of the lunch program for all students including the children at St. Ann's. A contract between the Couture School District #27 and the St. Ann's School Board was drawn up in 1970 whereby the district would assume the responsibility for educating St. Ann's grades one through four.[137]

The contract was renewed the following school year (1971–72). The Turtle Mountain Community Elementary School moved six third-grade classes to St. Ann's in lieu of the first grade. In 1972–1973, the contract was not renewed because new Armco buildings were erected to serve the Turtle Mountain Middle School. This alleviated some of the space problems for Turtle Mountain Community Elementary School.[138]

According to Tribal Resolution Number 725-905-73, St. Ann's continued to operate for the 1972–73 school term. Revenues generated by leasing classrooms and operating only four grades made this possible. However, the St. Ann's School Board sought to assume full responsibility for the school, and they looked for funding from the Federal Government. The resolution dated May 30, 1973, supported the board's effort to take over the responsibility for the operation of the St. Ann's School, and they endorsed the board's action to seek federal assistance. Hence, the 1972–73 school term brought to a close the Benedictines' role in Indian education on the Turtle Mountain Reservation.

## Tribal Contract School: Ojibwa Indian School

The Tribal Resolution dated May 30, 1973, granted total responsibility to the St. Ann's School Board for the operation and control of the school. Besides the sanction of the Tribal Council, it also needed the vote of the Turtle Mountain Indian people. In January 1974, the interim board (Kenneth Bauman, Louis Bercier,

---

[137] Jerome, Early Education Paper of Superintendent, December/1984, p.4.
[138] Jerome, Early Education Paper of Superintendent, December/1984, p.4.

Joseph Jerome, Vernon Gourneau, Richard Fairweather, and J. J. Monette) called an informal election for the purpose of determining the fate of the St. Ann's School. The people of the Turtle Mountain voted to continue St. Ann's as a mission school. The school operated at a loss in previous years and could not continue to do so. Understandably, many people had difficulty letting go of the school since it would mean the end of a sectarian school – which meant no religious instructions for the children in a school setting.

On March 20, 1974, an election was held to determine whether the people would sanction the take-over of the school by the board. The people passed the referendum with a vote of 657 in favor to 8 votes against. A favorable vote was also needed in an effort to obtain funding from the Bureau of Indian Affairs.[139]

The school was renamed Ojibwa Indian School on January 23, 1974. According to State documents, the Ojibwa Indian School, Inc. was issued its Certificate of Incorporation by the North Dakota Secretary of State April 4, 1974. The Articles of Incorporation of Ojibwa Indian School, stipulated that the interim board of directors would serve

Figure 6-3: Sister Judith Emge, first principal of the Ojibwa Indian School.

---

[139] Ojibwa Indian School files.

until the first annual meeting in 1975. The Articles of Incorporation, interestingly, had an even number of board directors. Apparently, this board had too many tie-votes and the number has since been changed to seven members.

The first newly elected Ojibwa Indian School Board had the vision of adding new teachers to the program and teacher aides to assist in the classrooms. Attracting qualified teachers meant an increased salary schedule. The board hoped to incorporate an up-to-date science program. They saw the need for a library and a full-time librarian and also had the

Figure 6-4: Mike Blue, principal of the Ojibwa Indian School.

foresight to plan for in-service programs for its staff. All that was needed was the money.[140]

In 1974, the Ojibwa Indian School, using the old St. Ann's facilities, offered classes for kindergarten through eighth grade. Kindergarten was added to the school system that year. There were 11 classrooms, a faculty room, kitchen and lunch area for the children, and a large gymnasium for physical education classes and other activities. The plan at the time was to keep the school at 250 to 275 students, and enrollment would be on a first-come, first-serve basis.

The Ojibwa Indian School was not even settled in before they began the process of moving out. The buildings they occupied had asbestos in the pipe insulation, floor tile and the old paneling. The Fire Marshall cited the buildings as a fire hazard – the halls were too narrow and the stairs were unsafe. In addition, the buildings

---

[140] Ojibwa Indian School files

were inaccessible to the handicapped. Several trailers were moved on to the grounds to be used as temporary classrooms. (In the school business "There is nothing more permanent than a temporary building." These temporaries will have been used for 30 years.) The gradual move began: first, from the four classrooms of St. Ann's; then from MaDonna Hall; and finally, from St. Joseph's Parish Hall. A total of twelve trailers were moved in to house the students. A metal administration building was completed in 1981 and another structure was built in 1995 adjoined to the gymnasium to accommodate the kindergarten program.[141]

## Ojibwa Indian School Funding

The Ojibwa Indian School is a contract school, and obtains its funding entirely from the BIA through the Tribe. Attorney Thomas Disselhorst, representing the Ojibwa Indian School, in his August 15, 1994, letter to Wayne Sanstead, Superintendent of Public Instruction for the State of North Dakota, questioned the possibility of State funding for OIS. Attorney Disselhorst argued that the Ojibwa School might be considered a Federal school, and may be eligible for funding from the State. The questions that Disselhorst posed needed an opinion of the North Dakota Attorney General.[142] The request for the opinion was through North Dakota State Senator Dan Jerome. Two questions were asked:[143]

1.  Is the Ojibwa Indian School a "Federal school" as that term is used in the North Dakota Century code with whom the school board of the Belcourt Public School District No. 7 may contract for the education of students who reside within its district?; and

2.  Does the school board of the Belcourt Public School District No. 7 have the power to contract with the Ojibwa Indian School to provide for the education of students within the Belcourt School

---

[141] Personal interview with John Frederick and Randy Jerome, May 25, 2006.
[142] Letter to Supt. of Public Instruction, ND, from Thomas Disselhorst, August 15, 1994.
[143] Letter to N.D. Attorney General, from Senator Dan Jerome, Legislative Dist. #9, August 25, 1994.

District under the general powers, authority and responsibility to provide free and open educational opportunities to all children within its district granted to it pursuant to various sections in Title 15 of the North Dakota Century Code and Article VIII of the North Dakota Constitution?

Attorney General Heidi Heitkamp's response explained that the term "'federal school' is not defined in North Dakota law." She further stated, "Generally, the law is what the Legislature says, not what is unsaid." She continued, "The Legislature must be presumed to have meant what it has plainly expressed. It must be presumed, also, that it made no mistake in expressing its purpose and intent. Where the language of a statute is plain and unambiguous, the court cannot indulge in speculation as to the probable or possible qualifications which might have been in the mind of the Legislature, but the statute must be given effect according to its plain and obvious meaning, and cannot be extended beyond it."[144]

The Attorney General felt that "only Bureau schools appear to have the potential for being federal schools under North Dakota law." Tribal Government operating schools and exercising control over the school, even with Federal funding does not qualify the school as a federal school.[145] However, Ojibwa Indian School could receive funding through Belcourt School District #7 if OIS agreed to come under the district's umbrella.

In a letter dated October 18, 1995, Senator Les LaFountain, State Representatives Merle Boucher and Gerry Wilkie asked for the North Dakota Attorney General to reconsider her 1994 opinion. Her response in part is quoted below:[146]

Only North Dakota public school districts organized and controlled under North Dakota law may receive state taxpayer provided foundation aid under N.D.C.C. ch. 15-40.1. Through other sections of

---

[144] Attorney General's Opinion to Senator Dan Jerome, October 25, 1994.

[145] Attorney General Opinion Letter to Senator Dan Jerome, October 25, 1994.

[146] Attorney General Opinion Letter to Senator LaFountain, Rep. Boucher and Rep. Wilkie, Nov. 22, 1995.

law, . . . those North Dakota public school districts, under the limited circumstances provided therein, may contract with a federal school to educate students of the public school district. Tribal governments and private school employees are not federal government officials.

The Attorney General's opinion remained unchanged. Therefore, the OIS could not receive foundation payments from the State.

## OIS Policies

To serve on the Ojibwa Indian School Board, one must win an election, which is conducted annually on the third Thursday in October. One must also have the following qualifications to run for a position:[147]

1. Parent and/or legal guardian of a student attending Ojibwa Indian School during school count week.

2. 21 years of age or older.

3. A high school graduate or passes a GED.

4. Any person receiving any form of monetary compensation from Ojibwa Indian School is ineligible.

5. Anyone holding a Tribal Council position is ineligible.

6. Not related by blood or marriage to a seated member of the board according to Turtle Mountain Band of Chippewa Indian personnel policy handbook.

7. Anyone convicted of a felony is ineligible.

The board member is seated within two days after the election, and will serve a three-year, staggered term of office. Board members are paid $50 per regular meeting and $25 for a special meeting not to exceed $100 monthly.[148]

---

[147] Ojibwa Indian School Board Handbook, SY 2005 – 2006.
[148] Ojibwa Indian School Board Handbook, SY 2005 - 2006.

# The Trail of Misgivings

For the 2005-06 school term, the board members are Robert Poitra (President), Ernest J. Lambert, Eric Dionne, Tim Hawk, Fred Gillis, Vicky Schroeder, and Stephanie Gillis.

### The Ojibwa Indian School Mission Statement:[149]

The Ojibwa Indian School will provide an educational program, which promotes the academic, spiritual, cultural, intellectual, social, emotional, and physical development of students who reside on or near the Turtle Mountain Chippewa Reservation through effective discipline, implementation of high education standards, continuous professional development and strong parent and community involvement.

## Ojibwa Indian School Today

Presently, the Ojibwa Indian School is located on leased St. Ann's Parish grounds. Twelve doublewide trailers sprawl over several acres located on the hillside. A newer steel structure was

Figure 6-5: Ojibwa Indian School in its present location on the side of St. Ann Mission's hillside. Madonna Hall in background upper left corner.

---

[149] Ojibwa Indian School Employee Handbook, SY 2005 - 2006.

built onto the gym and has two classrooms for kindergarten. Altogether there are twelve regular classrooms in these ill-suited structures. One trailer contains a computer lab adjoined to a music room. A bus garage and gymnasium are also leased from St. Ann's. The garage is used for bus maintenance as well as housing a fleet of eight buses. The school gym is used for physical education and other school functions. The dining and kitchen areas are on the lower floor of the gym. A second steel building located near the gym is used for administration offices.

The OIS enrollment for 2005–06 was 273 students for kindergarten through eighth grade. The staff consists of principal, counselor, librarian, twenty-two classroom teachers, eleven teacher aides of which five are parent aides, five office personnel, eight bus drivers (five drivers also serve as part-time janitors) and two full-time janitors. In addition, there are nineteen other support staff?[150] Educational services for handicapped students at OIS are provided through a cooperative effort with the Turtle Mountain Community School.

A new school was planned and construction began. However, problems developed that caused the BIA to shut down the project for approximately one year. The building would have been completed in August of 2005. The school is currently under construction. When completed, it will consist of 115,000 square feet at a cost of $27,000,000. The new structure will contain 32 classrooms, kitchen and dining area, science, home economics, computer laboratory, music room, gymnasium, and shop areas. The school design is in the shape of a hand with each finger containing a central work station and computer lab. Each of these areas will house the lower elementary, elementary, middle school and high school students. There will be a transportation building to house the eight buses. An athletic field is also part of the overall plan. The Ojibwa Indian School is planning to add the upper four

---

[150] Interview with OIS personnel, May 2006.

Figure 6-6: The new Ojibwa Indian School in the construction stage.

grades to their educational program when they move into the new structure. The completion date for the school is now set for August of 2007.[151]

## St. Ann's Native American School

The Society of Our Lady of the Most Holy Trinity (S.O.L.T.), Robstown, Texas, replaced the Blue Cloud Abbey Benedictines at St. Ann Parish in 1995. When Father Dale Craig arrived as pastor in 1997, one of his first endeavors was to reopen a Catholic school at the encouragement of Father James Flanagan, founder of S.O.L.T.

St. Ann's School reopened for the 1999–2000 school year. Father Dale opened its doors in September 1999, 26 years after having closed in 1973. The name given to the revived school is St. Ann's Native American School. The school uses the existing buildings. Some safety improvements had been made earlier. In

---

[151] Interview with OIS principal Mike Blue, May 15, 2006.

the beginning there were 25 students enrolled in kindergarten through third grade. Initially, the plan was to add one grade per year. The number of students peaked to 65 during the 2001–02 school year. In the following year, even though grade seven was added to the program, the number dropped to 59 pupils. St. Ann's numbers again dropped to 39 in the 2003–04 school term. In 2005, the school graduated its first students. With the decreased enrollment, the school personnel had to reassess its program, and are now operating only kindergarten through grade six. This school year (2005–06) the enrollment is 29 pupils. A lunch program is provided by the State of North Dakota and supplemented with commodities.

Figure 6-7: Father Dale Craig.

A small tuition fee is required; however, parents may work at the school in lieu of the tuition fee. No child is turned away. The school has a bus, but no driver.

St. Ann's Native American School Mission Statement:[152]

St. Ann's Native American School is dedicated to the spiritual, intellectual, emotional, and physical formation of the youth of the Turtle Mountain Reservation, and seeks always to assist the parents in their role as the primary educators of their children with continual focus on the kingdom of God.

Initially, the teaching and auxiliary staff were volunteer workers. Raymond Parisien, a local member of the tribe, was a volunteer principal for the first year. He was fully certified and held an Elementary Principal's credential from the State of North Dakota. The school now has a full-time principal, David Boyd,

---

[152]*New Earth,* Catholic Diocese of Fargo, November 2006, p. 1B.

Figure 6-8: Ray Parisien, first principal of St. Ann's NA School.

who volunteers part of his time. The teachers handle combined grades one through six. The kindergarten is self-contained. At present, the staff consists of four teachers, two are full-time volunteers, one volunteers half-time and is paid half-time, and the fourth teacher is paid a full-time salary. The school has seven other volunteers who serve in various ways. For example, the Sisters teach the music program. In addition to a solid religious educational program, they have music, arts, computer science, and the standard curricula prescribed by the State School Superintendent of North Dakota. Their sports program cooperates with the Ojibwa Indian School. They do have a problem with certification. Some teachers are certified in other states, however, they are not meeting the requirements for North Dakota certification.

Figure 6-9: David Boyd, present principal of St. Ann's NA School.

# Chapter 7

## Federal Takeover

The Continental Congress came into being in 1775. Since that time, there has always been a department within the government dealing with Indian Affairs. The Continental Congress had its commissioners, and the Congress of the Confederation had its superintendents. The United States found it necessary to create its departments and commissioners to deal with Indian Affairs. Most of these departments were established for a particular function – to negotiate, make treaties with the Indian Tribes and generally maintain a friendly relationship with them. Benjamin Franklin, Patrick Henry, and James Wilson were three of the men elected to these positions, which gives an indication of the importance of these offices.[153]

One of the first Acts of the United States Congress was to establish the War Department. The management of all affairs dealing with Indian Tribes became one of the functions of the Secretary of War.[154]

The United States maintained trading houses from 1796 to 1822. These trading houses were government-owned and were

---

[153] Felix S. Cohen, *Handbook of the Federal Indian Law with reference tables and Index,* United States Government Printing Office, Washington, 1945, 4th Printing, pp. 9-10.
[154] Felix S. Cohen, p. 9.

created to give the Indian Tribes goods and supplies at a fair market value and a fair price for their furs. The trading houses were set up in an attempt to keep the private white dealers honest. President Washington said as much when he recommended to Congress that trading houses be created, "in order to protect the Indians from the practices of private traders." The agents working in the trading houses were appointees of the President and were responsible to him. In 1806, the Office of Superintendent of Indian Trade was created by the President to work with the trading houses. His main responsibility was ". . . to purchase and take charge of all goods intended for trade with the Indian nations. . . and to transmit the same to such places as he shall be directed by the President." Agents and superintendents were to transfer their accounts to the Secretary of the Treasury. The Office of the Superintendent of Indian Trade was abolished in 1822[155]

With the abolishment of the Office of the Superintendent of Indian Trade, the Secretary of War, John C. Calhoun created the Bureau of Indian Affairs on March 11, 1824, within the War Department. Thomas L. McKinney was selected as its first department head. He was given, among other duties, the responsibility of the civilization fund, which was used in part for the purpose of educating Indian children. McKinney's staff consisted of two members – a chief clerk and an assistant. "His representative in the field included superintendents, agents, and subagents."[156]

Much confusion occurred between 1824 and 1832 when the Bureau of Indian Affairs was placed in the War Department. On July 9, 1832, the Congress passed an Act, which allowed the President to appoint, with Senate consent, a Commissioner of Indian Affairs. The commissioner was to assume responsibility for all Indian affairs. He remained under the supervision of the

---

[155] Felix S. Cohen, p. 10.
[156] Felix S. Cohen, p. 10.

Secretary of War, but ". . . subject to the regulations prescribed by the President."[157]

A second fundamental change occurred in 1834 known as the Organic Act of the Indian Service. It provided a reorganization of the field forces of the War Department. The status of the Bureau of Indian Affairs remained the same within the War Department. In 1849, the Bureau of Indian Affairs was placed in the Department of Interior.[158]

Nothing positive can be said about the early Indian Commissioners. The first commissioner recommended the building of schools to maintain the peace among the Indians. Commissioner William H. Crawford on the other hand thought the opposite, and said as much, "To teach a savage man to read, while he continues a savage in all else, is to throw seed on a rock. Manual labor schools are what the Indian condition calls for." The first commissioners were almost completely of one mind and were content with the national policy of moving the Indians west of the Mississippi River. Reports of the commissioners repeatedly supported the idea of civilizing the Indian by having them become individual landowners opposed to tribal ownership. Commissioner Crawford's remark on the subject was that "common property and civilization cannot coexist".[159]

The following quote blatantly reflects the sentiments of the secretaries and commissioners of the 1800's. Secretary Caleb B. Smith, who served as Secretary of Interior during Lincoln's Presidency, introduced his new policy as follows:[160]

> It may well be questioned whether the government has not adopted a mistaken policy in regarding the Indian tribes as quasi-independent nations, and making treaties with them for the purchase of the lands they claim to own. They have none of the clements of nationality; they

---

[157] Felix S. Cohen, p. 10.
[158] Felix S. Cohen, pp. 10-11.
[159] Fey and McNickle, p. 65.
[160] Felix S. Cohen, p. 16.

are within the limits of the recognized authority of the United States and must be subject to its control. The rapid progress of civilization upon this continent will not permit the lands which are required for cultivation to be surrendered to savage tribes for hunting grounds. Indeed, whatever may be the theory, the government has always demanded the removal of the Indians when their lands were required for agricultural purposes by advancing settlements. Although the consent of the Indians has been obtained in the form of treaties, it is well known that they have yielded to a necessity which they could not resist.

. . . A radical change in the mode of treatment of the Indians should, in my judgment, be adopted. Instead of being treated as independent nations they should be regarded as wards of the government, entitled to its fostering care and protection. . . .

The Office of Indian Affairs had this to say, "While treaties and wars had failed to break down the internal organization and culture of the Indian tribes, the allotment policy brought with it a growing roster of white superintendents, farm agents, teachers, inspectors and missionaries who superseded Indian leaders and to a large extent succeeded in destroying Indian culture."[161] A statement prepared by the Office of Indian Affairs in 1938 is quoted in part below and provides an interesting insight.[162]

The use of military force to control Indians was a dominant factor in United States policy from the 1820's until the 1850's and did not wholly disappear with the last of the Indian wars in the 1890's. This warfare materially handicapped the settlement of the West and proved costly to the Federal Government. It was officially estimated with probable correctness about 1870 that Indian wars had cost the Government in excess of $1,000,000 for every dead Indian.

This statement did not give the over-all cost of what the United States expended in waging wars against the Indians. It just gave a figure of the cost "for every dead Indian." Was it 100,000 or 10,000,000 Indians? The statement also did not say whether their numbers included women and children.

---

[161] Felix S. Cohen, p.28.
[162] Felix S. Cohen, p.28.

In 1924, the United States ironically granted citizenship to the Indian people. For various reasons, two-thirds of the Indian people were already citizens of the United States before the passage of the law. Many Indian people served in the armed forces during World War I. The Turtle Mountain people's patriotism and willingness to serve was carried forward to World War II (1941–45). Four hundred fourteen, or over nine percent, Indian men and women from the Turtle Mountain Reservation served during World War II. In comparison, 6.6 percent of the non-Indian men and women of Rolette County served. The percentages are derived from the total white and Indian population of the county – not of the eligible men and women within Rolette County. On the week of the Pearl Harbor attack by the Japanese, every male student from TMCS eligible to serve in the armed forces joined some branch of the military. The school was so drained of its male population that from 1944 to 1946 only two boys graduated from high school.[163]

## Federal Policy

The push was to get Indian children into public schools. Since the Indians were now citizens, the State was obligated to pick up the tab for any Indian child living in the district except for those Indian students who were living on the reservation attending federal schools. This relieved the Federal Government of having to educate the Indian child of school age who resided in a district off the reservation. However, when the district had a great number of Indian families living on non-taxable land in a particular district, a hardship was created for the district. The Federal Government did assist in these situations.

It has been, and still is, the policy of the Federal Government to enroll Indian children in the public schools wherever possible. The following document dictating policy dated March 9, 1929, was from the Commissioner of Indian

---

[163] D. F. Jerome, *Lilley-Dionne American Legion Post 262 History,* 1980, p.1.

Affairs addressed to the Turtle Mountain Agency Superintendent:[164]

> Wherever Indian children can find places in public schools according to instructions that have been sent out from the Department of the Interior to superintendents and supervisors in the Indian Service, they are to attend such schools instead of those institutions throughout the west that have been created especially for the purpose of educating them.

> Those children who live in isolated all-Indian communities will still go to Indian day schools and boarding schools. Care will be taken of those whose parents are so poor that they cannot provide proper food and clothes for them. At the schools, however, the effort will be made to increase the contact with the whites, to teach boys and girls to make a living as members of their communities, and to aid them to get money earning places when they finish school. Of the 103,000 Indian children, as reported by the federal census of 1930, 89,000 are enrolled in some schools of which number 50,000 are in public schools.

> The Secretary of the Interior, under the law, is authorized to make and enforce such rules and regulations as may be necessary to secure the enrollment and regular attendance of Indian children who are wards of the government in schools maintained for their benefit or in public schools. Thus the responsibility of determining which schools they shall attend is exercised by him through the Office of Indian Affairs. . .

According to this letter, the Bureau of Indian Affairs had accepted the responsibility of the education of the Indian children, and the letter emphasized the enforcement of compulsory school attendance. The letter further pointed out that the Federal Government must increase enrollment in public schools. Students were made to attend public schools, whether the schools were meeting the needs of the Indian children or not. The Indian Commissioner, who had some concern about the poor families, seemed to think that white contact was the key to making a living even in the Indian community.

---

[164] Robert Murray, pp. 35-36. U. S. Department of Interior, Bureau of Indian Affairs, Circular Letter from Commissioner of Indian Affairs to all Agencies, March 9, 1929.

## The Local Situation

When Agency Superintendent James H. Hyde arrived on the scene in 1926, plans for a new educational program got underway. He was not pleased with the operations of the educational system being conducted by the district boards. Examining the County Teacher Reports, Clerk and Treasurer's Reports, the contents tend to support J. B. Mortsolf's report quoted below. The takeover by the federal officials seemed justified. The boards, however, were not solely to blame. One point is worthy of consideration. In 1918, the federal officials had created a new day school inspector position as mentioned earlier. This watchdog, if you will, was to make certain that the districts fulfilled their obligations, which included all aspects of the educational program of the districts. The 1923 report from the Committee of One Hundred should have urged the inspector to monitor more closely into how well the districts were complying with their commitment to education.

A better understanding of the conditions of the educational program at the time the Federal Government was resuming the responsibility of education on the Turtle Mountain Indian Reservation is found in the report of Mortsolf, Day School Inspector, dated January 28, 1929: [165]

> The system of public education for these Indians is very unsatisfactory. The buildings are poor and have been allowed to run down. All are in need of paint and repairs, and equipment is in very poor shape. Attendance has been poor and is continually falling off. Parents are away a great deal, and in many instances, the larger pupils are kept out to work. The health of the pupils has been generally very good.
>
> Many visits have been made to Indian homes in the interest of better attendance, and the development of better interest in the education of the children. Poverty is the main excuse given for remaining out of school. In one of the schools, the teacher got a donation of clothing from his home town, which was distributed among the children, and which I am told was greatly appreciated, and resulted

---

[165] Robert Murray, p. 43.

in better attendance. In another school the teacher brings drinking water from his home three miles distant, every day, hauling it in a five gallon can. Mention was made in a previous report of slough water being used for drinking at one of the schools. A photograph is attached to this report, of this school, which as a building site and equipment is the poorest make-shift of a school that I have yet seen. If it were not for the fact that these children are probably drinking the same kind of water at home as they are getting in school, I would urge the immediate closing of this school.

Mismanagement in the past years in Ingebretson and Couture districts, which comprise the reservation has prevented them from building up the schools as should have been done, and could have been done, had the money been judiciously expended.

According to Mortsolf, funding was adequate to build more classrooms.[166] Student enrollment and their attendance for 1923 are in *Appendix B-1*. By today's standards, this table indicates that nearly all nine classrooms of Couture and Ingebretson were overcrowded, and the attendance for the 314 students was only 79.4 percent.[167]

The makeshift school building the inspector mentioned had to be one of the schools that the board added to the system. The choosing of the site was thoughtless and had not taken the students into consideration. The drinking water the report alluded to was bad, but people did drink slough water even in the 1950's. The need to boil it was necessary, but there was no excuse for not having a well at each school site.

Agency Superintendent Hyde's observation of the school is worthy to quote in full:[168]

I wish that I might say nothing but favorable things relative to the administration of the local schools under the school boards; but criticism thereof would not be entirely favorable. Suffice to say that on taking over the agency in 1926, I felt that they were improperly equipped to render a service comparable with the money that was being

---

[166] Robert Murray, p. 43.
[167] Robert Murray, p. 41.
[168] Robert Murray, pp. 83-84.

expended by the federal government on their behalf. The number of school children had grown rapidly until it was found that the local schools were unable to care for all the children living within their districts. Even increased enrollments in the non-reservation schools were inadequate to care for the situation. In 1926 it was found that over one-third of the enrollment was in non-reservation schools, and many hundreds of children were not attending any school, anywhere. Some reorganization was necessary to provide school facilities for all the children.

According to Murray, Hyde consulted with each of the parties involved in the education of the reservation. The Rolette County Superintendent, the State Officials, and the School Board members all agreed that the Bureau of Indian Affairs should once again head up the educational program on the reservation. Special legislation was needed by the State of North Dakota to grant a legal subdivision of the State to relinquish its educational responsibilities to the Federal Government. The North Dakota lawmakers passed an Act approving the takeover by the United Stated Government on February 25, 1929. The Act provided among other things that, ". . . the state tuition fund and the county tuition fund, which would otherwise be paid to the said district, if functioning, shall be paid to the United States provided that the compulsory school attendance laws of the state shall apply to and be enforced in such district and government schools."[169]

The new state law allowed an agreement to be made between the United States and Rolette County on April 11, 1929. The agreement stipulated that the state and county would make tuition payments to the United States Government when the responsibilities of educating the children within the school districts on the reservation are taken over by the United States Government. It also held that the United States comply with the provisions in the state law, which included compulsory education and educating all

---

[169] Robert Murray, pp. 47-48. Revised Code of North Dakota, 1943, Sec. 15-47-16 and 14-47-17.

students within the two districts even if they were non-Indian children.[170]

This agreement was signed on April 11, 1929; however, the Federal Government did not take over the educational program of the reservation until the beginning of the school term in 1931. That was the year the new building was completed. The takeover of the school system had been in the planning and construction stages since 1926. Why did the Federal Government wait nearly five years to take over the educational system that was so dissatisfying to them? The schools were in such a deplorable state, "and hundreds of children were not attending any school, anywhere." And yet what immediate action did the government take? No documents can be found stating anything that the Federal Government did, except to criticize and wait for the completion of the new construction. Murray's writings tabulated 1928-29 school statistics that were all negative, but wrote nothing about federal intervention to change the deplorable state of education.

## Federal Government Schools

The Turtle Mountain Community School was completed in the fall of 1931 at a cost of $150,000 to the Federal Government. The school dedication address given by Commissioner of Indian Affairs, Charles J. Roads on November 19, 1931, is as follows: [171]

> The dedication of the consolidated day school marks an advanced step in the education of Indians and whites together. It has been the policy of the Office of Indian Affairs for the past few years to secure the cooperation of the states in the education of our native sons and daughters. We have endeavored to break down the segregation of Indians in education, and today we are commemorating the success of our efforts in cooperation with the local community and state.
>
> The consolidated day school at Turtle Mountain is unique. It is the first instance in the education of Indian youth wherein the school has

---

[170] Robert Murray, pp. 49-50, Rolette County Commissioner Proceedings, April 1929.
[171] Robert Murray, pp. 86-87.

been built and is to be maintained by the Indian Service for the education of Indian and white children. The funds for the purpose of building the school were appropriated from the federal treasury by congress. The local community very cheerfully agreed to deposit in the treasury of the United States, for expenditures for the support of the school, the state allowances for payments for education of the children residing within the reservation in which the school is located.

The native residents of the Turtle Mountain Band of Chippewa have belonged here even before the days of the Louisiana Purchase. These native sons and daughters of the Chippewa tribe have been in contact with the white men since long before these United States came into being. Their first contacts were with the roving French voyageurs and trappers, a sturdy race who lent much color to the narratives of the early days, and northwest territory. Early in the history of our country the Northwest Company established trading posts in the country of the Turtle Mountain Chippewa, and from then on white settlers and white pioneers found friends among the native North Americans. The Turtle Mountain Chippewa have always eagerly absorbed the civilization and culture of the white man.

The building consisted of 36,762 square feet and had sixteen classrooms (eight on the main floor and eight on the second floor). A small gymnasium was on the main floor. The gym was not regulation size for high school basketball, and it had little room for seating spectators when games were played with other schools. At the east end of the gym was a stage. A classroom on the second floor was set aside as a medical room. A play area was on the south end of the basement. On the north side was a home economics area equipped for classes in cooking, sewing, and weaving, and a music room. There was a large kitchen and dining area and toilet facilities for boys and girls, and it also served as a bus garage. Norman Dauphinais, a shoemaker, occupied a little space in the storage area of the basement in the early school years. He repaired students' shoes while they waited. An office area was on the main floor.[172] A library was on the top floor in the front and central part of the building. The *Turtle Mountain Star* stated the library contained 3,000 volumes of a variety of books – novels,

---

[172] D. Jerome, *Early Education.* p. 2.

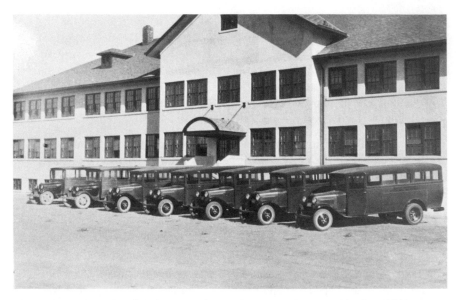

Figure 7-1: Old school and seven of the school bus fleet used in the 1930's.

fictions, non-fictions, children's books and references – in addition to periodicals, magazines, and newspapers.[173]

A separate building for the Shop and Arts and Crafts was completed shortly after the main school building.[174] The shop contained a wood working area. A table saw and drill press were the only power tools provided – the other tools were all hand tools. There was a forge for blacksmithing, a welding area, and a classroom where shop lectures and agriculture classes were conducted. The boys in grades seven through twelve were required to take these classes.

The west side of the building housed the Arts and Crafts center for older girls who did beadwork, ceramics, basketry and weaving under the National Youth Administration (NYA) program. This program was an attempt to preserve the Native American arts and crafts of the local people. The program also had a commercial aspect, and provided an opportunity for the students'

---

[173] *Turtle Mountain Star,* 1938 special edition, p. 25.
[174] Robert Murray, p. 124.

Figure 7-2: Bus garage that was added to the school in the early 1930's.

products to be sold. The program was discontinued because of a declining interest.[175]

A bus garage was then added to the south of the 1931-school building. This structure was used to shelter the buses and also provided mechanical space to repair or work on the buses and other government vehicles.

Hazel DeMontigny Franz, confirmed that home economics classes for students were held in the basement of the school building. In 1935, a shop and home economics complex was completed north of the school building. *St Ann's Centennial Book* pictures a building for home economics that should not be confused with the school facilities in this time period. It was later used for home economics, then the Agency Office. Later it was moved to the main street and became part of Turtle Mountain Community College facilities. President Roosevelt's Works Progress Administration (WPA) program was located in the building where clothing for needy families was sewn. It was later used for high school home economics classes.

---

[175] Robert Murray, p. 125.

Figure 7-3: Faculty of 1943. Front row (L→R): Charles Depoe (Band Leader), Leslie M. Keller (Principal of Education), John M. Byrd (Educational Field Agent), Albert B. Clark (Principal of High School), Oliven Sturla (Teacher of Agriculture). Second row: Frances M. Hart (2nd Grade), Mary K. O'Brien (Home Economics), Claire Wilcox (6th Grade), Esther M. Lowe (5th Grade), Mabel Richardson (3rd Grade), Lola Alice Zoldoske (Mathematics), Marian Taylor (Arts and Crafts), Melvie Reams (Primary), Edna G. Cupp (Secretary), Louise Wishmeyer (First Grade), Loleta Schrimsher (2nd Grade), Marguerite L. Dunnell (4th Grade), Hazel Z. Constance (English).

There is an Indian scene painted on the east wall of the 1931 gymnasium. (Originally there was a stage as described above, but it was later removed to add more space coupled with the fact that the school had not made use of the stage.) The painting is of the backside of a young brave facing a new horizon. The painting has been left intact, and has become the logo of the school. A reproduction of the logo is on the gymnasium floor of the present high school. This painting was a 1942 summer project by Miss Sunbeam Necklace. She was a Cherokee Indian, who taught what was one time called the beginner's class at the Turtle Mountain

Figure 7-4: Club building for single teacher housing circa 1931, which still stands today.

Community School. Miss Necklace's grandfather developed the Cherokee alphabet.[176]

In August of 1983, Albert Lee Ferris, a Métis from Belcourt, North Dakota, restored the original painting done by Miss Necklace. In the restoration process, Ferris added details to the painting which were more indicative to Ojibwa dress. Ferris also reproduced the painting on the circle of the gymnasium floor in the 1984 TMC High School.

The other paintings in the old gym that are near the ceiling on the south and north walls were done by John Brien. John was a fifth grade student when he painted those scenes in the 1941-42 school year.

Another addition to the school plant was a housing complex for single teachers built in the early 1930's. This structure is just about one hundred yards west of the school. The building provided individual rooms for the teachers, and contained a central

---

[176] Letter to Supt. Jerome, dated January 5, 1983, from Esther Lowe, former teacher at TMCS, 1941–47.

dining and kitchen area. Resident teachers hired their own cook or made other arrangements for their meals.

Fred Schindler recently related this story: "I used to go to the Kanick School, but they sent me to the new school [referring to TMCS]. They picked me up in a truck. They had two people with the truck—one to drive and the other to lift the kids on to the back of the truck. I enjoyed the ride. It was somewhat of a novelty. I was in char [chart] class at Kanick for a year, and they put me in the char [chart] class again." It is not known how many trucks were used to transport children to and from school or for how long it was done. Eight small buses seem inadequate for transporting 429 students even if one takes into consideration that some of the students were walk-ins.

That first year of 1931 ten percent of the 429 enrolled students were non-Indian.[177] The school offered academic classes for grades one through eight and continued to offer this course of study until 1938 when the school officials added a ninth year to the educational program.[178]

## Some Government School Regulations

One regulation in effect in 1931 for Indian schools stated the school year was to begin "on the first Monday in September and continue for a period of ten months, except when date of closing shall be otherwise indicated by the Commissioner of Indian Affairs."[179]

The English language regulation was enforced more in boarding schools than at the day schools. Murray also mentioned the regulation that "All employees must be able to speak English fluently. All employees must use English when on duty."[180] It is a known fact, that few local employees or students, if any, had

---

[177] Robert Murray, p.88.

[178] Jerome, *Early Education,* paper Dec/1984, p. 2.

[179] Robert Murray, p. 106.

[180] Robert Murray, p. 107.

problems with this regulation in school during the mid-1930's and 40's.

Another regulation required "the Indian Schools will conform with the 6-3-3 plan. This comprehends an elementary school of six years work, a junior vocational course of three years, and a senior vocational course of three years."[181] The Turtle Mountain Community School followed the vocational course work regulation very precisely. Students took shop and agricultural classes from their seventh through twelfth year of school. No doubt students did benefit from these courses; however, it might have had better holding power on the individual if alternatives were offered.

The regulation concerning enrollment was in part as follows:[182]

> . . . All healthy Indian children between the ages of 6 and 18 should be in some school, day, reservation boarding, non-reservation boarding, public or private. No Indian youth over 20 years of age shall be admitted to any Indian school except those maintaining senior high grades, when schools enroll up to 21 years of age for special vocational courses, without the consent of the Commissioner of Indian Affairs. No pupil over the age of 21 years of age shall be continued in school, except in senior high schools, without the approval of the Commissioner of Indian Affairs. Preferences in all cases shall be given to those children who (a) have a greater degree of Indian blood and (b) would be denied an education if not admitted to an Indian school."

In 1934, Congress passed the Johnson O'Malley Act (JOM) P.L. 74–815. The Secretary of the Interior now had the authority to contract with states and sub-divisions of the states (the local districts). These contractual agreements were made for the education of Indian children who lived in districts either on or off the reservation and on tax-free land.[183] School districts bordering

---

[181] Robert Murray, p. 108.

[182] Robert Murray, p. 109.

[183] Robert C. Andringa, Lee Antell, George Williams, *Indian Education Involvement of Federal, State and Tribal Governments, Sept. 1980,* p.11.

Figure 7-5: Belcourt students had to attend school in Rolla because of a lack of space in the Turtle Mountain School. From left to right: Rachel Roberge, Louise Montour, Elsie Ross, Romeo Grant, Russell Ross, Ernest Frederick, Mary Azure, Elizabeth LaPorte, Blanche Delorme, Herman Roberge, Roy Ferris, Eddie Ferris, Francis Maxwell – 5/26/32

the Turtle Mountain Reservation were among those that benefited by the Johnson O'Mallley Act.

## High School Added

Before the new school year got under way, eight teachers were hired, under the supervision of Dr. J. Arthur Anderson. They were chosen from a group of teachers who passed a Civil Service Examination. Each held bachelor degrees from various colleges and universities in the United States. [184]

The auxiliary staff consisted of a cook, dining room matron, laundress, janitor, clerk, mechanic and eight bus drivers. Bus drivers were assigned to bus maintenance, kitchen and dining work, and assisted with janitorial or other clean up duties when not driving buses.

---

[184] Robert Murray, p.89.

The original plan for the 1931 TMCS was to have a high school and an elementary program. The plan could not be carried out, however, due to lack of space. That first year, 429 grade school students showed up for classes. [185] This number of students filled the fifteen classrooms showing that the structure was already inadequate to handle that student population. According to the *Turtle Mountain Star*, it was necessary to reopened Roussin Day School in 1933.[186] Great Walker and Houle Schools were built in 1939 and 1940, respectively. At this time the government began to accommodate students who wished to attend a four-year high school within their own community. Prior to that, if they did not wish to attend boarding schools, they had to attend Rolla school.[187]

In 1940, a tenth year was added to the TMCS program. Each year thereafter, another grade was added. In 1943, the Turtle Mountain Community High School had its first graduates: Hazel DeMontigny, Mabel Grant, Marian Morin, Leona Poitra, and May Alvina Thomas.[188]

## Bureau Challenges

The commissioner delivered beautiful rhetoric in his TMC School dedication address; however, there were still many problems. The Bureau was better able to see the problems once school opened, and they were at the helm. With the new roads and the new bus routes, it should have been anticipated that new children would have been found who had never attended school before. Crowded conditions and the deplorable state for which they cited the school district still existed. The six years of not adding additional schools perpetuated the children lagging behind in learning skills. Murray stated, "many pupils 15, 16 or 17 years old could neither read nor write. Special classes for these retarded

---

[185] Robert Murray, pp. 88, 124.

[186] *Turtle Mountain Star*, June 23, 1938, p. 25.

[187] Robert Murray, pp. 119-126.

[188] Jerome, p. 2.

pupils had to be set up, . . .."[189] The Federal Government had eight teachers, fifteen classrooms, and 429 students. There were too few teachers for the number of students. Each teacher would have had 53 or 54 students. Stella Delorme Garcia, who attended Rolla School in 1934–1935, said of the Belcourt School ". . .they tried to push us out of school because it was so crowded." [190]

The depression of the 1930's created great hardships that wasted across the country. The poor were hit the hardest, but the devastation had no favorites and the hardships were not unique to the Belcourt area. Murray stated, "Many problems, not ordinarily encountered in schools were faced. Adequate clothing for school was a major problem. While not all of the families needed this help, the majority did." Different work programs were arranged with families so that they might work for clothing for their school-aged children. Some of the women worked at the school making

Figure 7-6: Snowplow with snow shoveling led by manual labor.

---

[189] Robert Murray, p. 90.
[190] Personal Interview with Stella Delorme Garcia, June 23, 2006.

clothing for needy families. Painting, repair work, maintenance and other jobs were available.[191]

An early snowstorm in the fall 1934, revealed how helpless even the Federal Government was. The snowstorm brought the bus system to a standstill. The snow removal equipment that the government provided was unable to clear the reservation roads for the buses. The officials closed the school to resume in the spring the following year. The school then operated on a spring-to-summer schedule until 1939 when the government was better equipped to handle snow removal.[192] However, Garcia commented about the school starting summer sessions at Belcourt in 1934. She stated that in 1933 they started the fall session, but were halted by

Figure 7-7: More snow shoveling adding up to no more than attempts to open the roads.

---

[191] Robert Murray, p. 90.
[192] Robert Murray, p. 92.

a winter storm. The short fall session was her seventh grade year as she moved to the eighth grade the following spring of 1934.[193]

Attendance was another challenge the federal officials had to face. There was an agreement signed between Federal and State Governments that stipulated the Federal Government would have to enforce State attendance laws. As was stated earlier, the educational goal of the Federal Government since the late 1800's and the early 1900's was to assimilate the Indian people into the dominant culture of America. The government attempted to accomplish this by sending children to far away boarding schools. They believed if the children were surrounded by white adult influence, the values and practical teaching learned would have a lasting effect on the children. At the same time, being absent from their parents and traditional-minded relatives, the government hoped the children would lose their Indian identity and become civilized. By the term *civilize,* the white man wanted to put the Indian into the white man's mold, so the Indian would be white in all aspects except color.

The Federal policy to accomplish this goal stated:[194]

> Sending a child to school out of State without consent – STATUTE – No Indian child shall be sent from any Indian reservation to a school beyond the State or Territory in which said reservation is situated without the voluntary consent of the father or mother of such child if either of them is living, and if neither of them is living without the voluntary consent of the next of kin of such child. Such consent shall be made before the agent of the reservation, and he shall send to the Commissioner of Indian Affairs his certificate that such consent has been voluntarily given before such child shall be removed from such reservation. And it shall be unlawful for any Indian agent or other employee of the Government to induce, or seek to induce, by withholding rations or by other improper means, the parents or next of kin of any Indian to consent to the removal of any Indian child beyond the limits of any reservation.

---

[193] Personal Interview with Stella Garcia, June 23, 2006.
[194] Aug. 15, 1894, ch. 290, Sec. 11, 28 Stat. 313; Mar. 2, 1895, ch. 188, Sec., 28 Stat. 906, 25 USC Sec 286 01/19/04.

The next government statute supported what was written earlier about withholding rations for nonattendance in schools:[195]

> The Secretary of the Interior may in his discretion, establish such regulations as will prevent the issuing ration or the furnishing of subsistence either in money or in kind to the head of any Indian family for or on account of any Indian child or children between the ages of eight and twenty-one years who shall not have attended school during the preceding year in accordance with such regulations. . . . The Secretary of the Interior may in his discretion withhold rations, clothing and other annuities from Indian parents or guardians who refuse or neglect to send and keep their children of proper school age in some school a reasonable portion of the year.

In another attempt to comply with the provision, the Secretary of Interior adopted the following policy:[196]

> The Secretary of the Interior is authorized to make and enforce such rules and regulations as may be necessary to secure the enrollment of the regular attendance of eligible Indian children who are wards of the government in schools maintained for their benefit by the United States or in public schools.

This particular policy refers to wards of the government. The Indian is not a ward of the government, but rather the Federal Government is a trustee of certain properties of the Indian.

In some cases the state law may be used to enforce the compulsory attendance of Indian students. Murray cited the Manual for Indian Service Sec. 58: [197]

> The Secretary of the Interior, under such rules and regulation as he may prescribe, shall permit the agents and employees of any state to enter upon Indian Tribal lands, reservations, or allotments therein (1) for the purpose of making inspection of health and educational conditions and enforcing sanitation and quarantine regulations or (2) to enforce the penalties of state compulsory school attendance laws against Indian children, and parents or other persons in loco parentis except that this subparagraph 93) shall not

---

[195] Mar. 3, 1893, ch. 209, Sec. 1, 27 Stat. 628, 635 – 25 USC Sec. 282.

[196] Feb. 14, 1920, ch. 75, Sec. L, 41 Stat. 410 – 25 USC Sec. 282 01/19/04.

[197] Robert Murray p. 94. Dept. of Interior, *Manual for Indian Service*, Sec. 60, The Sherman Press, Riverside, Calif. 1942, p. 41.

apply to Indians of any tribe with a duly continued governing body exists until such body has adopted a resolution consenting to such application.

The Turtle Mountain Tribal code has likewise adopted a compulsory attendance law:[198]

> Every parent, guardian, or other person who resides within the Turtle Mountain Jurisdiction and has control over any educable child of an age of seven years to eighteen who does not fall under the provisions of Section 5.1102 shall send or take such child to a public school each year during the entire time such school is in session.

The exception to the regulation refers to children who are over age 16, or finished high school, or in a private school or a parochial school, or needed at home to support family or the child has a mental or physical disability.[199] This section of the code probably has been in effect in some form longer than the given date of 1987, and perhaps was transferred over with the change of the new Juvenile Code.

Figure 7-8: Rabbit hunt, buffalo ersatz.

---

[198] Title 5, Turtle Mountain Children's Code, 5.1101. 8/4/87, p. 5-53.
[199] Title 5, Turtle Mountain Children's Code, 5.1102. 8/4/87, p. 5-54.

# Chapter 8

## Additional Schools

### Dunseith Day School

In 1912, the Federal Government took the responsibility for educating the Indian children off the reservation. They built a one-room structure about two and one-half miles north of the village of Dunseith for this purpose. A survey made the government aware of 80 other students that were not in school, and they added another room in 1933. These two classrooms housed an enrollment of 92 students at the time. Another addition had to be made in 1936 to accommodate the overcrowded conditions that existed. As things got worse, the Federal Government recognized that temporary buildings were not the answer. To meet the needs of Indian education, a larger facility was finally constructed in 1940. The building had four regular classrooms, a gymnasium, dining room, kitchen area, and a bus garage and the upper floor had two four-room apartments to house the teachers. One of the rooms in an apartment on the upper floor had to be made into a classroom in 1947 to handle the increased enrollment. A bussing system was established for those students who lived too far from the school to walk.[200]

---

[200] Robert Murray, pp. 116-117.

Figure 8-1: The old Dunseith Day School.

*Appendix B-2* shows the Dunseith Day School enrollment decreasing from 149 students to 137 students through the years 1949 to 1953. The teacher/student ratio of 1/37 was especially high in the 1949–50 school term. The school added another teacher for the 1952–53 school year, but even with the decreased enrollment the teacher/student ratio was still only 1/27. Students who completed the Dunseith Day School sixth grade were then bussed to the Turtle Mountain Community School for further schooling.[201]

Today, the Dunseith Day School offers academic programs from kindergarten through eighth grade. The kindergarten program was added in the 1972–73 school term. A new school was completed in 1992, and seventh and eighth grades were added in the 1992–93 academic year. Students who have completed the Dunseith Day School program tend to continue schooling at the Dunseith Public School rather than taking the long ride to Belcourt.

---

[201] Robert Murray, p. 128.

Figure 8-2: Today's Dunseith Day School.

Yvonne LaFountain St. Claire is the principal of the Dunseith Day School. She has held this position since 2002. Students are served by a staff of forty-four people consisting of the principal, one counselor, twenty-three classroom teachers, one librarian, five teacher aides, two secretaries, four janitors, eight support staff members – cooks and bus drivers. The school is both State and North Central accredited.[202]

Dunseith Day School is a modern block and brick structure built in the same vicinity as the original school. The building contains twenty-one classrooms, kitchen and lunch area, nurse station, staff lounge, gymnasium, library, office space, and storage space. According to the Bureau of Indian Affairs, Facilities Manager, Tim Demery, the structure consists of 49,319 square feet, and the estimated value of the school today is $5,079,856. The bus garage was erected in 1994 and consists of 3,707 square feet. The estimated value of the garage is $441,133.

---

[202] Interview with Pam Defender, 5/1/2006.

# The Trail of Misgivings

The Honorable Merle Boucher, State Representative, asked the North Dakota Attorney General for an opinion on the status of the Dunseith Day School receiving Foundation Payments. Representative Boucher asked two questions: (1) whether Dunseith Day School met the criteria of a federal school and (2) whose responsibility was it to educate students who were not eligible to be enrolled members of the Tribe, but attended school at Dunseith Day School. The Attorney General's opinion dated October 25, 1994 is in part as follows:[203]

> Concerning your question on the financial obligation for the education of certain students attending the Dunseith Day School who are not eligible to be enrolled members of the tribe, if the students are residents of a North Dakota public school district, the school district in question is responsible for the education of those children if they actually attend a public school of the district or the district authorizes their attendance at another North Dakota public school district either upon payment of tuition, tuition waiver, or by open enrollment. . . . Further, if the students in question attend school in the district as noted in the letter to Senator Jerome, then the public school district may contract with a federal school for their education. . . .

The Dunseith Day School was eligible to receive foundation payments through the Dunseith School District #1. They began receiving these payments in 1996.

## Roussin Day School

Roussin Day School, one of the typical one-room schoolhouses, was first built in 1905. The school was named after the former landowner. The building was a one-story structure. When first erected, it consisted of one classroom with a dining room next to a kitchen. A separate five-room house served as living quarters for a teacher and his family. According to Murray, an additional classroom was added only in 1940 after the Dunseith Day School was completely rebuilt. One of the newer buildings of the Dunseith Day School was moved to Roussin School to make it

---

[203] Heitkamp, Letter Opinion 94-L-291, 10/25/1994.

a two-classroom school. Murray further stated the bus transportation from the Belcourt School was altered to serve the needs of the Roussin Day School system. The enrollment of the school constantly fluctuated from forty to seventy students. With the additional classroom, the school now contained grades one through six.[204]

Roussin Day School had a staff of two certified teachers, a cook and a janitor, an active PTA, and the normal community services given to the other day schools on the reservation. Similar to the other schools, a large garden was raised to help feed the students during the school year. Potatoes, carrots, and other root crops were stored in a root cellar. All schools had storage areas filled with canned vegetables for use at the noon meal.[205] (In the 1940's, Belcourt School had a large root cellar built into the side of a hill west of the hospital road.) See *Appendix D* for more on victory gardens. According to Roy Malaterre, these schools were heated with fuel oil, and a well was nearby for a water supply.

Figure 8-3: Roussin Day School.

---

[204] Robert Murray, p. 120.
[205] Robert Murray p. 120.

# The Trail of Misgivings

The three schools in Couture and the four schools in Ingebretson were abandoned in 1931 after the Federal Government takeover of the educational program on the reservation. However, the Federal Government miscalculated the student population, and had to reopen Roussin Day School in August 1933. The *Star* reported that Roussin School had about 60 students in grades one through three for that year.[206]

Roussin Day School was fully accredited by the North Dakota Department of Public Instruction during the 1967–68 school term. The following year, however, a letter from James Bearghost, Education Program Administrator, Bureau of Indian Affairs, to Charlotte Lang, County Superintendent dated January 4, 1969, informed her that the education program at the Roussin Day School had been discontinued. The school actually closed December of 1968. Forty students were enrolled at the time of closure; thirty-three of these pupils were transferred to the Turtle Mountain Community School, two enrolled at the Dunseith Public School, and the remaining five students transferred to Great Walker Day School. The buildings were old and teachers were difficult to find because of the multi-grades they would have to teach. Transportation of the students to the various schools did not present a problem.[207]

The Turtle Mountain Tribal Council requested the school facilities be utilized as a community center by Tribal Resolution dated May 6, 1969. The tribe stated that the Council concurred with the closing of Roussin Day School. The Aberdeen area officials placed their stamp of approval on the request, and the tribe took over the ownership of the facilities.[208]

---

[206] *Turtle Mountain Star*, June 23, 1938, p. 25.

[207] District School Superintendent's Files.

[208] District School Superintendent's Files, Tribal Resolution No. 395-5-69, May 6, 1969.

## Great Walker Day School

In 1939, the Federal Government made another addition to the Turtle Mountain Reservation educational system. At a cost of $31,627, the Great Walker Day School was built and was named after the former landowner.[209] The school was located in the northwestern part of the Reservation approximately seven miles west of Belcourt in the Ingebretson Township, Section 8, NE¼ of the NW¼. The two-story white-framed building was more modern than previously built government facilities. A well was provided and water was pumped into the building supplying running water for drinking and bathroom facilities. There were two classrooms and a dining area with cooking accommodations to serve a noon meal to students. Minimal office space was also provided. Two four-room apartments were housed on the second floor.

The curriculum offered work for the first six grades. After completing grade six, the students went to the Turtle Mountain Community School at Belcourt. The Belcourt bussing system assisted in the transportation of these students to and from school. The staff included two teachers, a cook, and a bus driver who also served as janitor. The community services offered by the school were similar to the other day schools. Murray contended that in any given year, the enrollment varied between 60 to 80 children.[210] *Appendix B-2* of the Murray table does not indicate that variation in enrollment. It may have been as high as 80 students, but all the figures for the four years of his table are 58 and lower.

In 1969, grades five and six were moved to the Belcourt School system. David Burch, Education Program Administrator, spelled out the reason in his letter dated September 24, 1969, to Principal Daniel Jerome. Burch stated that three grades per classroom were rather outdated and needed to be cut back. He recognized that TMCS was also crowded, citing numbers of 85

---

[209] Robert Murray, p. 121.
[210] Robert Murray, p. 122.

students in grade five and 100 students in grade six. He reasoned that five additional students at each grade level would not burden the TMCS as it did Great Walker. The transfer of grades five and six was effective October 6, 1969.[211]

Figure 8-4: Great Walker Day School.

Great Walker School operated two more sessions 1969–70 and 1970–71 and received accreditation from the ND State Department of Public Instruction during those final years. The school was phased out, and in the 1971–72 school year, TMCS special education classes were held in the building.[212]

Harlen Wash, EPA for the BIA, notified the division of Property and Supply of the Bureau that Great Walker School would no longer be used as an education facility as of July 1, 1972. He requested the school building be removed from the education inventory. The second floor of the building still housed tenants in the apartments through the 1971–72 school year. The building was

[211] TMCS Superintendent Files.
[212] TMCS Superintendent Files.

ordered torn down in the summer 1972; however, during the process, the building suspiciously burned to the ground.[213]

## Houle Day School

The Houle Day School was built in 1940 at a cost of $35,830.40 to the Federal Government, and was named after Abraham Houle. The Federal Government purchased a tract of 22.5 acres from Houle.[214] The school was two miles north and one and a half miles east of Belcourt, located in the Township of Couture, Section 3, SW¼, SE¼, SE¼. Houle Day School was a two-story framed structure with three classrooms, dining room with an adjoining kitchen, office space, and was equipped with a medical room on the first floor. Two four-room apartments were provided for the teachers on the second floor. It was the largest of the three outlying day schools within the reservation boundaries. A two-stall bus garage was nearby.

Figure 8-5: Houle Day School.

---

[213] TMCS Superintendent Files.
[214] TMCS Superintendent Files.

Three teachers were needed at Houle school – one for each classroom. In later years, the teaching staff was reduced to two teachers due to lower attendance. [215] The auxiliary staff included a cook who served the noon meal to the students, and a bus driver who served as janitor and handyman as well. The bussing system at Belcourt assisted with transporting the students to school. The school served students from grades one through six. Students going beyond grade six were sent to the Belcourt School.[216] Compared with the other day schools, student average attendance from the 1949–50 school term to the 1952–53 school term was in the lower 90 percents, which was much better than the other day schools of the same period.[217] See *Appendix B-2*.

According to Roy Malaterre, a long time employee of the school, the basement was used as a mechanical and storage area. He mentioned that a well supplied water for indoor toilet facilities for both boys and girls. Roy said the well went dry, and he had to haul water daily to the school while it was in session and at times on weekends. He had a truck with a 1000-gallon tank, and made as many as three trips daily.

The Meriam survey of 1928, according to Fey and McNickle, was very critical of the Federal Government day schools. The survey (addressed earlier) recommended that these schools be used as community centers for adults as well as children.[218]

The day schools' officials on the Turtle Mountain Reservation took the recommendations seriously and carried them out well. There were movies, dances and other activities held regularly at the school.

Houle Day School was issued a non-accredited classification by the North Dakota State Department of Public Instruction in the

---

[215] Robert Murray, pp. 122-123.
[216] TMCS Superintendent Files.
[217] Robert Murray, p. 128.
[218] Fey and McNickle, p. 114.

1968–69 school term. The 1969–70 school year was the last year the school served students in grades one through six. During that term, the school received a provisional accreditation by the State. In October 1970, Harlen Wash informed the Director of School Food Services, State Department of Public Instruction at Bismarck, that Houle School was no longer in operation. The school was then used for special education classes for the Belcourt School system from 1970 through 1972. The school was non-operational after 1972, and in June 1977, it was turned over to the Turtle Mountain Tribe according to Bureau documents. A few years later the building was razed.[219]

## New High School building

The need for more space in the school cried out loud and clear in the 1950's. The 1959–60 school year total enrollment was 614 students with 227 students in grades nine through twelve. There were 132 students enrolled in the seventh and eighth grades and 255 in the lower grades. At last, a new high school building that was designed to house 400 students, grades seven through twelve was completed in 1961 at a cost of approximately $1,977,605. It provided an area of 56,503 square feet. According to Sandy Thomas, a freshman at the time, the students moved into the building in January of the 1961–62 school term. The January 27 article of the *Minot Daily News* has the move as January 18, 1962. The day they moved in, the enrollment for the upper six grades was 405 with a growing population. Grades one through six had an enrollment of 309, and they were housed in the older structure.[220]

The complex consisted of ten regular classrooms, two business classrooms, a home economics classroom suite, science room, library, reading room, a gymnasium with a seating capacity of 900 spectators and a regulation-size basketball court. There

---

[219] TMCS Superintendent Files.

[220] D. Jerome, Early Education, Dec. 1984, p. 3.

were two separate locker and shower rooms. The centralized kitchen and dining area had a seating capacity of 385. All TMCS grades one through twelve shared the same dining facilities. An inter-communication system was installed, which was new to the school. A 27-year-old shop building, separate from the high school building, continued to be used for practical arts and shop rooms. Office space for administration and guidance was insufficient. There were no provisions for music. Planning for library facilities, gym space, locker and shower rooms were entirely inadequate to accommodate the 400 students that it was intended to serve.[221] There were definite shortcomings with these new facilities.

Figure 8-6: The TMCHS built in the early 1960's.

This new high school was actually only a temporary fix for the space problem. Five years later the high school and the seventh and eighth grades exceeded the new plant's space capacity

---

[221] Jerome, Early Education, Dec. 1984, p.3.

by nearly 125 students, and the elementary population had grown to 577 in the 1966–67 school year. Improvised classrooms had to be set up in the basement of the 1931 school building.[222]

From 1969 to 1972, all outlying day schools were closed by the Bureau, and yet, the TMC school was in dire need of space. In response to the need to provide ongoing academic experience for the children coming through the Head Start Program, in the 1970–71 school term, the Bureau added kindergarten to its program with an enrollment of 145 pupils. This brought the kindergarten through sixth grade total enrollment to 907.[223] Planning for the kindergarten program began during the 1968–69 school term with hopes that it would be added the following year. The Head Start Program had 140 children enrolled at the Belcourt site and another 35 pupils in the Dunseith area. The majority of these children were from economically deprived and culturally disadvantaged homes. However, the planning was hampered by the space problem. It was estimated that there would be 170 children eligible for kindergarten within the reservation including the Dunseith area. The elementary school at the time (1968–69 school term) had an enrollment of 665 students grades one through six. In addition to regular classrooms, the students were also housed in makeshift classrooms and four trailers. The crowded conditions, makeshift classrooms, and the trailers all added to the problems. Too little for too long a time has been the problem and still haunts the school system today.

Plans for a new elementary building were underway in the early 1960's, and the building was finally brought to completion in 1972. The structure contained 67,600 square feet at a cost of approximately $3,380,000. The plant provided two levels of thirty open classrooms – fifteen on each level. The building contained a pod for four kindergarten units designed to accommodate 20 pupils per unit. This new elementary section provided an instructional

---

[222] TMCS records.

[223] School Records, Thomas/Sandy's Files.

materials center (IMC), a band and music room, office space, teacher preparation areas, bathrooms and storage space. The kindergarten units provided bathrooms, and space for play activities, group learning and privacy – all in a relaxed and comfortable atmosphere. Two additional units were added to the kindergarten in 1974 at a cost of approximately $720,000. The square footage added was 7,200.[224]

By the time these units were completed, the number of kindergarten students far exceeded what the units could accommodate. The 1970–71 school year was the year a contract was made with St. Ann's Mission School to handle the overcrowded conditions at the TMCS, whose total enrollment was 1,732 students. As mentioned earlier, seven first-grade classes were housed at St. Ann's.[225]

The old bus garage was razed to provide the necessary space for the elementary and kindergarten buildings. New garages for the buses were built in two phases north of the school. A four-stall garage was completed in 1972 and has a replacement cost of $178,700 as of 2006. In 1973, a fifteen-stall garage was completed with a welding and mechanical area to repair the buses. The replacement cost of this building as of 2006 is $1,105,601.[226] According to Pete Davis, Bus Garage Manager, the school district built another eight-stall garage in the 1980's to accommodate the many school-operated buses and vehicles.

Today thirty buses are in operation. Twenty-three years ago, transportation of students was handled by twenty-one buses.[227]

Community planning for another new Turtle Mountain Community High School began in October, 1970. Planning monies were obtained in FY1973, and the design funds followed in

---

[224] Jerome, Early Education, Dec. 1984, p. 4.
[225] TMCS records.
[226] TM Agency records.
[227] Couture/Ingebretson Proposed Reorganization planning, 1983, p. l.

FY1974. The construction funding did not come as promised by the Bureau of Indian Affairs officials in Albuquerque. The efforts of the school officials and staff would not be realized for another decade.[228]

The late 1960's and all of the 1970's were the years of temporaries and modification of buildings. Temporary metal buildings were erected and trailers were moved in to meet the demand of the ever-increasing enrollment. There were three trailers that housed some of the elementary students. The high school was also supplemented with two trailers to handle its overcrowded conditions.

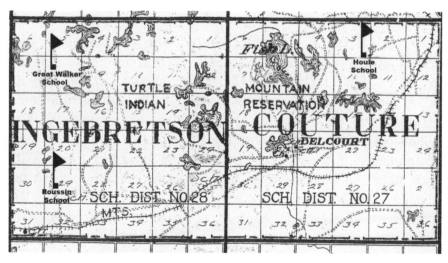

Figure 8-7: Additional Reservation schools from 1933 to 1970's.

---

[228] Jerome, Statement prepared to present to Senate subcommittee on Interior Appropriation, p. 9.

# Chapter 9

## Districts Developments and Rebuilding After the Fire

The Couture and Ingebretson School Districts were seemingly dormant since the federal takeover in 1931. Couture generated $7,611.11 in 1931 while Ingebretson brought in $8,067.75 from the State Government. The Bureau education officials used the money as needed in the school systems. The boards operated robot-like until the 1960's when Couture received State moneys in the amount of $13,000 in 1963 and 1964. With each student population surge upward in the district, so went the revenue. The money jumped to $30,000 in 1965 and 1966. The increase for Ingebretson was not as dramatic, but it was up to $14,694 in 1966. School Districts began paying salaries for several school personnel such as for Jon Eckerdt, a band teacher and Norma Good, a librarian in the 1962–63 school term. The following year Couture Board, without the consent of the Bureau officials, hired a school social worker to deal with attendance. In the 1966–67 school year, the Couture Board hired a high school principal. By 1967, the Couture District School budget was up to $68,552.75. In 1969, the Couture School District hired its first School Superintendent, Dan Jerome. As the budget continued to increase, more staff was hired to assist in teaching and other school tasks.[229]

The Districts helped in ways other than hiring school staff. In 1968, the Couture Board purchased 3.12 acres of land from Edward D. "Chick" Jollie and built four houses on the land for district school staff. This relieved the housing crunch the Bureau experienced at the time. The cost of the four teacher houses was $15,000 each for a total of $60,000. These homes were built just south of the elementary school and Highway 5. The next year the district added a four-stall garage for these sites at a cost of $10,000.[230]

Eighteen years later, the School District no longer had a need for the four houses and the land that was purchased from Jollie. They sold the buildings and land to Dave and Phyllis Jollie, at a price of $70,000.00. The board approved the sale during the 1986–87 school year.[231] The stipulation Chick Jollie had made with the District at the time of sale was that if ever the district wanted to sell the land it was to be offered first to members of the family.

In 1971, the Federal Government erected five temporary Armco metal buildings and moved in two trailers to accommodate grades seven and eight. These buildings were constructed on the hill, east of the 1962 high school building. The trailers provided one classroom and office space for the staff. The Federal Government paid $20,000 each for the Armco buildings. Couture School District paid for the site work and the pouring of the concrete slabs for the floors. The five metal structures were divided into two classrooms per building for a total of ten classrooms. These were to accommodate approximately 240 students.[232]

---

[229] Rolette County Records and TMCS files.

[230] Jerome, *Early Education*, p. 4.

[231] TMCS Supt. Reports 1986-87, p. 6.

[232] Jerome, *Early Education*, p. 4

# The Trail of Misgivings

Seventh and eighth graders moved into the metal buildings and trailers in the fall of 1971. Since this age group needed special attention, the middle school concept was explored and studied during the 1971–72 school year. It was thought that the middle school concept would lend itself for caring and educating these students of that age most satisfactorily.[233] The following school year the staff and students made the change to the middle school system. Darrell Ganarelli was designated principal of the new operation. The middle school concept gave the students a helping hand to make a smooth and practical transition from the lower grades to the high school setting. Middle school would not mirror high school like a junior high school. The staff had to dedicate themselves to the establishment of a two-year experience with these students, which would prepare them for the high school setting. The Middle School students were not classified as seventh or eighth graders, but students working through a non-graded status sequence. Each student was placed in an individualized instructional program according to his or her needs and interests.[234] However, the transitional phase of the Middle School Program was hampered with problems. Overcrowded conditions were no different than the problems in the rest of the schools.

In 1973, a sixth metal building was added to the middle school area at a cost of $28,957 to the Couture School District. This building was used as a reading and math laboratory. The following year an elementary reading lab was erected by the Couture School District at a cost of $47,375. This structure was located northwest of the old 1931 white elementary building. Each of these steel buildings contained 3,000 square feet of space and was equipped with bathroom facilities. The Districts and the Bureau were attempting to resolve space problems by rentals, improvising, and temporary buildings.[235]

---

[233] Jerome, *Early Education*, Dec. 1984, p. 4.
[234] Middle School Staff paper, *Mandate for Change*, 1971-72 acad. year, pp. 1-2.
[235] Jerome, *Early Education,* Dec. 1984, p. 7.

The bus garage was used as a physical education facility from 1973–75. These makeshift places, plus the gym facilities leased from St. Ann's, took care of the overflow of the physical education classes. A multi-purpose building for the TMC Middle School was needed and constructed in 1975 at cost of $206,000 to the Couture School District. It contained a regular size gym, lockers with shower facilities, and an activity room. This steel building was 70 feet by 120 feet with floor space of 8,400 square feet.[236]

There were 294 middle school students in the 1975–76 school term. They were housed in six temporary metal buildings; three ten-year-old trailers that were condemned by Bureau of Indian Affairs three years earlier; a trailer purchased by Title I to house the special education classes; a renovated bus garage used for part of the physical education classes; and gym facilities were leased from St. Ann's to take care of the remaining physical education classes. In addition, fifty percent of the seventh and eighth grade students used the high school shop facilities, which were already crowded with high school students. These 294 students shared both the elementary and high school library facilities.[237]

In an attempt to temporarily remedy the lack of space problem, the districts completed two more steel structures for the TMC Middle School in 1976 at the cost of $45,000. One building was for the administration and a second was an adjoining dining room area to accommodate the lunch program. Noon lunch was now catered to students from the main kitchen at the 1962 high school building.[238]

An accommodation for the Building Trades Vocational Program was constructed in 1976 at the middle school complex. At the same time, the district also had some remodeling done on

---

[236] Jerome, *Early Education,* Dec. 1984, p. 7.

[237] Jerome, Statement in support of a request for an Additional Appropriation for the BIA for FY 1976 for the Construction of a high school complex at Belcourt, North Dakota, 1975, p. 6.

[238] Jerome, *Early Education,* Dec. 1984, pp. 7-8.

the old shop to be used for welding. The cost of both the building and remodeling was $92,000. This vocational building did ease some of the pressure placed on the TMC High School.

In that same year, a 35-by-60-foot district school administration building was erected north of the elementary school. The Couture District cost was $31,000. It provided office space for the School Superintendent, Assistant Superintendent, Finance Director, Title I Director, Title IV Director, and the Business Office. The building eased some of the overcrowding at the high school.[239] Two additions were added to the administration building in 1979 and 1980. These were two additional offices (20 by 35 feet) to the west of the building and a boardroom (20 by 35 feet) to the east. The cost of the additions was $33,000. This building became a source of controversy in later years.[240]

An addition was also added to the middle school administration building in 1980 at a cost of $17,000 to the Couture School District.[241]

The middle school was a poor climate for any school setting with its sprawled-out metal buildings and trailers. Daily, students traveled to nearly each building within the middle school compound to attend various classes in all kinds of weather. They also had to trek to the high school for their shop, library, and music classes. The bus garage was used as a gymnasium, and the buses had to be moved out during the day. During cold weather, it was necessary to start all the buses so that they would be warm and ready to go when school was dismissed. These facilities were not designed for the purpose of holding physical education classes. Limited sanitary facilities in the building made it necessary for students to return to their regular classrooms without showering. The garage was a distance from the middle school campus, which

---

[239]Jerome, Statement to U.S. Legislative Committees, p. 7.
[240]Jerome, *Early Education,* Dec 1984, pp. 6-7.
[241]Jerome, *Early Education*, Dec 1984, pp. 6-7.

necessitated that the students be bussed to and from their physical education classes losing quality class time.[242]

The 1962 high school building was to accommodate 400 students in a traditional classroom setting. In the 1975–76 academic year, there were 529 high school students enrolled. As mentioned earlier, no provisions were made for music classes in the high school building. Library facilities, gym space, locker and shower rooms were inadequate to serve 529 students. All 1,732 students (K-12) shared the band and music room in the 1972 elementary building.[243]

To further emphasize the squeeze on facilities at the Turtle Mountain Community School, the following excerpts were taken from the Team Evaluation Report, North Dakota State Committee, North Central Association Commission on Secondary Schools, March 11 and 12, 1973:[244]

> In spite of all the positive aspects of the school and its program, problems do exist. The needs of the Turtle Mountain Community School are many. The facilities although in sound condition and state of maintenance, are inadequate in terms of the program being offered and in terms of the projected enrollment increase for the next five years. Plans for a new facility are being created at the present time which, when realized, will enhance tremendously the intended program for this high school.

The new high school was completed and ready for occupancy in the fall of 1984. The building had 92,000 square feet of space at a cost of $8,200,000. The new high school plant was designed to accommodate 525 students and was equipped with a music area, which it lacked in the first high school setting. Besides music, the building accommodated the following disciplines: Math-Science, Humanities, Business and Career Education, Industrial Arts, Art-Home Economics, and Physical Education. It contained

---

[242] Jerome, Statement to U.S. Legislative Committees, p. 7.

[243] Jerome, Statement to U.S. Legislative Committees, p. 4.

[244] TMCS Superintendent's Files, 1973.

administration offices, guidance area, a library, dining/commons area, and a gymnasium with a seating capacity of 1,200 spectators.[245]

The school year got off to a good start August 22, 1984. The high school had moved to its new facilities, and the middle school had moved to the old high school. All the moving took place during the summer months. The enrollment for each grade was as follows:[246] These are beginning and ending year figures, which may differ from *Appendix B-3*.

### Table 9-1A: TMCES Attendance

| Grade | Beginning | Ending |
|-------|-----------|--------|
| K | 117 | 118 |
| 1 | 107 | 110 |
| 2 | 126 | 122 |
| 3 | 121 | 120 |
| 4 | 82 | 82 |
| 5 | 86 | 87 |
| Elementary Totals | 639 | 639 |

### Table 9-1B: TMCMS Attendance

| Grade | Beginning | Ending |
|-------|-----------|--------|
| 6 | 97 | 98 |
| 7 | 91 | 98 |
| 8 | 85 | 84 |
| Middle School Totals | 273 | 280 |

---

[245] TMCS Superintendent's Files.
[246] TMCS Superintendent's End of Year Report 1984-85, p. 2.

**Table 9-1C: TMCHS Attendance**

| Grade | Beginning | Ending |
|---|---|---|
| 9 | 126 | 124 |
| 10 | 93 | 81 |
| 11 | 100 | 88 |
| 12 | 99 | 88 |
| High School Totals | 418 | 381 |
| | | |
| Combined Schools TOTALS | 1,330 | 1,300 |

The Belcourt Learning Center (BLC) was brought into existence by the Board of Education of the newly reorganized Belcourt School District No. 7 in 1984. This center was an alternative school, which operated in conjunction with the high school. It was designed for students who had difficulty functioning in the regular high school setting. Jon Fimmel served as BLC principal. The center operated through the 1984–85 academic year. It was discontinued because of students' lack of interest and could not generate the funding required to keep it in operation. The center had an enrollment of fifty-eight students. Eighteen of these students earned transcript credits and three received high school diplomas.[247] (May 28, 1985, 81 students graduated from the eighth grade).[248]

## The Big One

Friday morning, October 26, 1984, a fire was discovered at the middle school. Belcourt firemen were called to the scene shortly after 5 a.m. Rolla firemen who were summoned at 5:27

---

[247] Superintendent's Report, 1984 – 1985, p. 8.
[248] Superintendent's Report 1984 –1985, p. 2.

a.m. arrived on the scene before six o'clock. Firefighters from St. John, Rolette, and Dunseith joined the group of firefighters shortly after six that morning. Rock Lake, Bottineau and Bisbee arrived at the scene after 8 a.m. Despite the efforts, the fire continued to spread through the building.[249]

Figure 9-1: TMC Middle School fire, which swept through the building just after daybreak.

Throughout the day, the fire continued to burn before the firefighters from Belcourt and seven neighboring communities had it under control. Flare-ups throughout the weekend occurred and a constant fire watch was maintained for several days. Damage was extensive. Two home economics rooms, coach's office, nurse's area, photo lab, art room and instructional media center were totally destroyed by the fire. The area lost was approximately 32,325 square feet. The gymnasium, south wing (which contained 12 classrooms), dining and kitchen area, elementary administration

---

[249] *Turtle Mountain Star,* October 29, 1984. p. 1.

and counseling offices, and the band room received smoke, water, and fire damages in various degrees. These areas included approximately 36,750 square feet.[250]

Figure 9-2: TMC Middle School fire.

Within the elementary, the old gymnasium received extensive smoke damage. The classroom areas suffered considerable smoke and water damage. Fifteen classrooms in the upper level received the most damage and even the carpeting had to be removed. The lower level that also contained fifteen classrooms suffered smoke damage to a lesser degree. This area contained 58,900 square feet.[251] The fire was ruled as deliberately set. To date no one has been charged.

The fire caused 950 students – kindergarten through eighth grade – to be displaced. However, on the following Monday, October 30, 1984, the students were back to school on split shifts –

---

[250] Superintendent's Report 1984 – 1985, p. 3.
[251] Superintendent's Report 1984 – 1985, p. 3.

kindergarten and grades one, two, nine, ten, eleven, and twelve were attending classes from 7:00 a.m. to 12:00 noon. Grades three, four, five, six, seven, and eight were in school from 12:15 p.m. to 5:15 p.m. The elementary students were housed in the old 1931 white elementary building and the middle and high school students were housed in the new 1984 high school plant.[252]

Figure 9-3: TMC Middle School fire.

At the beginning of the second semester of the school term (January 14, 1985), classes resumed their regular schedule. The high school students finally settled in the new high school facilities. The middle school students moved to their old setting of Armco metal buildings. The elementary students moved back into their regular facilities including the old school building of 1931. The elementary gym was used for the dining area for the elementary students. Sandwiches, instead of the regular hot lunches, were served to the students during this crisis period.

---

[252] Superintendent's End of Year Report 1984 – 1985, p. 3.

There was obvious overcrowding and a decrease in some services. For example, the physical education program had to be reduced because the dining program monopolized the gym area.[253]

Figure 9-4: The temporary space for the middle school was once again made temporary.

Almost immediately after the fire, the planning began for a new middle school building. Several planning meetings were held locally, and on November 19, 1984, education officials from Washington, Aberdeen, Albuquerque, and Belcourt met in Aberdeen, South Dakota to discuss the educational needs at Turtle Mountain. On January 12th and 13th of 1985, two architects, Frank Lotta from Washington, D.C. and Wallace Ashley from Albuquerque, New Mexico, met with Bureau of Indian Affairs and School District education officials to discuss the preliminary functional requirements of the Turtle Mountain Community

---

[253] Superintendent's End of Year Report, 1984 – 1985, p. 4.

School. Summary of estimated construction costs was (1) Overall site work clean up, etc. $900,000, (2) Middle School Construction $6,100,000 for a total cost $7,000,000.[254]

In the fall of 1989, five years after the fire at the TMC Middle School, the new facility was ready for occupancy. The eighth graders who once watched their school burn were already out of high school. The building had another deck added to it. This upper floor contained ten regular classrooms. Later, the science area was divided into two classrooms. The Instructional Media Center (IMC) was renovated, and six more classrooms were added west of it. Special education classrooms were also a feature of the new building. The construction included a large multi-purpose room used for physical education and various activities. The total cost of the entire project was $8,822,723.[255]

## More Fires

The first fire was in 1984 that did considerable damage to the TMCMS. A second fire scare occurred at TMCES approximately 6:30 p.m. on December 3, 1986. The fire started in a second grade classroom on the upper level. It was determined that the fire was deliberately set. The police questioned several suspects, but not enough evidence was found for prosecution. Sam Laducer, janitor, discovered someone had broken into the building. He then found the other janitor on duty. Meanwhile, the fire alarm was activated. They found the fire and snuffed it out before the fire department arrived. State Fire Marshall was in the area that evening, and he made his investigation before 9:00 p.m. Damage was slight, and the smoke cleared that evening. There was no delay of school.[256]

On January 11, 1987, at approximately 5:30 in the evening, Louis Dauphinais discovered a second fire of that school year in

---

[254] Introduction and Summary Planning for Middle School Construction, November/1985, p. 8.

[255] Superintendent's End of Year Report, 1988-89, p. 43.

[256] Superintendent's End of Year Report, 1986-87, p. 10.

## *Insert to* **The Trail of Misgivings**

Page 22: Red Thunder is documented as a Cree Indian. Judy Kakenowash Azure claims ancestral lineage to Red Thunder, and stated (11/17/2006) that Red Thunder was Ojibway (Ojibwe). Charlie White Weasel's "Pembina and Turtle Mountain Ojibway (Chippewa) History," indicates Red Thunder to be Cree on page 148.

Page 224: a picture of Larry Belgarde (first TMCC president) was omitted (right). His name is also misspelled when first used on this page.

Chapter 17 is missing the pictures of the Superintendents Wayne Keplin (below) and Viola Champagne LaFontaine (lower right).

Missing in chapter 17 was Roman Marcellais (left), TMCS elementary principal, presently assistant superintendent.

Appendix E: correction in the Belcourt school board members:

2004: Allan Malaterre (President), Richard Schroeder, Wanda Laducer, Will Grant, Kurt Peltier, Jim Parisien, Curtis L Poitra.

2005: Richard McCloud (President), Allan Malaterre, Wanda Laducer, Will Grant, Kurt Peltier, Jim Parisien, Curtis L Poitra.

2006: Richard McCloud (President), Allan Malaterre, Wanda Laducer, Will Grant, Kurt Peltier, Jim Parisien, Curtis L Poitra.

Bibliography: mention of Charlie White Weasel's documentary, *Pembina and Turtle Mountain Ojibway (Chippewa) History* (undated), is missing.

On the last page of the book two bus drivers' names were misspelled in the caption: *Lloyd Martin* and *Walter Davis*.

Edited November 20, 2006

the Middle School. There was a forced entry to the home economics area. The State Fire Marshall ruled out an electrical fire. Once again, it appeared that the fire was deliberately set. The Middle School home economics classes were conducted in one of the BIA houses for a period of two weeks during the reconstruction of the fire-damaged area. Bureau and District personnel met and decided that a security watch would be set into operation immediately.[257]

---

[257] Superintendent's End of Year Report, 1986-87, p. 10.

# Chapter 10

# Couture and Ingebretson Reorganization

James Bearghost, Education Program Administrator, Bureau of Indian Affairs, addressed a letter to Charlotte Lang, County Superintendent of Schools, on January 25, 1969 and stated Roussin Day School was closing. In a letter Lang wrote to the Rolette County Commissioners, dated March 4, 1969, she requested a spring meeting with the County Reorganization Committee for the purpose of the reorganization intentions of the Ingebretson and Couture School Districts. That Committee took no action. In 1977, Lang promised if Couture Board would increase its membership, she would again make an effort to reorganize the Couture and Ingebretson School Districts into one district. The Couture School Board voted to add two more members to make it a five-member board. Again her intentions fell short. Reorganization was definitely within the realm of the County Superintendent of School's authority to initiate. In fact, State law says it was her duty to exercise that power when a district does not have a school in its district boundaries. Ingebretson had not had a school within its territorial limits for eight years. County Superintendent of Schools Lang was acutely aware of this fact. County records indicate a Rolette County Reorganization Board meeting was held August 25, 1978. Neither the TMCS Superintendent nor the presidents of the boards had been informed. According to the minutes, the meeting of the Rolette County Reorganization Board studied plans of the school districts of Rolette County.[258] Lang mentioned nothing about the agreement she made with Couture District board and their reorganization plan. The minutes read in part: "Couture School District #27 and Ingebretson School District #28: As there is only one school in these two districts and the children from both districts attend this school, sometime in the future they should become one district, when this becomes the desire of the people."[259] The reorganization board was quite willing to proceed with reorganization if some county official present would have set the process in motion.

By reorganizing the districts, duplication of work would be eliminated for the office staffs of the districts. The school administration was still determined to accomplish the task of reorganization. The Tribal Chairman, Richard LaFromboise, was consulted on the subject. He contacted the State Department of Public Instruction, and reorganization of the districts was again on the agenda.[260]

Couture School District Board held a special meeting Monday August 1, 1983. Members present: Ray Trottier, Ed Herman, Tiny Brien, and Lynn Davis. Susie Wilkie was absent. Others present: Bob Abrahamson, County Superintendent of Schools, and Dan Jerome, School Superintendent. The Ingebretson School Board was also in attendance and in session. All members were present: Yvonne St. Claire, Judy Delonais, and Stanley Gourneau. Howard Frederick and Rochelle Gourneau, clerks of the Couture and Ingebretson Boards, respectively, were also present.[261]

---

[258] Dan Jerome, *History of the School Districts on the TM Reservation,* Summer of 1984, pp. 2-3.

[259] Rolette County School Reorganization Board Meeting Minutes, August 25, 1978, p. 1.

[260] Jerome, Summer of 1984, p. 3.

[261] Jerome, Summer of 1984, p. 4.

# The Trail of Misgivings

Ingebretson School District met to study the reorganization plan. September 15, 1983, Couture School District met to review the same reorganization plan. At a later meeting, both boards conducted sessions at the same time and place. They selected the Belcourt School District to be the name of the reorganized district. The number 7 was chosen and attached later to the new district. They also opted to have seven members on the new board.[262]

The boards reached an agreement and voted to carry-over members. The decision was that Ray Trottier, Tiny Brien, and Stanley Gourneau would serve the two years remaining in their terms of office. Ed Herman and Yvonne St. Claire would serve the one year remaining of their three-year term. Two additional members would be required to run for a three-year term at the next election.[263] (Six months later Mike Nelson and Lynn Davis were voted in as the sixth and seventh members of the new Belcourt School District #7 Board.)[264]

Even though State law did not require a public meeting, a meeting was held September 22, 1983 at the TMCHS cafeteria. Very few people turned out, but the plan was discussed and accepted by those in attendance.[265]

The Rolette County Reorganization Board met and approved the reorganization plan October 6, 1983. There was no opposition to the proposal. The Findings of Fact of the Rolette County Committee for Reorganization of School Districts Couture and Ingebretson were as follows:

1. No school is presently located in the Ingebretson School District and none has been in that district for the last twelve [fourteen] years.

2. Ingebretson School District students have been attending the schools within the Couture School District.

---

[262] Dan Jerome, Summer of 1984, p. 4.

[263] Dan Jerome, Summer of 1984, p. 4.

[264] School Superintendent's files.

[265] Dan Jerome, Summer of 1984, p. 4.

3. The School's accounting system will be less complex and more efficiently operated.

4. Operation of the school system would be less cumbersome.

The State Board of Public School Education approved the reorganization proposal submitted by the Couture/Ingebretson Boards on November 2, 1983. But the new district still needed a vote of approval from its constituents. An election was called by County School Superintendent Abrahamson to be held on December 19, 1983. The electors had to approve the plan by a majority vote in each district before the new district could be formed. According to Rolette County records the Couture voters approved the plan by 120 yes votes to 9 no votes. Ingebretson voters cast 77 votes in favor of the plan and none opposed.[266]

The reorganization plan went into effect July 1, 1984. The new legal description of the Belcourt School District # 7 is: Couture Township, 162 North, Range 70 West; and Ingebretson Township, 162 North, Range 71 West in Rolette County. The plan required the property, debts, and liabilities of the two districts - Couture and Ingebretson – to be turned over to the reorganized district and that all existing agreements by either board remain in force except where agreement might conflict with state law. The first meeting of the newly formed district was held in July 1984 to discuss planning for the new school year.[267]

## Annexation of Shell Valley

According to the Turtle Mountain Housing Authority records, 50 housing units were built and ready for occupancy September 30, 1978. The housing project was built in the township of Shell Valley on Tribal land and contiguous to the Turtle Mountain Reservation. Rolette School District #29 received about $20,000 in tuition apportionment moneys generated by the students living in the Shell

---

[266] Rolette County Records.

[267] Dan Jerome, *History of the School Districts on the Turtle Mountain Reservation,* Summer/1984, p. 5.

157

Valley Housing Project. However, the Belcourt school system provided all the educational needs of these students.

In 1984, the residents living in the Shell Valley Housing area petitioned the County and the State to annex the land to the Belcourt School District. There were 119 signers on the petition. The map of Rolette County on Figure 10-1 outlines the tract of land cited in the petition. The tract consisted of about 240 acres.[268]

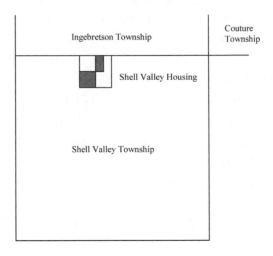

Figure 10-1: Map of Shell Valley Annexation.

Testimony was given at the annexation meeting with the Rolette County Reorganization Committee on May 14, 1985. Minutes of the meeting are quoted in part:[269]

Testimony in favor of the petition:

a. Dan Jerome – Supt. of the Belcourt School
   1. No indebtedness involved with this annexation.
   2. No taxable valuation involved because land is federally owned.
   3. Shorter bus route to Belcourt.

[268] Rolette County Records; Superintendent Reports, 1984-85 and 1985-86.
[269] Minutes Shell Valley Annexation Hearing Rolette County Courthouse, May 14, 1985.

4. Culturally relevant curriculum.
5. Low income students from Shell Valley would benefit from breakfast program, full kindergarten, complete special education program.
6. Students now attend Belcourt.
7. People of Shell Valley cannot vote in school elections.
8. Parents can become more involved in their child's education because of distance factor.
9. Public Health Service is available in Belcourt.
10. Most parents consider Belcourt their hometown.
11. Busing after extra-curricular events.
12. If annexation is approved, Belcourt could claim P. L. 874 money.

b. Howard Frederick – Clerk and Finance Director
1. Explained 874 money – can't claim Shell Valley students for 874 money because they don't reside in Belcourt School District.
2. $110 – $115 thousand that neither district is eligible for.

c. Richard LaFromboise – Tribal Chairman
1. Education is very important to tribe.
2. Tribe wants to provide quality education to all Tribal Members.

d. Tony Hovet – Resident of Shell Valley
1. Would like to vote and have right to hold school board position in Belcourt School where his children attend school.

e. Cindy Hawk – Resident of Shell Valley – Aide at Belcourt
1. Approved annexation would benefit the students monetarily.
2. Wants to vote and hold school office.

f. Howard Frederick
1. Reason cost per pupil is so high is because of all the extra programs at Belcourt.
2. Rolette wouldn't have had any of these students if Shell Valley Housing wasn't built where it was.

## Testimony against petition:

a. Merrill Krueger – Rolette Supt. of Schools
1. Rolette also provides a quality education.
2. Rolette would stand to loose revenue from State Tuition Apportionment of approximately $20,000.00.
3. This annexation does not fit the Comprehensive Plan – irregular boundaries.

# The Trail of Misgivings

The Rolette County Reorganization Board approved the petition at that annexation meeting. The North Dakota State Board of Public School Education approved the petition the 15th day of July 1985. The annexation went into effect the same day.[270]

Errors on the land description were made during the annexation and the following corrected legal description was received from the State by the County Superintendent of Schools on September 18, 1987: Lot 2 and the SW¼ of NE¼ and the SW¼ of Section 4, Township 161 North, Range 71 West.[271] This description consists of 240 acres instead of the 80 acres indicated on the plan.

---

[270] Rolette County Records; Superintendent Report's 1985-86.
[271] Letter from State Board of Public School Education, September 21, 1987.

# Chapter 11

# Types of Schools and Funding Sources

One is easily convinced that the Belcourt School District funding is complicated with the various revenues from the State and Federal Governments. Contract schools and cooperative agreements add to the dilemma of understanding the system. Imagine what funding sources were like when there were two separate school districts. Today, the total funding for the Belcourt School District is more than $20,000,000.

It was discussed in earlier chapters that the Bureau regulations conflicted with the state law. Bureau regulations stated that the government would fund no Indian child if the child's parents worked for the Federal Government because the parents were taxpayers, and their children should be the responsibility of the State. This policy conflicted with North Dakota State Century Code 15–40–14 which stated in part, " There shall be paid from the county equalization fund to all school districts operating high schools, to school districts contracting to educate high school pupils in a federal Indian school. . . . However, no payment shall be made for Indian pupils in districts in which the school facilities are being provided, maintained and staffed wholly or in part by the Federal Government for the education of the Indian pupils."[272]

---

[272] School Laws of North Dakota – 1967 Supplement – Vol. 3, p. 85.

# The Trail of Misgivings

The North Dakota Attorney General's opinion dated May 2, 1963, in response to a question that the Department of Public Instruction posed concerning an agreement between the School District and the Turtle Mountain Indian Agency is stated in part as follows: "You then call our attention to House Bill No. 685 passed by the 1963 Legislature, which will become law July 1, 1963, and which contains, amongst other things, the following language:"[273]

> The school board may make arrangements for the education of pupils in a Federal Indian school and contract with the superintendent of the Indian agency for the payment of tuition for these pupils.

The Attorney General's opinion mentioned that the contract does not state provision for tuition payments. Instead it stated it would contribute $6,500 for a teacher's services and other school costs. The contract specified other responsibilities for the education of district students at TMCS. "You then ask, does this contract meet the requirements of House Bill No. 685? . . . . We deem the term 'tuition' to be used in its broad sense and that it does not necessarily require the payment of money for the education of children at the Indian school. Payment in kind would be permitted under such term. . . . We therefore conclude that the proposed contract is within the provisions of House Bill No. 685."[274]

The correspondence that had transpired between the Bureau and State officials brought about State law changes and concessions. A letter from the State Department dated August 14, 1963, to the Bureau office in Aberdeen, South Dakota, reads in part: "The 1963 session of the legislature amended the foundation program law to permit payments to school districts that educate children in a Federal Indian school. This is an exception to the rule in that the law otherwise only provides for payment to the school districts in which the children are actually being educated." The letter further states, "It is imperative that only those children who are the responsibility of the school district be included for

---

[273] Attorney General, State of North Dakota, Opinion May 2, 1963.
[274] Attorney General, State of North Dakota, Opinion May 2, 1963.

foundation program payments. In fact, the law so stipulates. . . . In addition to this, the Bureau has a regulation that no child of an employee of the Bureau can be educated at Federal expense. We, therefore, have accepted as eligible for payment those children who are of one-fourth Indian blood or more but whose parents are employed by the Bureau of Indian Affairs."[275]

This change of law and the understanding between the State and Bureau officials now opened more funding for the reservation districts. The 1950 Public Law 81–874 provided money for school districts impacted by federal activities. This law did not immediately affect Indian children living on the reservation, but in 1953, the law was amended to include Indian children living with parents residing and/or working on Indian lands held in trust by the Federal Government or a reservation. Children had to be one-fourth degree Indian. Money generated by these children went into the general operating budgets of the Couture and Ingebretson School Districts. Later the law was amended to include all Indian children who lived on land that is not taxable regardless of where the parents worked.[276] This law gave the Districts more control in the education of Indian children. More importantly the law gave the Tribe a stronger voice in how the funding for education of their children was spent.

In 1934, Congress had passed Public Law 73–815 known as Johnson-O'Malley (JOM). This law was designed to help school districts near Indian lands, or that had federal activities operating on tax-free lands, and provided funds for school construction.[277] The

---

[275] Ltr. of Dept. of Public Instruction, Bismarck, ND, to BIA, Aberdeen Area Office, Aberdeen, SD, 8/14/63.

[276] Indian Education Involvement of Federal, State and Tribal Governments, Education Commission of the States, Denver, Colorado, Report No. 135, September 1980, p. 11.

[277] Indian Education., Involvement of Federal, State and Tribal Governments, Education. Commission of the States, Denver, Colorado, Report 135, September 1980, p. 11.

St. John School District was assisted with JOM funds for their recent school building completed in 1995.

In 1967, another problem erupted with regards to the funding of the Districts. According to Howard Snortland, Director of Finance and Statistics for the North Dakota State Department of Public Instruction, someone challenged the funding of the foundation payments to the Ingebretson School District. Snortland called the Aberdeen Education Office and spoke to Leslie M. Keller, Acting Area Director.[278] Both Couture and Ingebretson School Districts had cooperative agreements with the Bureau of Indian Affairs. These agreements specified which students each district would be responsible for educating, and to what educational costs the Districts would contribute. The children in question were those who had parents working for the Federal Government in Belcourt – Bureau of Indian Affairs, U. S. Public Health Service, U. S. Post Office, and the William Langer Jewel Bearing Plant in Rolla, North Dakota.

The definition of a cooperative school is: ". . . a school operated under a cooperative agreement between a School District and the Bureau of Indian Affairs in conformance with State and Federal school laws and regulations."[279]

A letter dated November 28, 1967, was written to the Commissioner of Indian Affairs, Washington, D. C. by Leslie M. Keller, Acting Area Director at Aberdeen, South Dakota. The letter indicated that Ingebretson School District listed 25 students and Couture School District claimed 226 students who had parents employed by the Federal Government. Since the State Finance Director might have to get an opinion from the North Dakota Attorney General, he needed information providing clarification

---

[278] Letter Mr. Snortland, dated Dec. 14, 1967 from Leslie M. Keller, BIA, Acting Director, Aberdeen Area Office, Aberdeen S.D.

[279] Code of Federal Regulation, Title 25, Section 31.0 (b), revised as of April 1, 2004, p. 128.

that would "explain why children of Indian Federal employees are not eligible for education at Federal Government expense."[280]

Glenn C. Lundeen, Chief Branch of Public School Relation, responded to Keller stating that 31.1 (a) and 31.1 (b) of the Code of Federal Regulation (CFR), Title 25 applied. Keller responded to Howard Snortland in a letter dated December 14, 1967, and enclosed Lundeen's letter. [281]

(a) Enrollment in Bureau-operated boarding school is available to children of one-fourth or more degree of Indian blood who reside within the exterior boundaries of the Indian reservations under the jurisdiction of the Bureau of Indian Affairs or on trust or restricted lands under the jurisdiction of the Bureau of Indian Affairs when there are no other appropriate school facilities available to them or when they are from broken or unsuitable homes. Enrollment may be available also to children of one-fourth or more degree of Indian blood who reside near the reservation when a denial of such enrollment would have a direct effect upon Bureau programs within the reservation.

(b) Enrollment in Bureau-operated day schools is available to children of one-fourth or more degree of Indian blood who reside within the exterior boundaries of Indian reservations under the jurisdiction of the Bureau of Indian Affairs or on trust or restricted lands under the jurisdiction of the Bureau.[282]

An opinion was solicited and the ruling of the North Dakota Attorney General came in January of 1968. Needless to say, it was not in favor of the Districts. North Dakota Century Code 15–40–14 as cited earlier clearly stated that "no payment shall be made for Indian pupils in districts in which the school facilities are being provided, maintained and staffed wholly or in part by the Federal

---

[280] Letter dated Nov. 28, 1967, from Leslie M. Keller, Acting Area Director, Aberdeen, South Dakota, to Commissioner of Indian Affairs, Washington, D.C.

[281] Letter dated Dec. 14, 1967 from Leslie M. Keller, Acting Area Director, Aberdeen, South Dakota, to Howard J. Snortland, Director of Finance and Statistics, State Dept. of Public Instruction.

[282] Letter dated Dec. 11, 1967, from Glenn C. Lundeen, Chief, Branch of Public School Relations, Washington, D.C., to Martin N.B. Holm, Area Director, Aberdeen, South Dakota.

Government for the education of the Indian pupils." *Déjà vous* has come to haunt the Indian.

Art Raymond of the *Grand Forks Herald* writes, "Educationally, because of peculiar finances, the 355 [Indian students] are unwanted by the Bureau of Indian Affairs and by the state."[283] The article includes the number of children affected in other reservations of North Dakota as well as Turtle Mountain. At that time, the foundation payments of $198 were allocated for each elementary student, and each high school student received $290.40. According to the *Grand Forks Herald*, Couture and Ingebretson Districts lost $35,065.80 on this ruling. Snortland stated that, "We have been making Foundation payments on the basis of an old law. . . . This goes way back to the days before the Foundation program. It was called the high school tuition program then. The law was so written school districts could contract with the superintendent of the agency for the education of children in the district and district became eligible for payments." The Districts would receive some revenues from the state.[284] There might be some discrepancy in the figures the article used as Couture had an operating budget of $128,035.02 in 1968 and Ingebretson had $17,435.98 for that same year.[285]

The goal for the Districts was to change the North Dakota law in order to receive the full amount of foundation payments. Many meetings attended by the school superintendent, school board members, local Bureau personnel with State officials including the North Dakota Attorney General brought about the change that was made in the 1971 session:[286]

15-40.1-07   HIGH SCHOOL PER-PUPIL PAYMENTS – AMOUNT –
PROPORTIONATE PAYMENTS. – There shall be paid each year
from the county equalization fund to all school districts operating

---

[283]*Grand Forks Herald*, Grand Forks, ND, 1-18-68.
[284]*Grand Forks Herald,* Grand Forks, ND, 1-18-68.
[285] Rolette County Records.
[286] North Dakota Century Code.

high schools, to school districts contracting to educate high school
pupils in a federal school, subject to adjustment as provided in
section 15-40.1-09, payments as follows: . . . .

15-40.1-08  ELEMENTARY PER-PUPIL PAYMENTS – AMOUNT.
– There shall be paid out of the county equalization fund to school
districts of the county operating elementary schools and to school
districts contracting to educate elementary pupils in a federal
school, employing teachers holding valid certificates or permits,
payments based on the number of registered students at the
beginning of each school year, adjusted as provide in section 15-
40.1-09, as follows: . . .

It should be noted that the words "Indian pupils" are now
completely omitted from the text in the North Dakota Century
Code.  Therefore, payments could finally be made from State funds
to Indian students who were attending a federal school facility and
whose parents worked for the Federal Government.  Furthermore,
all Indian students living on a reservation could be claimed for
foundation payments provided the federal school had a contractual
agreement with the School District, and the School District was in
control of the education program without interference from Tribal
Government.

In a 1979 opinion, the North Dakota Attorney General alluded
to a response to similar questions about the law.  He cited the 15-
40.1-07 and 15-40.1-08 laws quoted above stating, "Under the
language of these sections the duty of the state to pay school aid to
school districts educating pupils in a federal school arises only if a
contract has been made."[287]

Another problem with the State and funding occurred after
discussions about the space problems of the elementary school and
the financial problem of St. Ann's.  The Couture School Board
assumed the responsibility to educate the first grade students and to
rent space at St. Ann's.  The State questioned the amount of
students the Couture School District had claimed for both

---

[287] North Dakota Attorney General Opinion letter, March 14, 1979, p. 4.

foundation payments and moneys under Public Law 874. In a letter, Howard Snortland, now Assistant Superintendent, N. D. Department of Public Instruction, stated that, "Our office is now in a quandary as to which students are eligible under Public Law 874 and since the original agreement also defines these as public school students, for which students foundation program payments should be made. It was our understanding that this agreement was binding on all three agencies. . . ."[288]

Peter Schmidt, Assistant Area Director (Education), addressed a letter to Fayes Albert, President of the Couture School District, January 21, 1971, about Snortland's concern. He wrote that Snortland was under the mistaken impression that the district was working from a cooperative agreement and that was not the case. Schmidt alluded to a meeting of July 1, 1970, with the Couture School District officials, Turtle Mountain Community School officials, Glenn Lundeen, Chief, Division of Public School Relations, Dan LeRoy, Director of Indian Education for North Dakota and himself, "an inquiry was made as to the manner in which your district could assume greater responsibility for the education of all the children in your district." At that July 1970 meeting, a discussion was held about a gradual takeover assuming responsibility for the first and second graders, then another grade or grades until eventually the entire school would be taken over by the District. Schmidt stated that, "This is in keeping with the Bureau's policy to transfer programs when Indian people feel such a transfer is beneficial to them." It was also assumed at the meeting that finances would come from both State and Federal sources if this method of gradual takeover was used.[289]

Schmidt emphasized that this was not a cooperative agreement between the District and the Federal Government, but the District

---

[288] Letter from N. D. Dept of Public Instruction, to U.S. Office of Education, Washington, D. C., 1/5/71.
[289] Letter from Assistant Area Director (Education), to President of Couture School District, 1/21/71.

was assuming responsibility for the first grade students. The Bureau would not "interfere with the rights and responsibilities of any school district to educate any of its children (Indian and non-Indian) when it is their wish to do so."[290] The State withheld foundation payments to the Couture School District until this scuffle was settled. In the end, the District received State Foundation Payments from the State that year for those students in the first grade and others.

In 1972, the Couture budget surpassed the one million-dollar mark. The revenue for Couture School District in 1974 was nearly one and a half million dollars and the following year it was $1.7 million. The Couture and Ingebretson Districts contributed more than two million dollars to the TMCS system.[291] Money is power. Consequently, both Districts assumed more responsibilities, and the Federal Government, living up to its policy, was happy to give them more control. The sources of the Districts' school funding came from Bureau mini contracts, state foundation payments, Public Law 874 moneys, and Title programs (Federal and State). The Bureau sources of revenue were from the Indian School Equalization Program (ISEP) formula and Bureau Title programs.

During the 1970's and early 1980's, the Federal Government 874 officials allowed the Districts to count more students. Indian families on the reservation impacted the Districts by living on tax-free land. Parents of Indian students generated more money if they resided and worked on federal or trust lands. Children of a parent who lived on the reservation and did household work qualified for the full 874 payments. The Districts claimed only those students that the State and Federal Governments allowed them to claim.

The Federal Government took a closer look at the 874 funding with all cooperative schools in October of 1985. The local School

---

[290] Letter from Assistant Area Director (Education), to President of Couture School District, 1/21/71.
[291] Rolette County Treasurer Reports.

Superintendent and the Finance Director had a conference call with Robert Farning, Director of 874 in Washington, D. C. He had questions concerning duplication of funds. The federal officials began reaffirming that their policies of 874 payments were dependent on a district receiving State Foundation Payments. The Federal Government was concerned that the District was also getting a third funding, which were ISEP moneys.[292]

On November 25, 1985, the Bureau/State/School Board and the School Administration held a meeting in Belcourt. In attendance were Alton Koppang, DPI Director of Finance and Reorganization/School Construction and Transportation; Rolland Larson, DPI, Director of Compliance and Evaluation – Chapter I; Dennis Fox, Assistant Director of Indian Education, Washington, D. C.; Belcourt School District #7 Board Members; TMC School Administrators, Chuck Dunlop, Rolette County Superintendent of Schools; Philip Berude, District State Senator; and W. Larry Belgarde, Agency Superintendent for Education. The purpose of the meeting was to determine where the Belcourt School District and the TMCS stood with regards to funding. The cooperative school-funding concept had been under attack by the Bureau of Indian Affairs for the past four or five years.[293]

More recently, the State Government has been questioning the duplicate funding given to cooperative schools. Koppang quoted a section of North Dakota law 15-40.1-07, "However, no payment should be made for whom federal agencies provide education." Koppang made it clear that the State would take full responsibility for the education of students who were not funded by a federal agency.[294] This appeared only in the high school section of the law not the elementary school section.

---

[292] TMCS, School Superintendent's Report, 1985-86, pp. 11-12.
[293] TMCS, School Superintendent's Report, 1985-86, p. 13.
[294] TMCS, School Superintendent's Report, 1985-86, p. 13.

Fox did not seem concerned with the duplication of funding, and said he would grant ISEP funding to the District at maximum level as long as the pupils were of ¼ Indian descent. Koppang assured the TMCS group that foundation payments would be made for this year and next (1986–87). He further stated there was precedence established and everything had been done above board; funding would continue unless the legislature changed the law. Koppang also assured the group, if the foundation program were to be cut, a plan of gradual reduction in funding would be made with school officials.[295]

Both the Federal Government and State Officials were helpful. They were interpreting their policy and law correctly. After more meetings with Federal Officials and U.S. Senators Burdick and Dorgan, the District received 75% of the impact aid amounting to $1,337,342.01 on May 23, 1986. Of course, the money came with a stipulation that it may have to be returned. However, the new regulation changes did not affect the school funding for the 1985–86 school year. Therefore, the District kept the entire entitlement.[296]

The Belcourt School District approved a Future Funding Committee to study and plan for the decrease in district funding December 5, 1986. The committee consisted of Howard Frederick, Finance Director, Jim Davis, Agency Superintendent for Education, Dan Jerome, District School Superintendent, Patty Allery, School Board Director, Duane Schindler, High School Principal, Louis Dauphinais, Middle School Principal, and Teresa Delorme, Elementary School Principal.[297]

Mandaree and White Shield of the Fort Berthold Reservation, as well as the TMCS were all affected by the North Dakota law. The meetings held at Bismarck usually included officials from those

---

[295] TMCS, School Superintendent's Report, 1985-86, p. 13.
[296] TMCS, School Superintendent's Report, 1985-86 p. 16 and TMSC, School Superintendent's Report, 1986-87, p. 10.
[297] TMCS, School Superintendent's Report, 1986-87, p. 11.

areas as well. The Belcourt school officials involved ND State Senator Allen Richard, State Representatives Gerry Wilkie and Pat DeMers from District 9 to help with the law change.

Meanwhile, the State issued notice on April 10, 1987, that they would give the District foundation aid payments as in the past for the next year only.[298] That meant the State law had to be changed if the District would receive foundation moneys after the 1987–88 school year.

A planning meeting was held April 5, 1988, at Bismarck. As a result of this meeting, the Department of Public Instruction stated they would draft a bill that would change the language in the law which would pay foundation payments to all Indian students, but they thought that they could better support a bill if it were introduced by someone else. It was agreed that Senator Richard would be asked to introduce the bill. The question of when would be the appropriate time to present the bill to the legislature was discussed. Some wanted to wait-and-see the make-up of the legislature in the November election. At the time, there were twenty-two democrats and twenty-six republicans in the Senate, and forty-five democrats and sixty-one republicans in the House. Reservations normally voted for the democratic candidate.[299] The TMCS representatives were all democrats indicating Turtle Mountain would have the support locally. This was not the case with Mandaree and White Shield.

Another question for discussion was whether a change in the law should be requested. It could red flag the elementary and middle school pupils. The schools were still eligible for foundation payments for these students. Whether it was an oversight by the legislature that the foundation payments should still be paid to the elementary and middle schools students and not the high school

---

[298] TMCS, School Superintendent's Report 1986-87, p. 11.
[299] TMCS, School Superintendent's Report 1987-88, p. 9.

pupils was not known.[300]   Judging by the April 10, 1987, notice received from the Department of Public Instruction, they too were not aware of the difference until the TMCS Superintendent mentioned it.

November 16, 1988, another meeting was held at the State Capitol.   That was the year the schools would not receive the foundation payments.  Howard Frederick, Dan Jerome, Lynn Davis, Belcourt School District board member, Al Koppang of DPI, State Representatives Gerry Wilkie, Pat DeMers, Diane Ness, and Bob O'Shea, ND State Senators Allen Richard and Layton Freborg, Dennis Whitebear and Superintendent Ron Hauf from Whiteshield, and Superintendent John H. Ruegamer of Fort Yates were present. Koppang reported that DPI had hesitated to ask the Attorney General for an opinion on the law regarding foundation payments to Indian students to the Districts involved.   He would continue payments for this school year (1988-89), but the law must be changed.[301]

Koppang drafted the bill.   The bill was co-sponsored by Representatives Wilkie and DeMers and Senator Richard from District 9, Rolette County, Representatives Bob O'Shea and Diane Ness, and Senator Layton Freborg from District 8.   January 27, 1989, the House passed House Bill 1232 by a vote of 95–0.  March 9, 1989, the bill passed in the Senate by a vote of 49–1.   The Governor signed the bill into law March 15, 1989.   The law was changed and the foundation funding was secured.[302]   In the spring of 1989, the Turtle Mountain Community School Superintendent and the Finance Director met with Koppang to discuss the claiming of kindergarten students.   Approval was given and the kindergarten count was added to the total student count.[303]

---

[300] TMCS, School Superintendent's Report, 1987-88, p. 9.

[301] TMCS, School Superintendent's Report, 1988-89, p.17.

[302] TMCS, School Superintendent's Report, 1988-89, pp. 18-19.

[303] TMCS, School Superintendent's Report, 1989-90, p. 25.

# The Trail of Misgivings

However, the 874 funding was still in jeopardy. The District received $630,000 in 874 funds for the 1986-87 term, which was one-third of the entitlement. An audit determined that the District was only entitled to $250,000. The excess of $380,000 that the District received had to be returned. An agreement was made that an offset of the entitlement over a three-year period would be satisfactory to the Federal Government. A seven-percent interest charged was added to the $380,000. Since the District's entitlement was $250,000, it meant that the District would receive less than $125,000 from 874 moneys for the next three years unless some change in funding was made.[304]

Today, the District cannot claim 874 payments for the same student for which the bureau claims the ISEP funding. Whatever students the District claims for foundation payments through the State, the students may also be claimed for 874 payments.

Throughout this whole ordeal of getting reorganization and the funding squared away at the time both Districts and Bureau administrations worked well together. However, the Bureau staff and the districts staffs were not as compatible because they had different pay schedules and different benefits, and so on. These anomalies had to be constantly taken into consideration by attempting to balance the work inequalities.

---

[304] TMCS, School Superintendent's Report, 1987-88, p. 8.

# Chapter 12

## The 638 Issue

The Couture School Board had been paying out-of-district tuition for children of Bureau of Indian Affairs employees who sent their children to the nearby town of Rolla for an education. There were twelve or thirteen students attending the Rolla School for whom the District paid about $6,000. In 1965, the board challenged those tuition payments by refusing to pay. They told the Rolette Arbitration Commission they could not justify the amount of money to be paid out each year by the board when a State accredited school existed just a few blocks from the employees' homes. The decision came quickly settled by an all-white arbitration commission, which ruled that the District must pay tuition payments. No reasons were given. The following year twenty-three students attended the Rolla School and again asked the Couture School District to pay the tuition, which was now about $12,000. The District again refused to pay, but this time the board hired Clyde Duffy, a well-known attorney from Devils Lake, to make their case. The outcome of this hearing was that the District had to pay tuition for one student who took a foreign language that the Belcourt School did not offer.[305]

Some non-Indian teachers at TMCS felt that it was important to be a community member and succeeded. These teachers realized

---

[305] Letter from D.Jerome, Supt. of TMCS to Commissioner of Indian Affairs, Wash. D. C. 10/24/76, p. 1.

the asset that their children were to the school system. They wanted to help create the spirit of, "If our school is good enough to work in, it is certainly good enough for our children to attend." Others still wanting the good salary moved from the reservation and commuted to their place of work. Those bureau teachers seemingly never understood the problem or cared to try. In sporting events, they sat on the opposite side of the bleachers cheering for their new hometown community while the students they taught were left in wonderment. They seemed to have neither feelings nor warmth for the students they spent the day teaching, even though they must have felt the strained relationship. The problem did not go away. In fact, the problem grew worse in many ways.

To put it bluntly, some non-Indian Bureau employees became a burden to the Districts – they were hired to teach within the system because they brought a particular skill with them other than their major subject such as coaching wrestling, football, etc. After a year or two, they decided to drop the coaching activities but remained on staff as a teacher. This conundrum caused the school districts to hire more teachers who had that particular skill the Bureau teachers decided they no longer wanted to use. Eventually, when enough Bureau teachers found it too much of a strain to take on the extra responsibilities, the Districts ended up hiring other teachers just to pick up all the odds and ends that Bureau teachers refused to do. The school system depended on teachers to assist with student activities. However, many Bureau teachers never had the time since they had to attend other school activities in which their children were involved in the neighboring community.

James Henry, Tribal Chairman, during this ordeal was aware and informed of the existing problems with the high school faculty. He was willing to take the initiative in resolving the dilemma. Ken Davis, Acting Education Program Administrator, was the driving force from the Bureau. Both Couture and Ingebretson board members and their administration supported and staunchly backed the movement in resolving the conflict.

This led to the next step that the Tribe, Bureau, and Districts took in the fall of 1977. Under Public Law 93-638, the Turtle Mountain Band of Chippewa Indians contracted the education of the TMCHS with the BIA on October 19, 1977.

In a special meeting January 27, 1978, the Couture School District #27 (now Belcourt School District #7) subcontracted the education of the TMCHS with the Tribe, which took effect February 14, 1978. The amount of the contract was $150,000 for the remainder of the 1978 fiscal year, which ended September 30, 1978. One stipulation the ND State Department required was that the District must have control of the operation of the school.[306]

The Sunday *Forum Fargo-Moorhead* headlines were: "Chippewas seeking control over Belcourt High School." They wrote that the reservation people were moving toward a takeover of the Turtle Mountain Community High School. They wrote that the loss of jobs were by 12 Bureau teachers who were white. The *Forum* mentioned the tension in the community. A teacher at the middle school during that time made two statements for the *Forum*. Her first statement was "They don't hire white people anymore." And the second comment the *Forum* writes, ". . . is not surprised by the Indian move toward a takeover, saying it had been expected for some time. And, she notes, Indian control of the grade school and junior high is probably not far behind."[307]

The contract did cause change in the high school personnel. BIA employees had options to resign or accept other Bureau assignments elsewhere. Some accepted the transfers offered by the Bureau of Indian Affairs. The Ingebretson School District hired four. Some chose to test the legality of Public Law 874 and brought suit against Fred C. Gillis, Superintendent, Turtle Mountain Agency, BIA, U. S. Government, Reginald J. Brien, Jerilyn Decoteau, Raphael Trottier, Edward Herman, Richard Frederick,

---

[306] Jerome, *638 Contract*, June 1885, p. 1.
[307] *The Sunday Forum, Fargo-Moorhead*, October 23, 1977.

members of the school board of Couture School District, Edward J. Henry, Tribal Chairman, and Cecil Andrus, Secretary of Department of the Interior.[308]

An order enjoined the Couture School District from hiring replacements for the BIA staff during this period. The board was unable even to hire some of the former Bureau teachers. The order also temporarily withheld foundation payments from the District. The cases were all dismissed in March 1978 with prejudice and without costs to any party.[309]

The 638 takeover came about and jobs were lost only if a BIA teacher did not accept employment elsewhere. More white people were hired to teach in the high school setting. It is 29 years later, and white people are still being hired. Some people have the mistaken impression that local control is good only for white communities. At the time of the takeover, the TMC Elementary and Middle Schools were operated by a cooperative agreement where the Districts and the Bureau had joint control over these schools. Both schools continue to operate in the same manner today.

---

[308] Jerome, p. 2.
[309] Jerome, pp. 2-3.

# Chapter 13

## Special Programs

The TMCS took advantage of the many educational programs made available to assist Native American communities. These programs were Future Indian Teachers (FIT), Teacher Corps, Follow Through (FT), Title 1, Title III, Title IV, and Title VII.

### Future Indian Teachers

On June 17, 1969, the Couture School District #27 and the University of North Dakota, Grand Forks, filed a joint proposal to provide training for local people to become certified teachers. The proposal was filed in the Career Opportunities Program (COP) under the Education Professions Development Act.[310]

The Couture School Board selected fourteen candidates for the work-study program planned by the applicants who were already working in a classroom setting as teacher aides. These first FIT interns were: Agnes T. Belgarde, Gaylene Belgarde, Marcenia A Brunelle, Flora Delorme, Shirley M. Dionne Decoteau, Myrtle R. Gillis, Shirley A. Herman Allery, Delcie R. Jerome, Elizabeth C. Keplin, Delores M. Monette, Cecelia S. Olson, Rose A. Slater,

---

[310] Career Opportunities Program FIT proposal 6/27/69.

Barbara A. Thomas, and Teresa Delorme. This group was the pilot group for the FIT[311]

These fourteen women began a two-week summer session in 1969 at the University campus. Additional academic work was scheduled for the interns during the regular school term. The interns spent part of the school year at their work sites and part of their time attending classes at the University. They had four three-week sessions of academic studies at the University each school term. The interns were enrolled in 12 semester hours per semester plus eight hours during the summer. Summer sessions were not always at the University, but were scheduled at the Belcourt site as well.[312]

In the summer of 1973, these FIT interns received their Bachelor of Arts degrees from the University of North Dakota. Elizabeth Keplin, the oldest of the group, was 52 years old. She retired from teaching in May 1984. Gaylene Belgarde, Director of Special Education Programs at the TMCS, retired at the end of the 2005–06 school term. Flora Delorme (deceased) worked as a teacher at Dunseith Day School. Shirley Dionne Decoteau also retired from teaching kindergarten at the TMCES this year. Shirley Allery is teaching in TMCES. Delcie R. Jerome, who is now retired, was first the assistant, then Director of Student Activities at TMCHS. She later taught and was Cultural Director at the Ojibwa Indian School. She returned to TMCES first as the Cultural Consultant and later as a team teacher. Myrtle Gillis is a classroom teacher in the TMCMS. Barbara Thomas was a teacher at the TMCMS; she is now retired. Teresa Delorme has since earned her doctorate in education and is principal at Solheim Elementary in Bismarck. Marcenia Brunelle (deceased) taught at TMCES.

---

[311] Letter to Duane C. Moxon, Agency Superintendent from David N. Burch, Acting Reservation Principal, TMCS.

[312] *Insights, New School*, Behavioral Studies in Education, UND, Grand Forks, p. 2.

The Career Opportunity Program also offered graduate work for teachers. Ida Solberg, Dorothy Cwach, Rita Brown, and Helen Guilbert were selected from the Bureau of Indian Affairs staff, and Dorothy Gustafson Guderjohn was a participant from the Couture School District. This program focused on master degrees in elementary education for the graduate participants. Only Guilbert, Guderjohn and Solberg received their master degrees from the program. Guilbert worked as an education specialist for several years in the elementary system then transferred to the middle school where she taught mathematics until her retirement August 20, 1982. Dorothy Gustafson continues to teach in the TMC Elementary School. Solberg worked in the Belcourt elementary as an education specialist until her retirement February 13, 1985. People at the graduate level received $4,800 stipends for the school year and $600 for the summer sessions. The teacher interns received their regular teacher aide pay on and off campus. They received travel expenses and money for board and room while at the UND campus.

In the summer of 1970, a second group of teacher interns prepared for the fall session at UND under the COP. There were thirteen in this group: Marie Arpan, Agnes Azure, Addie (Delores) Jerome Brunelle, Alice Decoteau, Josephine Decoteau, Ramona Decoteau, Doris Demery, Barbara Frederick, Karen Gourneau, Christine Knight, Marie LaFontaine, Kay LaVallie, and Linda Morin.

Nine of the second group graduated in the spring of 1974. Doris Demery and Kay LaVallie completed their work in elementary education in 1975. Marie Arpan is still teaching in the TMC elementary school. Marie LaFontaine taught in the elementary at Dunseith Day School and is now retired. Addie Brunelle taught at the TMCES until she retired in 1989. Alice Decoteau and Karen Gourneau also taught in the elementary area and are now retired. Christine Knight was teaching in the elementary until illness forced her retirement in February 2006.

Linda Morin is still teaching in the elementary school. Ramona Decoteau Klein taught in the elementary school for a time and then earned her doctorate in education in 1986. She is currently doing consultant work. Doris Demery taught in the middle school and now works in the Bureau education office. Kay LaVallie, is on disability retirement, she taught in the elementary school for a while and transferred to the Dunseith Day School. She is presently living in the State of Missouri.

## Teacher Corps

A Teacher Corps proposal was submitted jointly by the University of North Dakota, Grand Forks and the Black Hills State College at Spearfish, South Dakota on December 15, 1969. The objective of this program was to train people of Indian descent to teach Indian children. Dr. Donald K. Lemon of the University of North Dakota was instrumental in writing the program and became the director of the project. Five North Dakota Indian communities became involved in the venture: Belcourt, Dunseith, Solen, Cannon Ball and Fort Yates [313]

Couture School District #27 served as the contracting agency for the Belcourt School. The contact person for the District was Dan Jerome, TMCS Superintendent. David Burch was the Reservation Principal with the Bureau of Indian Affairs. [314]

Five interns from each community were allowed for the Teacher Corps program. The interns had to have at least two years of college credits to qualify. The Belcourt site selected four local Native Americans: Margaret Bearking, Viola Carlson, Ray Grandboise and Leigh Jeanotte and Susan Fund who was from out of state and non-Indian. Rita Brown, a teacher at TMCES, was the team leader whose responsibility, among other things, was to coordinate activities for the interns. [315]

---

[313] Dan Jerome Papers, June 1983. p. 1.
[314] Dan Jerome Papers, June 1983. p. 1.
[315] Dan Jerome Papers, 1983, p. 1.

Teacher Corps interns began their training at UND during the summer of 1970. Stipends and family allowances were paid to the interns. The cost to the local school district was the staff time contributed to the program. The federal cost was $176,646. The program was a success from the standpoint that all interns graduated. However, it did not meet its objective of training Indian people to teach Indian children. Only two participants, Margaret Bearking and Viola Carlson, taught in elementary school.[316] Later, Margaret Bearking was the Reading Specialist for the TMC Elementary School for a number of years before she retired at the end of the 2002–03 school year.

This first group of interns at Belcourt was called the fifth cycle. The seventh cycle began in the summer of 1972. In this particular cycle six interns were selected. Five were Native Americans from the Belcourt area – Sammy Azure, Lyman Bercier, Dennis Blue, Lynn Davis, and Roman Marcellais. The sixth person, a non-Indian, was Don Davis from the St. John area. The team leader again was Rita Brown. Dan Jerome, Superintendent, was the contact person for the contracting district.[317]

This program was a success with all interns graduating in the summer of 1976, and Turtle Mountain Community Elementary School acquired three people who went through the program. Roman Marcellais taught in middle school for two years. He became the BIA Chapter I Coordinator, and worked there for fifteen years. He was the TMCES Principal for nine years. He is presently working as the Assistant School Superintendent at Belcourt. Don Davis taught several years in the Belcourt elementary before he took the position of Assistant Principal at the middle school. He is presently Superintendent of Schools at St. John, North Dakota. Lyman Bercier worked for a time as Title IV Director before moving onto other non-school related employment.

---

[316] Dan Jerome Papers, 1983, p. 2.
[317] Dan Jerome Papers, 1983, p. 2.

Sammy Azure is presently the Principal at the United Tribes Technical School in Bismarck, North Dakota.[318]

In the 1978–79 academic school term, the district participated in the 11th cycle of Teacher Corps. This was a five-year program. The final program, under the direction of Dr. Lemon, was a joint venture between the University of the North Dakota and the Turtle Mountain Community School. The team leader was Anna Morrow, a member of the TMCMS teaching staff. Loretta Delong, Viola Champagne and Rosie Henry Davis, all of Indian descent from the Turtle Mountain Reservation, and June Lowery were the four interns who met the entrance requirements of the University of North Dakota. Loretta Delong and Viola Champagne received their doctorate degrees in education at the end of the five-year program.[319]

## Follow Through Program

The U.S. Office of Education announced in a letter dated March 20, 1970 to Cooper, Acting Reservation Principal, that the Turtle Mountain Community School had been nominated as a candidate to participate in the Follow Through project in the 1970–71 school year. According to the information received, Turtle Mountain Community School was one of ten schools chosen for the coming school year. The selection was made jointly by the North Dakota Department of Public Instruction and the Economic Opportunity Agency. One hundred forty communities in the United States were involved with the Follow Through Program. April 3-4, 1970, Sister Bridget Brochin attended an informational meeting in St. Louis, Missouri. She was instrumental in writing the first application for the Couture School District #27.[320]

The Follow Through project was originally authorized in 1967 under the Economic Opportunity Act. The project was later

---

[318] Dan Jerome Papers, 1983, p. 2.
[319] Dan Jerome Papers, 1983, p. 3.
[320] Dan Jerome Papers, summer of 1973, p. 1.

extended through the Community Service Act of 1974. The purpose of the program was to sustain and supplement "in the early grades the gains made by low-income children who have had a full year's experience in a Head Start or comparable pre-school program." It focused on all aspects of the child's learning and development and had to include instruction, medical and dental health, nutrition, psychological services, social services, staff development and career advancement.[321]

During the first year, a participant school was required to select a program sponsor. The U.S. Education Office provided a list of sponsors for universities, regional educational laboratories or other agencies that had developed a new approach or model for education. The Couture School District Board, with input from the Bureau and District personnel, selected the University of Pittsburgh to serve as the sponsor of the Follow Through project at Belcourt. The Learning Research and Development Center at the University was to provide the model and orientation training for the staff of the Belcourt project. "The sponsor's model consists of an individual instructional system having selected curriculum areas, diagnostic tests, materials for instruction, and a management system for instruction, and a management system for implementation."[322]

Sister Kerstin Van Ryan was hired as Coordinator of the project during the summer of 1970. Three education specialists were already employed by the schools: Ida Solberg, Helen Guilbert, and Shirley Motis. These four were to be trained in all aspects of the program model during the spring and summer of 1971.[323]

The school district requested $192,591 for the 1971–72 Follow Through Program. Salaries headed the list with $179,497. The salaries were for the additional personnel such as the

---

[321] Dan Jerome Papers, summer of 1973, p. 1.

[322] Dan Jerome Papers, summer of 1973, p. 2.

[323] Dan Jerome papers, summer of 1973, p. 4.

coordinator, secretary, three education specialists, music teacher and two floating aides, sixteen teacher-aides, nurse, social worker, parent coordinator, parent education aide, and substitute teachers. A total of twenty-nine new people were added to the operational staff of the program.[324]

The Follow Through Program included kindergarten through grade two in its first year. At the TMCES, there were four kindergarten classrooms, seven first grade classrooms and seven second grade classrooms. Since the Ojibwa Indian School was included in the program, two more classrooms were added. Ojibwa did not have a kindergarten program at the time so one first grade class and one more second grade class were added to the project. Third grade classrooms were added to the program the second year.[325]

One component of the Follow Through Program stipulated that para-professionals employed in the program had to be given an opportunity for career development and advancement. In order to fulfill these requirements, the University of Pittsburgh teamed up with the Turtle Mountain Community College. The TMCC was in its infancy stage, and the program was a boost to them. The program mandated a five-member Policy Advisory Committee (PAC) to serve as an advisory board that was to be involved in all aspects of the program. Two members were to be parents and three were to be community members. The first PAC members were: Bill McCloud (Chairman), Estelle Jerome Trottier, (Secretary/Treasurer), Gerald Jeanotte, Francis LaFromboise, John Lattergrass, Ken Bauman, and Clarence Frederick.[326]

## Title Programs

Different Title Programs have been with the school since the incorporation of the Elementary and Secondary Education Act of

---

[324] Dan Jerome papers, summer of 1973, p. 4.
[325] Dan Jerome papers, summer of 1973, pp. 5-6.
[326] Dan Jerome papers, summer of 1972, pp. 7-8.

1965. The funding for Title I comes from both the State and Federal Governments. These programs were written for those students needing extra help in reading, mathematics, and language. The 1984–85 school term moneys contributed by the Federal Government amounted to $487,337 while $177,062 was funded by the State.[327] Below are samples of the distribution of funds through the years.

In the 1984–85 school year, Title IV was funded with $201,524. The funds were used for drug and alcohol prevention programs, homebound project, recreation, cultural, and tutoring. All of funds came from Part A of the Title IV Program. Part B moneys were approved for the 1985–86 school year. The total allocation for the new school year was $242,118 of which $71,548 was Part A moneys.[328]

Title VII funded a bilingual program for kindergarten through the third grade. The total funding for the 1984–85 school year was $234,817.[329] The total allocation from these programs amounted to $1,100,740.

Five years later, the Federal Government approved $647,899 for the TMCS Title I program. These funds provided school-wide services to 604 students. The State Chapter I Program approved $197,985. These funds were earmarked for remedial services in the areas of reading, math, and language for students in grade two and math services to students in grade six. Both State and Federal Chapter I funded early childhood and dropout prevention programs. Twenty-two teachers, eleven aides, parent person, education specialist, and business technician were hired through the Title I Program.[330]

---

[327] Superintendent Report, 1984-85, school term. p. 12.

[328] Superintendent Report, 1984-85 school term. p. 12.

[329] Superintendent Report, 1984-85 school term. p. 12.

[330] Superintendent Report, 1989-90 school term. p. 4.

# The Trail of Misgivings

Title VII, funded at $183,843, was a supplementary program that focused on raising the English language proficiency of students in grades four through eight. It provided a microcomputer lab in the elementary area and employed a director, secretary, and three teachers.[331]

Title V was funded at the beginning of the 1989–90 school term for a cost of $181,434. The funds were used to hire a full-time Director, full-time secretary, Alcohol and Drug Abuse Counselor, Alcohol and Drug Education Resource Person, Cultural Resource Person, and Alternate Activities Coordinator. The program also had a Peer-Tutoring component. A second grant of $136,502 was received under the Secretaries Discretionary Fund for Drug Free Schools and Communities. The BIA added to the Fund bringing the total to $168,951. Title V also applied for a State Drug Free Schools and Communities grant of $13,253. The total amount generated by Title V for that school year was $363,638.[332] Revenues from Title Programs for the 1989–90 school term was $1,393,364.

Today, all the Titles are now under one program. Presently, Debbe Poitra is in charge of this consolidation of Title Programs. Schools may opt for school-wide programs if forty percent or more students qualify for free lunch or reduced price lunch. In 1995, the TMCS met the stipulation and elected to come under a school-wide Title Program. This allows the funding to be spread to the general population of the school. Titles I, IIA, IIB and IV are written under a single application which must be done electronically. The present funding for the school system is at the $3,000,000 mark. Ten percent of the moneys received must be set aside for professional development. Another five percent is mandated by the State to be set aside to upgrade the teachers in their core subject areas to meet the requirements for the No Child Left Behind Amendment to the Education Act. The program provides

---

[331] Superintendent Report, 1989-90 school term. p. 4.
[332] Superintendent Report, 1989-90 school term. p. 5.

188

after school tutoring for students and pays salaries for twenty-six teachers, aides and other staff in the TMCS system.[333]  A total of thirty-seven staff members serves 1,642 students.

## KEYA Radio Station

In 1974, the Couture School District #27 launched the KEYA Radio Station, as a component of Part IV of Title III of the Communication Act of 1934.  A federal grant of $50,437 was awarded to the district to establish a public radio station.  The main objective of the radio station was to provide broadcasting experience for students of the Turtle Mountain Community School. Educational programming and selected programs of special interest were to be offered to the people in the local area.

Figure 13-1: KEYA Radio Station, which started broadcasting in 1975.

Dallas A. Brien was selected as General Manager to get the station off the ground.  Jay Silverheels, a well-known personality as Tonto in a television series, *The Lone Ranger*, was present for

---

[333] Personal Interview with Debbie Poitra 5/15/06.

the dedication. KEYA meaning "you" in the Métis or Cree language became the station call letters. There are variations of the spelling such as *kiya* or *keyah*.

The District first rented an old building on Main Street about fifty yards east of Ox Creek for the KEYA office. Before the station became a reality in 1975, the operation had moved to the old hospital that has since been torn down. In the beginning, there was a staff of six people. Broadcasting was from 6 a.m. to 10 p.m. Monday through Friday, and from 8 a.m. to 10 p.m. Saturday and Sunday. Today, KEYA operates on a nineteen-hour daily schedule from 6:00 a.m. to 1:00 a.m. The station has had two homes since then. Both are less than one-fourth of a mile north of the Turtle Mountain Mall.

In October 1985, the Belcourt School District fulfilled its commitment to construct, operate, and maintain the station for a period of ten years. This stipulation was specified in the provision of the Title IV program. At a regular school board meeting held on March 10, 1987, the radio station was cut from the district budget for the 1987–88 school year.[334] Twenty years later, KEYA is still on air and doing well under the management of Kimberly Eller Thomas.

Kimberly is a 1981 graduate of the Turtle Mountain Community High School. She first learned about radio through the courses taught at the TMCHS. She worked her way up through the ranks with various jobs at the station. She has now worked for the station twenty-six years – the last ten years as the manager. The managers before her were, Dallas Brien, Tim McCartney, Debbie "Chook" Keplin, Vicky Short and Betty Hamley.[335]

The current budget for the radio station, according to Thomas, "is about $330,000 to $350,000 and that's a bare minimum." The majority of the funding is from Corporation for Public

---

[334] Superintendent's Report 1986–87, pp. 3-4.
[335] Interview with Kimberly Thomas, May 11, 2006.

Broadcasting (CPB). Thirty percent of CPB funds are restricted funding for National programming. KEYA generates some revenue with underwriting advertisements and sponsoring gaming programs.[336]

Originally, the radio station was to devote some time to educational and instructional programming. Training in radio station operation is still provided for high school students, and there are about six students a year from the surrounding areas (mostly from the local high school, but Rolette and Rolla have sent students for training). Some of the students have gone on to receive degrees in Communication and Radio Broadcasting.[337]

The present day structure is 4,800 square feet and was funded with a grant through U.S. Department of Agriculture, Rural Development, in Bismarck, North Dakota. KEYA received a grant of $270,000 and a loan of $90,000 to build the station. They moved into the building in the year 2000.[338]

Five full-time employees operate the station with the help of ten other volunteers. KEYA is governed by a board of directors consisting of seven people. They are Ron Peltier, Clark Peltier, Richard Turcotte, Lambert Azure, Marilyn Poitra, Richard Thomas, and Kevin Keplin.[339]

The initial effort of the school district and its personnel to establish a radio station in the community has borne much fruit. As a result, the people who presently operate the station are making their own decisions, and the community and surrounding area continue to enjoy KEYA airwaves.

---

[336] Thomas Interview.

[337] Thomas Interview.

[338] Thomas Interview.

[339] Thomas Interview.

# Chapter 14

# Curriculum Policies and Student Enrollments

In 1934, the Bureau emphasized meeting the needs of local Indian communities instead of a standard curricular policy for all tribes. The statement is as follows:[340]

> There is no uniform curriculum for Indian schools, and federal schools are not subject to state courses of study of the areas in which they are operated. Programs of instruction suited to the needs of each particular area should be developed by the personnel of that area in the light of the general principles set out in this manual – not dictated by college entrance requirements. However, Indian schools may be accredited by the state department of education, or other accrediting agencies, when the recognition is based upon a sympathetic attitude which permits the development of a legitimate educational program suited to the needs of the area.

The curriculum for the local area was prepared in a series of in-service training sessions for the educational personnel given by the Washington office. Willard Beatty, Director of Indian Education, from 1932 to 1951, had much influence on the type of education program each area would have.[341] Even though the local school staff had input in what the curriculum would be, the Washington officials shaped the program.

---

[340] 79 U.S. Dept. of the Interior, Manual of Indian Service, p. 21, Robert Murray, p. 110.
[341] Robert Murray, p. 111.

In the early 1950s, the federal course of study, besides emphasizing that students have experience in livestock management, gave preparatory training to interested students to meet standard requirements for college entrance. This training even had as a goal, "To give students an understanding and appreciation of the cultural contributions their own tribal arts have made to the literature, art, music and folklore of the nation."[342]

Presently, the federal mission statement for Indian education is in part as follows:[343]

> Recognizing the special rights of the Tribes and Alaska Native entities and the unique government-to-government relationship of Indian Tribes and Alaska Native villages with the Federal Government as affirmed by the United States Constitution, U.S. Supreme Court decisions, treaties, Federal statutes, and Executive Orders. . . . it is the responsibility and goal of the Federal Government to provide comprehensive education programs and service for Indian and Alaska Natives. . . .The mission of the Bureau of Indian Affairs, Office of Indian Education Programs, is to provide quality education opportunities from early childhood through life in accordance with the Tribes' needs for cultural and economic well-being in keeping with the wide diversity of Indian Tribes and Alaska Native villages as distinct cultural and governmental entities. The bureau shall manifest consideration of the whole person, taking into account the spiritual, mental, physical and cultural aspects of the person within family and Tribal or Alaska Native village contexts.

Today, the Federal Government requires that a student complete 20 units of instruction in a four-year high school program before receiving a high school diploma. If the State in which the federal facility is located has standards that exceed the Bureau standards, then the State standards will apply. The Bureau requires 15 units be as follows: four units in language, three units in mathematics, three units in social studies, two units in science, one

---

[342] Robert Murray, pp. 112-113.

[343] Code of Federal Regulations Title 25, Revised as of April 1, 2004, p. 131.

unit in physical education, one unit in practical arts, and one unit in fine arts.[344]

Staffing requirements of the federal schools must not exceed the following ratios in a self-contained classroom: one teacher to twenty students in kindergarten, one teacher to twenty-two students in grades one through three, and for grades four through high school: one teacher to twenty-five students.[345]

These are just a few of the requirements that are clearly spelled out by the publication of the Code of Federal Regulation (CFR) Title 25. The Bureau has set up some excellent standards for the operation of a school system. The policies appear to be appropriate and reflect what is best for the students and the community that the school is intended to serve. School administrators should make a thorough study of the detailed Bureau policy and recommendations for the education of Indian children.

In 1977, the North Dakota Indian Education Association (NDIEA) advocated Indian studies as a requirement to be a certified teacher in North Dakota. These studies were a meaningful attempt to make teachers aware of the Indian children within their classrooms. After a series of meetings and discussions, the North Dakota Teachers Professional Practices Commission (TPPC) gave some positive consideration to the suggestion of an Indian studies course being added to the certification of North Dakota teachers. The North Dakota Association of Colleges for Teacher Education (NDACT) also became involved.[346]

---

[344] Code of Federal Regulations Title 25, revised as of April 1, 2004, p. 145.

[345] Code of Federal Reg. Title 25, revised as of April 1, 2004, p. 141.

[346] Cheryl Rose Marion Kulas, A Thesis Submitted to the Committee on American Indian Studies in Partial Fulfillment of the Requirements for the Degree Master of Arts, In the Graduate College The University of Arizona, 1989, pp, 61-63.

On July 19, 1979, the Director of Certification, Ordean Lindermann of the Department of Public Instruction approved the Indian studies course. NDACT, NDIEA, and other organizations took the responsibility for disseminating information of the requirements to educational institutions.[347] The North Dakota law supporting Mr. Lindermann's actions above was 67-02-03-04:[348]

> All teachers certified or renewed for certification after April 1, 1982 shall have two semester or three quarter hours of college credit in North Dakota Native American Indian Studies, or the equivalent inservice pursuant to approval by the Department of Public Instruction.

In the study that Cheryl Marion Kulas had completed, the results were less than positive as she stated: "The findings suggest that the course is not having a positive effect on the attitudes of heightening teacher sensitivity toward stereotypes and there is an apparent indifference to adjusting curricula to reflect cultural diversity."[349]

In addition to the North Dakota Native American Indian Studies initiative in 1982, the Office of Indian Education Programs was established by the North Dakota Department of Public Instruction. The duties of the office, among other things, were to promote "the concept of race and sex equity in North Dakota schools." Originally, Project Equal (Sex Equity Program) was contracted with the North Dakota State University at Fargo. Later, in 1984, the North Dakota Office of Indian Education assumed the responsibility of administering the Sex Equity Program.[350] Kulas is the current Director of North Dakota Indian Education.

## The Analysis of Schools' Indian Student Enrollments

A trend of sending students to boarding schools increased up to the mid 1900's then began to decrease to only a few students attending today. The trend also indicated that the student

---

[347] Kulas, p. 62.

[348] Kulas, p. 64.

[349] Kulas, Abstract, p. 6.

[350] Kulas, p. 59.

population in Rolette County public schools had increased. An analysis of the student enrollment records during various school years reveals the growing Indian population on the Turtle Mountain Reservation and surrounding areas.

Murray has a table (*Appendix B-2*) listing the enrollment of the various reservation day schools including the Dunseith Day School. The table shows the number of teachers per school. The figures for TMCS show an increased enrollment from 445 students for the 1949–50 school term to 530 students for the 1952–53 school term. Average daily attendance was about 78 to 80 percent for those four years, and the number of teachers increased from sixteen to eighteen. The teacher/student ratio was 1/28 in the 1949–50 school year, and did not improve as the student population increased. In the 1952–53 school term the teacher/student ratio was 1/29. Of course, the number of classrooms did not change. These figures are evidence that the building had reached its student capacity. Murray makes no mention of any plans for building. However, the new building for the high school was constructed about ten years later.

During the 1952–53 school term, the non-reservation schools had an enrollment of 233 children from the Turtle Mountain area for grades one through twelve. Chemawa, Oregon, had four students and Haskell, Kansas, had three students from the area. Wahpeton, North Dakota had the majority of the students. The Wahpeton Indian School served only elementary students grades one through eight, and housed 143 Indian students from the Rolette County area. Fort Totten, North Dakota had 67 students in grades one through twelve, from the Turtle Mountain Reservation.[351] From 1972 to 1986, the Turtle Mountain enrollment at the Wahpeton Indian School decreased from 190 to 61 pupils.

---

[351] Robert Murray, p. 132.

Presently, there are only four TM students at Circle of Nations School (formally Wahpeton Indian School).[352]

Flandreau, South Dakota had 16 students from the area in grades one through twelve in 1952–53.[353] The Flandreau Indian School remained steady with about 38 students from 1976 to 1986. School records indicate only 12 students were from Turtle Mountain in 1981–82.[354] Today, there are five enrolled TM students at Flandreau. One student is from the reservation, and the others are from the Grand Forks, New Town, Bismarck and Aberdeen communities.[355] There are presently 31 TM elementary students enrolled at Pierre Indian Learning Center, Pierre, South Dakota.[356]

During this same period (1952–53), mission boarding schools educated 194 students from the Turtle Mountain. Stephan, South Dakota, had an enrollment of 50 students grades one through twelve; Chamberlain, South Dakota, enrolled 32 Indian children grades one through eight; St. Michael, North Dakota, housed 56 children grades one through six; and Marty, South Dakota, had 56 pupils grades one through twelve.[357] A total of 427 students from the Turtle Mountain community were attending government and mission boarding schools in the 1950's.

The local Bureau officials did not have to worry about the 303 students attending St. Ann's plus the 427 attending boarding schools. These 730 children plus the 530 attending the TMCS totaled 1,260 students who were eligible to attend school at the TMCS. Without St. Ann's and the boarding schools (mission and federal), the Belcourt School System could never have met the

---

[352] TMCS Records and recent telephone conversation with area boarding personnel.
[353] Robert Murray, p. 132.
[354] TMCS Records.
[355] TMCS Records and recent telephone conversation with area boarding personnel.
[356] Letter from Pierre Indian Learning Center dated 2/16/2006.
[357] Robert Murray, p. 33.

needs of the growing population of Indian children in the Turtle Mountain area without making some drastic building changes.

Other interesting statistics from the Department of Public Instruction and from Rolette County Records emphasize the ever-growing Indian population on the reservation. These are contained in Table 12-1.[358]

## Table 12-1A: 1955-56 School Term

|  | Total Enrolled | Indian Enrolled | % of Indian Students |
|---|---|---|---|
| Dunseith | 268 | 57 | 21.3 |
| St. John | 260 | 76 | 29.2 |
| Mt. Pleasant (Rolla) | 380 | 44 | 11.6 |
| Rolette | 294 | 26 | 8.8 |
| Total | 1,202 | 203 | 16.9 |

## Table 12-1B: 1965-66 School Term

|  | Total Enrolled | Indian Enrolled | % of Indian Students |
|---|---|---|---|
| Dunseith | 672 | 284 | 42.3 |
| St. John | 269 | 120 | 44.6 |
| Mt. Pleasant (Rolla) | 629 | 67 | 10.7 |
| Rolette | 429 | 50 | 11.7 |
| Total | 1,999 | 521 | 26.1 |

The tables indicate an increase in enrollment in all schools for that ten-year period. The Indian population increased in the public schools by just over 156 percent while the non-Indian population

---

[358] Department of Pubic Instruction, Dept of Indian Education, Bismarck, ND

increased by 48 percent. Dunseith and St. John made the largest gains in the enrollment of Indian students.

**Table 12-2: Enrollment Numbers for Rolette County**

|                        | *1975-76* | *1985-86* | *1995-96* | *2005-06* |
| ---------------------- | --------- | --------- | --------- | --------- |
| **Total Students**     | 3,819     | 3,277     | 3,882     | 3,320     |
| **Total Indian Students** | 2,678  | 2,405     | 3,111     | 2,789     |
| **% of Indian Students**  | 70     | 73.3      | 80        | 84        |
| **Non-Indian Students**   | 1,141  | 872       | 771       | 531       |

The above table shows the continued growth of Indian students in Rolette County.[359] The table also reflects a steady decline of non-Indian students in the County.

The following table (12-3) indicates that the Ojibwa Indian School and the Dunseith Day School had 100 percent Indian students attending for the 1999–2000 school term. Dunseith Public School – not TMCS – had the next highest percentage of Indian students in attendance in 2000. Dunseith Public School had an Indian population of 93.8 percent while the TMCS had 90.6 percent. St. John had 72.6 percent pupils of Indian descent attending its school while Rolla had 35 percent and Rolette had 20.8 percent Indian children. This table indicates the non-Indian student population had stabilized at about 700 students while the Indian student count had leveled off to about 3850.[360]

---

[359] Department of Public Instruction, Bismarck, ND
[360] Rolette County Records

## Table 12-3: Rolette County Nationality Breakdown

| | 1995-96 Ind | 1995-96 non- | 1995-96 Total | 1996-97 Ind | 1996-97 non- | 1996-97 Total | 1997-98 Ind | 1997-98 non- | 1997-98 Total | 1998-99 Ind | 1998-99 non- | 1998-99 Total | 1999-00 Ind | 1999-00 non- | 1999-00 Total |
|---|---|---|---|---|---|---|---|---|---|---|---|---|---|---|---|
| Dunseith | 467 | 59 | 526 | 465 | 48 | 513 | 465 | 51 | 516 | 474 | 38 | 512 | 528 | 35 | 563 |
| St. John | 188 | 82 | 270 | 199 | 96 | 295 | 198 | 99 | 297 | 228 | 90 | 318 | 207 | 78 | 285 |
| Mt. Pleasant (Rolla) | 106 | 323 | 429 | 135 | 270 | 405 | 146 | 236 | 382 | 157 | 243 | 400 | 136 | 250 | 386 |
| TMCS | 1592 | 121 | 1713 | 1761 | 90 | 1851 | 1762 | 120 | 1882 | 1739 | 158 | 1897 | 1676 | 174 | 1850 |
| Rolette | 51 | 190 | 241 | 53 | 194 | 247 | 52 | 188 | 240 | 55 | 163 | 218 | 37 | 179 | 216 |
| Ojibwa Ind School | 455 | 0 | 455 | 368 | 0 | 368 | 366 | 0 | 366 | 348 | 10 | 358 | 341 | 0 | 341 |
| Dunseith Day | 254 | 0 | 254 | 227 | 0 | 227 | 245 | 0 | 245 | 217 | 0 | 217 | 212 | 0 | 212 |
| Totals | 3113 | 775 | 3888 | 3208 | 698 | 3906 | 3234 | 694 | 3928 | 3218 | 702 | 3920 | 3137 | 716 | 3853 |

**Table 12-4: Turtle Mountain Indian Student Enrollment**

End of year for 2004 - 2005 school term[361]

| | *Total* | *No. of Native American* | *Percentage of NA* |
|---|---|---|---|
| **TMCS** | | | |
| K-5 | 679 | 674 | 99.3 |
| 6-8 | 410 | 399 | 97.3 |
| 9-12 | 560 | 537 | 95.9 |
| **TMCS Subtotal** | 1,646 | 1,610 | 97.8 |
| **Ojibwa School** | | | |
| K-8 | 282 | 277 | 98.2 |
| **Dunseith Day** | 178 | 160 | 89.9 |
| **St. Ann's NA School** | 39 | 38 | 97.4 |
| **Rolla** | 293 | 110 | 37.5 |
| **Rolette** | 177 | 33 | 18.6 |
| **St. John** | 306 | 263 | 85.9 |
| **Dunseith** | 445 | 437 | 98.2 |
| **Total of all schools** | 3,366 | 2,928 | 87.0 |

---

[361] US Dept. of the Interior, BIA, TM Agency, Belcourt, ND, p. 8.

# Chapter 15

# Turtle Mountain Community School System Today

The Turtle Mountain Community School is the largest federal Indian School in the Nation.

The mission statement for the Turtle Mountain Education System is "Ensure excellence in education and respect for the local culture." The system's vision statement is, "Excellence in academics, community and cultural education, where every employee is a teacher, every parent a partner, every child a winner." The high school vision statement is "Quality learning for all."[362]

The TMC Schools are neatly spread over several acres of federal land. As of May 18, 2006, the total enrollment for the TMCS kindergarten through twelfth grade was 1,643.[363] The

---

[362] Turtle Mountain Community High School, 2005-2006 Student Handbook, p. 3.
[363] TMCS records.

Elementary and Middle Schools are separated from the High School complex by two softball playing fields, four basketball courts, and a track and football field. Construction is underway for the new TMC High School being built east of the present 1984 high school structure.

## Turtle Mountain Community High School

There have been numerous Federal Government principals at the TMCHS over the years. Dan Jerome was the first high school principal under the District rule followed by: Les Fettig, Jon Fimmel, Florence Crouse (BIA), Ron Witt, Ernesto Jimenez,

Figure 15-1: The TMCS High School completed in 1984.

Duane Schindler and Rose Mary Jaros. Jaros is the present head of the Turtle Mountain Community High School. She arrived in 1978 to teach and then became principal in 1991.

The 2006 TMC High School enrollment is 572 students. There is a principal, assistant principal, personnel officer, fifty-two

Figure 15-2: Rosemary Jaros, present day High School Principal.

teachers, thirty-two teacher aides, five counselors, a librarian, office staff, three custodians, and twenty-two other support staff.[364]

The High School offers a complete and comprehensive educational program including college preparatory courses. The curriculum also contains special education and individualized programs plus an alternative school program. The Career Technical Education program (vocational education) currently offers: construction technology, welding technology, auto technology, family consumer science, health occupations, business and office education, information technology, and career development.[365]

According to Duane Poitra, Finance Director, the vocational building was built with borrowed money from Dacotah Bank. A loan of $500,000 was from the Qualified Zone Academy Bond Loan at zero percent interest. This loan was the first of its kind for North Dakota schools, and the first loan to an Indian school. The vocational building was completed in two phases from 1997 to

Figure 15-3: Duane Poitra, Finance Director.

---

[364] TMCS records.
[365] Personal interview with Kelly Thomas Hall, TMCHS Director of Career and Technical Education, July 17, 2006.

2001. The first phase positioned the four walls. The second phase resumed the project in 2000 and brought it to completion in 2001. The building consists of 10,000 square feet. The welding and auto classes are taught in the building.[366]

School District requirements for high school graduation are a minimum of twenty-one credits (Bureau standards require twenty units). These units must equal or exceed the requirements set by the State of North Dakota. The following units apply: Language Arts – four and one-half credits, Mathematics – two credits, Social Studies three and one-half credits, Laboratory Science two credits, Physical Education one credit, Health one-half credit, Driver Education one-half credit, and Electives seven credits.[367] (Agriculture courses are no longer offered).

The high school has been fully State accredited since 1940.[368] However, in the 1984–85 school year, conditional accreditation was given because the principal was unable to obtain his credentials from the State Department. He was asked to resign and did so at the end of the school year.[369] During the 1972–73 academic year, the TMC High School applied for and received North Central Accreditation.

The Turtle Mountain Community High School athletic teams have had some good years in both boys and girls basketball. The boys placed second in Class B State Tournament in 1970. The girls placed second in Class A State Tournament in 1989. In 1997 the boys were runner-ups in the Class A State Tournament. One athlete placed first in the State javelin event. Individual wrestlers have placed first in State Wrestling. Tribute must be given to the 1971 State Wrestling Championship Team. The team was coached

---

[366] Personal Interview Belcourt school District # 7, Finance Director, Duane Poitra, 5/5/2006.

[367] 2005-2006 Student Handbook, p. 5.

[368] Robert Murray, p. 124.

[369] Superintendent's Report, 1984-85, p. 11.

by George Schlager and members of that team were at 98 lbs. - Duane Falcon, first place; 105 lbs. – Logan Davis, first place; 112 lbs. - Mickey Decoteau, first place; 119 lbs. – George Falcon, fourth place; 126 lbs. – Steve Peltier; 132 lbs. – Howard Azure; 138 lbs. - Larry Azure, third place; 145 lbs. – Gerald Davis, second place; 155 lbs. – Pat Delorme; 167 lbs. – Victor Baker; 185 lbs. – Alex Albert; Heavy weight – Fred Schindler. Duane Falcon was the youngest member on the team at age fourteen.[370]

## Turtle Mountain Community Middle School

The Middle School is comprised of grades six through eight and has an enrollment of approximately 400 students. There is a principal, assistant principal, forty-one teachers, twenty-two teacher aides, two counselors, librarian, eight office staff, five custodians, and twenty-five other support staff.[371] The sixth grade

Figure 15-4: Middle School today after the renovation.

---

[370] Personal Interview with Duane Falcon, May 2006.
[371] TMCS records.

Figure 15-5: Louis Dauphinias, Middle School Principal.

moved to the Middle School in 1984. They moved back with the elementary section after the 1984 fire. They reentered the Middle School program in 1989 when the renovation was completed. The sixth grade classes are self-contained. Seventh and eighth grades are departmentalized. The TMC Middle School gained North Central Accreditation in 1988.

At the time the TMCHS applied for and gained North Central Accreditation in 1973, the middle school was located in metal buildings east of the high school (built in 1962), and the administration did not wish to apply for accreditation until the school moved to a more appropriate accommodation and environment. Upon completion of the high school in 1984, the middle school moved into the older high school complex. The middle school will again move to the 1984 high school structure when the new high school is completed in 2007.

## Turtle Mountain Community Elementary School

The TMCE School has 671 students, kindergarten through fifth grade. There is a principal, two assistant principals, eighty-two teachers, twenty-four teacher aides, one counselor, three librarians, five office staff, a school nurse, three

Figure 15-6: Dave Gourneau, Elementary School Principal.

other support staff.[372]  The TMC Elementary School gained North
Central Accreditation in 1975.

Figure 15-7: The Elementary School that was built in 1972 and has served in the
same capacity since then.

The school will soon occupy the entire complex that currently
houses the middle school in addition to their present structure.
(The 1931 building is slated to be demolished – the local people
are still attempting to salvage it as a historical land mark.)

## The District Administration Building

It was mentioned earlier that in 1976 the District built the
Administration building south of the Turtle Mountain Agency at a
cost of $31,000.  In 1979 and 1980, two additions were built one to
the west and one to the east of the building at a cost $50,000 for
both add-ons.  Offices were placed to the west and a boardroom to
the east.  In 2005, the Bureau needed space and confiscated part of
the District building by a technicality.  Either the Board did not get

---

[372] TMCS records.

proper permission to build on federal land, or the building was inadvertently placed on federal inventory. Records show that at times Harlen Wash, EPA, would shift federal funds and workload to the District. Such moneys would be used for different programs that had to be implemented by the school or a building that the school needed. Never, however, did he shift $81,000 for the District Administration Building. It should be mentioned that during his tenure, Wash used the district to get certain projects accomplished because he had good working rapport with them, and it was efficient and convenient. Today, however, there seems to be less harmony between the two entities. The conflicts continue.

The Bureau has a recent Historical Background publication that profiles the Turtle Mountain reservation. The Sweet Corn Treaty of 1858 is discussed in the document that relates a separate story of a Chippewa/Dakota agreement thirty-three years earlier. They agreed to abide by the boundaries established, but further mutually agreed to allow the other to hunt beyond the boundaries if the game was depleted on their side. They also agreed to return all the horses and property they stole from each other. The two chiefs involved in the treaty making were Chief Waanatan (He Who Rushes On), Dakota, and Chief Emay das Kah (Flat Mouth) of the Chippewa Tribe. According to the oral history, to seal the treaty, the tribes exchanged members, and concluded "We will not make war against our grandchildren." However, it is known that border skirmishes and battles continued between the Chippewa and the Sioux breaking the treaty.

This story parallels with the disagreement about the Administration Building. The handshake of the people of the past dies when they leave office. The people in charge today seem to care less about what was previously agreed on by others or carelessly ignore it. One is reminded of President Jackson who said, "He made the decision let him enforce it," alluding to a Justice Marshall court decision in favor of the Cherokee. And the fight goes on. And history repeats itself.

The Belcourt School District is constructing another new building again on federal land to house the District administration and business center. The completion date is set for May 1, 2007. The building will be 6,800 square feet at a cost of about $1,000,000. This money comes from the Bank of North Dakota, Bismarck, under the North Dakota Public Finance Authority. It is a capital finance program set aside for North Dakota Municipalities.[373]

Figure 15-8: The old TMCS Administration building from the 1970's, which has more recently been a point of inflammation between the District and Agency.

## No Child Left Behind

The Elementary and Secondary Education Act was first approved by Congress in 1965. No Child Left Behind (NCLB) was an amendment to the Act in 2001. NCLB has high standards and great expectations that every child kindergarten through the twelfth grade will have an opportunity to succeed in any public

---

[373] Personal Interview, Finance Director, May 5, 2006.

school.    The Act "is built on four common-sense pillars: accountability for result; an emphasis on doing what works based on scientific research; expanded parental options; and expanded local control and flexibility."[374]

In compliance with NCLB, the State of North Dakota defines an Adequate Yearly Progress (AYP) for each school by establishing "a 'starting point' that is based on the performance of its lowest-achieving demographic group or of the lowest-achieving schools in the State, whichever is higher." A level of student gain was determined to indicate AYP.    The level of student achievement is changed periodically.[375]    Students from all public schools must be proficient in reading and mathematics by 2014.

A school must take corrective action if it fails to make adequate progress within four years.[376]    Since the TMCS system has been in a school improvement program more than three years, the school was placed in the fourth year for the school term 2002–03.  Consequently, TMCS was placed in "Corrective Action" since it failed to meet its AYP.   The district must initiate corrective action plans designated by the No Child Left Behind Act.[377]

The Federal Government recommendations for corrective action are: "Replacement of staff relevant to the failure; Implementation of a new curriculum; Extension of the school year or day; Appointment of an outside expert; [and] Restructuring of the internal organization."[378]

The State has its own consequences for schools not meeting AYP.  The second year a school must implement a program for school improvement.  To not meet AYP the third year, the school has the option of setting aside ten percent of Title funds for

---

[374] No Child Left Behind, A Parents Guide, US Dept of Educ. 2003, p. 1.
[375] No Child Left Behind, A Parents Guide, US Dept of Educ. 2003, p. 8.
[376] No Child Left Behind, A Parents Guide, US Dept of Educ. 2003. p. 9.
[377] Sandy Thomas, paper summer of 2003,  pp. 3-4.
[378] Sandy Thomas, paper summer of 2003, pp. 3-4.

Professional Development (PD) for staff or updating and implementing a Program Improvement Plan Technical Assistant (TA). By the fourth year, if the school still has not reached the objective, they must continue with its TA and the ten percent set aside for PD. They must update and implement a Program Improvement Plan, and the school must offer supplemental services. By the fifth year, if the school has not yielded the needed results, the school must continue with what was done in the fourth year. They will also have an option of replacing key staff, or offering a new curriculum, or getting new management, or extending the school day or year, or restructuring and increasing State Oversight. In the sixth year of not meeting AYP, they must continue with the school choice and what was done in year five. They also must plan for alternative governance.[379]

In compliance with these stages of corrective actions as listed above, the TMCES has re-established the team-teacher approach. There are now two certified teachers per class in grades one, two and three.[380] The District also hired Roman Marcellais as a full-time assistant superintendent in 2004.[381]

At the end of the 2005–06 school year, the TMCS completed the sixth bracket year but in reality is in the third NCLB year. According to the Elementary Principal, Dave Gourneau, TMCES met AYP this school year. The school will remain on a program of improvement since it is their first year of making AYP. If they make AYP again next year they will be removed from the program improvement status. The TMC High School and Middle School did not meet AYP, and must continue with their consequences for not making Adequate Yearly Progress.

---

[379] ND DPI, *Consequences for Schools NOT making AYP*
[380] Personal Interview with TMCES Principal David Gourneau, 6/2006.
[381] Personal Interview with TMCS Ass't Supt. Roman Marcellais, 5/2006.

## Teacher Negotiation and Belcourt Association of Improvement Teaching (BAIT)

In the 1970's, teachers and school districts' representatives became involved in negotiations pursuant to the provisions of North Dakota Century Code 15–28.1 and 15.1–16–13. The teachers and board representatives were to meet and negotiate in good faith the terms and conditions of teacher employment. When an agreement was reached, the teachers took the proposed agreement back to their organization for approval while the board representatives presented the proposal to the board members for their approval. If each side agreed to the terms of the negotiation, a contract would be drawn up. The terms within the contract would determine for what period of time the contract covered. It could be one, two and more years.[382]

If an agreement could not be reached, an impasse was declared. The parties would seek mediation or refer the disagreement to the State fact-finding commission. Normally, parties reached an agreement before it went that far.

The first representatives for the district were Harlen Wash, Jack Adams, and Dan Jerome. K. W. Simons, Fern Marrara, and Chuck DeRemer were some of the first members who negotiated for the teachers' unit.

These negotiations between the board and the teacher organization are still carried out today.

## Special Boards

The Belcourt School District #7 Board, the 100 – 297 High School Grant Board, and the Bureau of Indian Affairs govern the Turtle Mountain Community School system. As mentioned earlier, the Belcourt School District is a seven-member board elected by the voters of the district. The recent 100 – 297 High School Grant Board is made up of the same elected members of the

---

[382] North Dakota Century Code.

district, plus two other Reservation at-large members appointed by the Tribe.

A Bureau school board was formed in 1978 by Public Law 95–561. The purpose of this board is to involve the local people in education. Harlen Wash, EPA, for the Bureau of Indian Affairs, allowed the regular school district boards to serve in this capacity and thus avoided unnecessary boards. Bureau records indicate that this arrangement lasted for nearly 22 years.

In 2000, Loretta Delong, EPA, decided since parents outside the district proper were not allowed to vote in the school district elections, they did not have input into the school system. A letter dated August 21, 2000, was written to the parents to advise them that an election of a seven-member 95–561 board would be held on August 25, 2000. However, after the election, only four members were placed on the board.[383] No explanation was given as to why the original number of seven was changed. In reality, the board membership was cut to three members, but since there was a tie vote between Richard Marcellais and Lynell Pays, both were allowed to serve making it a four-member board. The other two elected members of the 561 board were Carla Peltier, and Tyler Grant. These four people served both the elementary and middle schools. According to Carla Peltier, a change was made to a five-member board about three years later. Today, two separate 561 boards serve the elementary and the middle schools. Members of the elementary school board are Richard Marcellais, Carla Peltier, Lynell Pays, Barbara Azure and Tony Vandal. The Members of the middle school 561 board are Richard Marcellais, Carla Peltier, Mike Laducer, Tony Vandal and Barbara Azure.

## BIA Realignment

"The initial discussions on realigning the field-based Education Line Offices (EL0) began early in 2003. Reasons for proposing realignment focused on changes in legislative

---

[383] BIA education records.

requirements for schools such as the Government Performance and Results Act (GPRA for both K-12 and post-secondary schools) and

the No Child Left Behind Act (NCLBA for K-12 schools). Also significant changes in the Education Amendment of 1978 have affected the range of responsibilities and authorities of the Education Line Officer. In the 1970–80's, less than one-third of all BIA-funded schools were operated as a Tribally controlled contract/grant school by Tribal authorities. By 2003, more than 120 or two-thirds of the BIA-funded schools are operated by Tribal authorities. There has been no corresponding realignment of Education Line Offices to address such a shift in the types of schools and programs being administered."[384]

Figure 15-9: Rose Henry Davis, ELO.

As a result of the planning meetings held for realignment of the field-based ELO, Minot, North Dakota was designated as the site to handle the schools in the North Dakota area. Rose Davis was selected for the line officer position and will be responsible for thirteen schools: the three TMC Schools and Ojibwa Indian School at Belcourt, Dunseith Day School at Dunseith, Four Winds at Fort Totten, Standing Rock Grant School at Fort Yates, Circle of Nations at Wahpeton, Theodore Jamerson School at Bismarck, Twin Buttes at Halliday, Mandaree and White Shield at Fort Berthold, and Trenton. The realignment was to go into effect August 2006.[385]

---

[384] TM Education Agency files.
[385] Personal Interview with Betty Poitra, BIA, Education Specialist, 6/8/2006.

# The Trail of Misgivings

The Tribe has filed an injunction against the Bureau in an effort to keep the BIA Education Agency office on the T. M. Reservation. Ken Davis, Tribal Chairman, in his July Report indicated the closing of this office is temporarily on hold. Davis stated, the Bureau "was not honest with the Tribe," regarding their rules of "meaningful consultation." So far the courts have ruled in the Tribe's favor.[386] Realignment of the ELO is another subtle move of the Bureau of Indian Affairs moving farther away from their responsibilities.

---

[386] *Turtle Mountain Times*, August 7, 2006, p. 2A.

# Chapter 16

## Special Education Program, Head Start, Turtle Mountain Community College

The Head Start Program sponsored the first Special Education Program in the Turtle Mountain area in 1966. Two years later the Belcourt School District began a program funded by Title I. Congress passed Public Law 94–142 in 1975 making it mandatory that all handicapped children have a right to receive a free public education.[387]

Today both the Bureau of Indian Affairs and the State of North Dakota fund the Special Education Program. The District receives approximately $235,000 from the State. The school also works with the Peace Garden Special Education Program and generates anywhere from $30,000 to $60,000 annually.[388]

The Director of the Agency Special Education Program for the TMCS system has worked with nine Bureau, District, Tribal contract schools – Three Turtle Mountain Community Schools, Dunseith Day School, Ojibwa Indian School, Mandaree, Twin Buttes, Trenton, and White Shield. In addition, to these nine schools, the Agency program operates a preschool special education program in conjunction with the Turtle Mountain Head

---

[387] Notes of Gaylene Belgarde, January 2006, pp. 1-2
[388] Notes of Gaylene Belgarde, January 2006, pp. 1-2.

Figure 16-1: The Special Education building, which is next to the Head Start facilities.

Start Program. The preschool special education program serves eleven children from the Head Start Program with five children attending in the morning and six in the afternoon. These students are housed north of the Head Start building in the former Heritage Center leased from the Tribe. The Turtle Mountain Community Schools program provides services for children that are Educable Mentally Handicapped, Trainable Mentally Handicapped, Specific Learning Disabled, Emotionally Disabled, Speech and Language Impaired, Visually Impaired, Mentally Handicapped, Other Health Impaired, Traumatic Brain Injured, and Orthopedic. The Agency Special Education Program works with 628 students of which 455 are from the five local schools. The program has a staff of 100 people – forty teachers, thirty-seven para-professionals and twenty-three ancillary personnel including administration, psychiatrist, psychologist, counselors, office staff and other professionals.[389]

---

[389] Notes of Gaylene Belgarde, January 2006, p. 1, and addendum sheet.

A Cooperative Agreement Unit (CAU) was authorized by the Office of Indian Education in 1993. "The purpose of the CAU is to consolidate common or certain Exceptional Education functions at the Turtle Mountain Agency Schools using Exceptional Education Programs Funds." The five schools involved are the three Turtle Mountain Community Schools, Ojibwa Indian School, and the Dunseith Day School. Each of the five schools hires their own special education teachers; however, they contract through the CAU for special services.[390]

The five schools enter into an annual cooperative agreement, which binds the schools to consolidate moneys for the funding. Funds generated by this endeavor are used to hire professional staff to serve disabled students. The CAU will absorb the administrative, training and technical assistance, material, supplies, and transportation costs of the program. [391]

OIEP, Division of Compliance Monitoring and Accountability, approves the annual budget of the CAU. Each school is apportioned funds according to the number of the disabled children they serve. The agreement provides services for physical therapy, occupational therapy, business technician, transportation and vehicles, travel, supplies, material, test supplies, extended school services, school psychologist, counselor, social workers, psychiatric nurse practitioner, special education coordinator, and field education specialist. The field education specialist addresses school reform to be in compliance with IDEIA, and provides assistance services to No Child Left Behind (NCLB). Special education staff adheres to the Individuals with Disabilities Education Improvement Act (IDEIA) regarding due process and the rights of parents.[392]

---

[390] *Turtle Mountain Exceptional Education LEA Cooperative Agreement*, TM Schools, Belcourt, N.D. 1/20/06, prepared by Gaylene Belgarde, SEC, p. 7.
[391] *Turtle Mountain Exceptional Education*, p. 7.
[392] *Turtle Mountain Exceptional Education*, pp. 7-8.

Louis Dauphinais (BIA), TMC Middle School Principal, has the overall responsibility for the CAU. The school principals are responsible for the administration for their Special Education Programs.[393]

## Turtle Mountain Head Start

Originally, Head Start began as a pilot program at St. Mary's Church north of Dunseith in 1965. Myrtle Hansen was in charge during its inception. She served the program temporarily until Sonya Banish was hired as the first director in 1966. Then in rapid succession came Diane Schroeder, Sr. Mary Daniel Schlomer, OSB, Richard (Jiggers) LaFromboise, and Jennifer Ramey who took charge in 1972. Ramey has been in the position for the past thirty-four years.[394]

Figure 16-2: The Head Start building, which was once known as the CAP building.

---

[393] *Turtle Mountain Exceptional Education*, pp. 8.
[394] Ronald Poitra, Informational Paper on Head Start, 4/18/06, p. 1.

## Special Education Program, Head Start, Turtle Mountain Community College

The Head Start Program began serving children in the Belcourt and St. John areas in 1966. Two half-day sessions were held at both sites. At Belcourt, there were 18 children in the morning and 18 in the afternoon. The first teachers for the Belcourt center were Jean Bonn, Diane Schroeder and Pam Williams. The first classroom for the Belcourt site was a trailer located near the TMC Elementary School. The children had lunch in the TMCS cafeteria. Evelyn Langan was the lone teacher at the St. John site and Donna Bryant was the cook.[395]

Presently, the Belcourt Head Start Center is in the former Community Action Program (CAP) building that was erected in the mid 1960's. There are eleven classrooms to accommodate 196 children. The Head Start program operates a full day schedule for children ages three to five years. St. John, Shell Valley and Dunseith have 20 children each in their centers. There are 58 pre-school children at the North Dunseith Center. This is a grand total of 314 children at the five sites. It also employs seventy-five full-time and part-time staff that includes thirty-four teachers, seventeen teacher aides, five part-time bus drivers, seven bus drivers/janitors, eleven food service people and other auxiliary staff.[396]

## Turtle Mountain Community College

After years of dreaming and planning, on behalf of a hand full of local people driven by Carol Monette Davis, Turtle Mountain Community College became a reality in 1972. The institution had neither funding, nor official staff, nor building. It was necessary for the Turtle Mountain Community College to link with another higher education institution for accreditation purposes. NDSU-Bottineau Branch served in this capacity from 1973 to 1983. The ND Board of Regents insisted that the reservation institution be known as the Higher Education Enrichment Center during that

---

[395] Ronald Poitra, p. 1.
[396] Ronald Poitra, p. 2.

period. TMCC became an independent entity when it obtained its accreditation in 1984.[397]

Figure 16-3: The old downtown campus of TMCC. The school still uses some of these buildings.

Governance for the TMCC was set up as a two-tiered system. The Tribal Council appointed a nine-member Board of Trustees with a lifetime appointment for the chairman. The Board of Trustees' membership consists of two community members, two tribal council members, two students, and two members of the local educational institutions. The first Board of Trustees were: Jack Fiddler (Chairman), Frank X. Morin (Secretary), Lynn Davis, Mike Laducer, Gregory King Davis, Janice Schlenvogt, Russell Davis, Jr., Roger Decoteau and Patricia Gailfus. The Board of Trustees, in turn, selects a five-member Board of Directors. The

---

[397] St. Ann's Centennial Book, pp. 184-185.

first directors were Carol Davis (Chairman), Wayne Keplin (Secretary), Donna Poitra, Mike Keplin and Lance Azure.[398]

The Boards of Trustees and Directors selected Larry Belgarde and Twila Martin to head the college as co directors in 1973. In 1974, Martin left the institution. With this vacancy, the NDSU-BB and the Board of Directors made a change in the administrative structure. Larry Belgarde became the director of the TMCC/Enrichment Center and Gerald "Carty" Monette became an assistant director.[399] In the fall of 1973, the Turtle Mountain Community College conducted their first classes. Several of the local students who had been attending NDSU/Bottineau transferred their registrations to the TMCC. Some students, sponsored by the Couture District #27's Follow Through Program, were Leonard Azure, Louis Dauphinais, Betty Ann Laducer, Joyce C. Morin, Barbara B. Poitra, Elaine Rodland, and Mary Ann Slater.[400]

The first year there were 64 students registered for the nine college courses offered. Larry Belgarde, Marlin Belgarde, Jace Cuney, Dennis Demontigny and Father Guy Gau were the instructors.[401] The offices and the classrooms for the College were in the Community Action Program (CAP) building in Belcourt. In the 1974–75 academic year, the college found a temporary home at the Queen of Peace Convent about two miles west and south of Belcourt. The college moved again to the old hospital for the 1975–76 school term. Before the school term had ended, flooding caused another move to a building on Main Street.[402] Parts of the TMC High School facilities were also used in the evening as classrooms for the college.

---

[398] Wayne J. Stein, *Tribally Controlled Colleges, Making Good Medicine*, pp. 80-81
[399] Stein, pp. 83, 90.
[400] St. Ann's Centennial Book, pp. 184-185
[401] St. Ann's Centennial Book, p. 184.
[402] Personal Interview with Dr. Larry Belgarde.

The first building the college owned was on Main Street. The Board purchased the old tribal building for $10,000.[403] A conglomeration of buildings (sixteen in all) eventually became the college campus and some are still being used today.

In 1977, Belgrade resigned as the director of the Enrichment Center, and accepted the Board appointment of acting president of TMCC. This appointment drew opposition from NDSU/BB.

Figure 16-4: The new college campus located on the shores of Fish Lake, north of Belcourt.

Monette then became director of the Enrichment Center, and the power struggle heated up between he and Dean Johnson of the NDSU/BB. After deliberating for nearly a year, the Board of Directors appointed Belgarde as the college's first president and then focused their efforts on Monette's clash with NDSU/BB. The TMCC bargaining power with NDSU/BB gained momentum when TMCC became a candidate for North Central Accreditation on July

---

[403] Personal Interview with Larry Belgarde.

24, 1978. The Board immediately seized control of the Title III funding.[404]

Figure 16-5: Jim Davis, present TMCC president.

November 29, 1978, Belgarde was granted a leave of absence and did not return. In 1980, Monette, the acting President, was named President of the college. Monette served until his resignation in 2004.[405] Carol Davis served as interim President of the College until the installation of James Davis on November 7, 2005.

Within a ten-year period, the college enrollment was nearly 300 students and offered 85 classes. The staff had grown to twenty-nine full-time and twenty part-time instructors.

The college began construction on its new facilities two and a half miles north of Belcourt on March 10, 1997. Twenty-six months later TMCC moved to a permanent campus by the east shore on the north end of Fish Lake on 114.3 acres of land.[406] The legal description uses the lake shore as its western boundaries with the SE¼, and the tip of NE¼ of the SW¼, Section 5 of Township 162 N, Range 70 W, Rolette County.

The building contains 105,000 square feet of general classrooms, math lab room, science rooms, library and archives, mechanical rooms, weight room, administrative office space, student service area, gymnasium with an indoor track above the gym, cafeteria, student support area, bookstore, business office,

---

[404] Stein, pp. 90-91.
[405] Stein, pp. 90-91.
[406] TMCC Records.

and learning center. This was the first phase of construction. The cost of phase one totaled $9,913,000 plus a 6% Architect and Engineering (A/E) fee. The second phase of the construction began in April of 2002 and was completed in 2003. The new construction provides an additional 40,000 square feet of space contains a 1,000-seat fully furnished auditorium, music and arts rooms, boardroom, business office, and computer lab. The cost of phase two amounted to $4,885,500 plus the A/E fee. The total cost of the college complex is $15,686,410.[407]

There were 1,480 full-time/part-time students of whom 1,349 were of Indian descent in the 2005–2006 academic year. The College also has responsibility for the General Equivalency Diploma (GED) Program. Last year (2005–2006), 225 students passed through this program.[408]

The Turtle Mountain Community College Board of Trustees present members are Jim Lindgren, Resa Rivard, Yvonne St. Claire, John Frederick, Dwight Trottier, with Troy Decoteau and Curtis Davis, representing the Tribal Council, and two student members Jeff Grant and Bineeshi Azure. Lance Azure (President), Francis "Fatty" Davis, John Trottier, Jerry Gourneau and Ronald Peltier serve as the Board of Directors.

---

[407] TMCC Records.

[408] U.S. Dept of the Interior, BIA, TM Agency, Belcourt, ND, p. 8.

# Chapter 17

## Turtle Mountain Community School Administrators

In the early days, the Reservation Education system was in the hands of the Farmer in Charge. E. W. Brenner was the first to serve from 1887 to 1904. E. E. Jones held the position from 1905 to 1907. William P. Schwab replaced Jones and was here until the Turtle Mountain Agency Superintendents assumed the role in 1910.

The list of the Agency Superintendents is as follows:[409]

| Agency Superintendents | From | To |
|---|---|---|
| Stephen Janus | July 1910 | April 1914 |
| R. C. Craige | April 1914 | September 1919 |
| J. J. McQuiggs | September 1919 | August 1926 |
| James H. Hyde | September 1926 | March 1931 |
| Charles H. Asbury | March 1931 | May 1932 |
| Francis J. Scott | July 1932 | September 1934 |
| John B. Balmer | October, 1934 | February 1939 |
| Fred W. Boyd | April 1940 | September 1943 |
| James D. Crawford | January 1944 | September 1947 |

---

[409] *St. Ann's Centennial –1885-1985 100 - Years of Faith,* p. 102.

| Harold E. Bruce | October 1947 | September 1948 |
|---|---|---|
| C. H. Beitzel | October 1948 | September 1951 |
| Peru Farver | October 1951 | December 1953 |
| Knute H. Lee | December 1953 | November 1954 |
| Harold W Schunk | November 1954 | July 1957 |
| H. P. Mitlelholtz | July 1957 | June 1961 |
| Leonard O. Lay | July 1961 | October 1964 |
| William A Mehojah | November 1964 | June 1968 |
| Duane C. Moxon | June 1968 | June 1971 |
| Frank X. Morin | June 1971 | October 1974 |
| Fred E. Gillis | March 1975 | May 1982 |

Shortly after Gillis took office, the Education Branch became a separate entity from the Agency Superintendent. Reservation Principals or Education Program Administrators were then Bureau Administrators in charge. J. Arthur Anderson was the first administrator of the 1931 consolidated school (Turtle Mountain Community School). How long he served is lost in time in some government documentation warehouse. Barnes was Education Principal in the late 1930's and early 1940's to the best of Hazel Demontigny Franz's recollection. *The Chipaway 1943* indicates that Leslie M. Keller, Principal of Education, was here during the 1942–43 school term (though he could have been earlier). He served until 1945.[410] The list continues below:

Leslie M. Keller

---

[410]The identity of the principals and the education program administrators was validated by TMCS alumni diploma signatures.

| *Principals of Education[411]* | *Years* |
|---|---|
| Glenn C. Lundeen | 1945 – 1947 |
| Olaf Nelson | 1947 – 1949 |
| I. L. Nichols | 1949 – 1951 |
| Clarence Ashby | 1951 – 1954 |
| A. V. Kirk | 1954 – 1955 |
| Lawrence T. Mickelson | 1955 – 1965 |
| James Bearghost (EPA) | 1965 – 1969 |
| David Burch | 1969 – 1970 |
| Harlen Wash | 1970 – 1980 |
| Ken Davis | 1980 – 1980 |
| Larry Belgarde | 1980 – 1985 |
| James Davis | 1985 – 1990 |
| Loretta Delong | 1990 – 2002 |
| Betty Poitra (Acting EPA) | 2002 – 2003 |
| Paige Baker (Acting EPA) | 2003 – 2004 |
| Rose Henry Davis (ELO) | 2004 – present |

Daniel Jerome

The Couture School District hired Dan Jerome as its first Superintendent for the Turtle Mountain Community School in 1969. He also served in this capacity for the Ingebretson School District through the reorganization of the Districts, which formed the Belcourt School District #7 in 1984. Jerome retired as superintendent in 1990. Wayne Keplin served from 1990 to 1995 followed by Viola Champagne LaFontaine who is the present School Superintendent.

---

[411] Some pictures of these and following administrators are through the courtesy of the Chipaway and Agawase Yearbooks.

# The Trail of Misgivings

Verona Cover

The first Bureau Principal for Turtle Mountain Community Elementary School was Verona Cover from 1955 to 1970. The Elementary Principals have been Bureau personnel, though with the cooperative agreement, there have been both Bureau and District Assistant Principals and staff. A list of her successors follows:

| Elementary Principals | Years | Affiliation |
| --- | --- | --- |
| Russ Miller | 1971 – 1972 | Bureau |
| Elner C. Monson | 1972 – 1984 | Bureau |
| Jerry Woody (Acting) | 1984 – 1986 | Bureau |
| Dr. Teresa Delorme | 1986 – 1990 | Bureau |
| Roman Marcellais | 1990 – 1999 | Bureau |
| Denise Lajimodiere | 1999 – 2000 | Bureau |
| David Gourneau | 2000 – present | Bureau |

The first Bureau of Indian Affairs Principal for Turtle Mountain Community Middle School was Darrell Gannarelli (1971 to 1982). Gannarelli took ill during his administration and Louis Dauphinais, who was assistant principal, became acting principal of the Middle School. He then became Principal in 1982 and has held that position to the present time.

Darrell Gannarelli

Albert Clark

The first Principal of the Turtle Mountain Community High School was Albert Clark. He was Bureau and served in that capacity from 1942 to early 1949. Most of the high principals were bureau administrators until the Couture School District subcontracted the high school under PL 93–638 in 1978. Clark's successors were:

| High School Principals | Years | Affiliation |
| --- | --- | --- |
| A.V. Kirk | 1949 – 1952 | Bureau |
| Robert Murray | 1952 – 1954 | Bureau |
| L.A. Russell | 1954 – 1958 | Bureau |
| David Fischer | 1958 – 1962 | Bureau |
| Samuel Feld | 1962 – 1964 | Bureau |
| Paul Melchior | 1964 – 1965 | Bureau |
| David Burch | 1965 – 1968 | Bureau |
| Daniel Jerome | 1968 – 1969 | School District |
| Darrell Gannarelli (Actg) | 1969 – 1972 | Bureau |
| Lester Fettig | 1972 – 1974 | School District |
| Jon Fimmel | 1974 – 1975 | School District |
| Florence Crouse | 1975 – 1976 | Bureau |
| Ron Witt | 1976 – 1984 | School District |
| Ernesto Jimenez | 1984 – 1985 | School District |
| Duane Schindler | 1985 – 1991 | School District |
| Rosemary Jaros | 1991 – present | School District |

Jim Davis verifies that Fischer began the 1962–63 year stating that Fischer was in his school football picture. Fischer may have left during the school term because Dwain Jerome graduated in 1963; his high school diploma is signed by Samuel Feld. Some of the administrators that came through the years are seen below.

## Principals of Education

David Burch
Glenn C. Lundeen
Harlen Wash

## Elementary Principals

Russ Miller
Elner C. Monson

# Turtle Mountain Reservation School Administration

## High School Principals

Florence Crouse
Lester Fettig
Jon Fimmel
Duane Schindler
Ron Witt

233

## Administration Staff

Connie Baker
(Superintendent Secretary)
Stan Campbell
(Computer Center Director)
Betty Peach Poitra
(Field Education Specialist)
Sandy Thomas
(Financial Systems Director)
Dwight Trottier
(Personnel Director)

# Chapter 18

## A Vision

### The Trail Ahead

Despite betrayals and misgivings, we, the Turtle Mountain people, have endured skepticism, doubt and the forceful ways that were used in an attempt to mold our way of life, which began with the white man's ever increasing want for land. We are encouraged because "Those that sow in tears will reap rejoicing." (Psalm 126). We have adapted and preserved our culture they wanted to destroy. We have made significant achievement in today's society by taking advantage of the educational opportunities available throughout the years. There are numerous certified Native American teachers in the classrooms, Native American administrators are leading our schools, and local members of the school boards have control. We, the Turtle Mountain people, have made progress in determining our own destiny.

We, the Turtle Mountain people, have much for which to be grateful. Two new schools will soon be a reality (TMCHS and OIS). This is the first time ever that there have been two large government school construction projects simultaneously going on in the same year. The Tribal Council, the Bureau, the Belcourt School District and the Ojibwa Indian School Board are to be commended for this remarkable achievement. With the present educational facilities and the new schools being constructed, we shall finally be adequately prepared to house our student population. Since the laws and policies of State Government, which blatantly prevented the funding of Indian students, have been changed through the efforts of our local elders, we have had the financial resources. The Turtle Mountain Community College has been one of our Tribe's achievements. Local business owners contribute much to the advancement of the community and take an active leadership role in reservation affairs.

However, there are still challenges on the trail ahead, and we must not be complacent. It is imperative that parents take an active role in their children's education. The No Child Left Behind Act (NCLB) is both a motivator and a blessing to the community and the school system. The Act holds schools accountable for student progress. We must inspire students to accomplish what they are capable of achieving. We need to teach our students to be responsible for their academic learning. Students must be in attendance. Some teachers will be forced to dismiss the attitude that "Indian children can't learn." More creativity must be put into their teaching styles with results, or teachers must leave the system. It is fortunate that NCLB will pressure the neighboring schools to be more attuned and sensitive to Indian students. We are challenged to search for new ideas and solutions in educating our children.

Contrary to the Career Opportunity Program, Teacher Corps and other program philosophies of producing "Indian teachers to teach Indian children," not everyone is cut out to be either a teacher or an administrator. A college degree alone does not fill all the requirements. Some people have degrees and others have the know-how; teachers must have both. Don't misunderstand the statement – many good Indian teachers have come through these programs. Indian preference may get one's foot in the classroom door, but once in, if you can't teach, your "preference" means nothing. The danger looms when our leaders fail to recognize that not all Indians can be educators. A teacher must have a love for children and must have the desire, the drive, the knowledge, and the techniques to teach. Teaching is a committed profession that is continually changing, and requires educators to keep abreast with current practices.

There are issues in our community that deeply impact education. We must be managers of our problems. We must be problem solvers. Why do we have a dropout problem? Why do we have a high teenage pregnancy rate? Why do we have drugs, harmful smoking and chewing, and alcohol problems? A recent study indicated that most people conclude that peer pressure is the cause of children using drugs, but that is not the case according to the study. The use of drugs and alcohol by children come from the home as a learned behavior. They see parents using cigarettes, alcohol and drugs. Parents show indifference toward this or just don't speak to their kids about it being harmful. The home may have a medicine cabinet full of pills and capsules. Children see these and conclude drugs must be okay. How the medicines are used and why must be explained to the children. They have to say "NO" to drugs – a TV commercial nowadays calls parents, "the anti-drug."

Figure 18-1: Terry Jerome.

In a recent interview with TMCHS North Dakota Licensed Addiction Counselor, Terry Jerome, he emphasized, "Just to say 'No' carries no weight. It is easier said than done." Parents must take the responsibility to be the antidote, and break their denials and then become the "anti-drug." This attitude for changing requires the efforts of the entire community through intervention and education. Community denial is our biggest enemy. We are denying the spiritual, moral and physical aspects of certain damaging behaviors and the consequences. Some parents have a drinking or drug problem, and while under the influence, conceive children causing damage to their children from the beginning. Families must make the effort to get a healthy balance back into the community mainstream inter-relationships gene pool. Healthy children are more apt to be in the mode to learn.[412]

Our values and education begin at home; therefore, it is not solely a Bureau or District responsibility. A Tribal effort must be made; the Bureau, District, families, parents, students, and the community must work together in harmony. Jealousies must be squelched as fighting amongst us hinders our efforts.

To wallow in bitterness over what happened in the past is fruitless. Racial injustices may be a fact of life for us, but we can and must rise above it. We are well aware that prejudices still exist today, not only from the white community, but also from and within our own tribe. As mentioned earlier, our people have physical traits that range from dark skin and dark eyes to light skin and blue eyes. Even these differences bring out the prejudices amongst us. This too is not a "their problem" but an "our problem," that together we must deal with and resolve. Harassment must cease.

Our schools have had their dark sides – log shacks too small to accommodate the Indian children who wanted an education; children shipped away for years at a time to boarding schools; constant overcrowding due to inadequate facilities and money shortages. We have been in the darkness – we are now coming into the light that whispers the vision of our need for an education. The ideal attitude of learning rests within each of us.

We must not remain captives of the past either in our own land or within ourselves. We must reconcile the misgivings and

---

[412] Personal Interview with Terry Jerome, LAC, 7/2006.

hurts. We must forgive the unforgiven. We must preserve our integrity that we have retained for the struggles that lie ahead. We are a proud people capable of meeting the challenges that confront the global community in which we live today. We have endured *the trail of misgivings – a scourging journey.* Though it has been a long, arduous one, it has made us who we are today. We have vision, and we shall survive and thrive.

I attended the first school board meeting in sixteen years on May 17, 2006. It was impressive to observe the school board members begin the meeting with prayer calling upon the Almighty for guidance. What a beautiful example to set for our children trusting in Him that in all things He may direct our steps as we walk in faith along the way. What a vision to behold.

Figure 18-2: TMCC 2006 Graduates Zane & Kyle Zaste. President Jim Davis in background. Courtesy of Kathe Peltier Zaste.

# Appendices

## Appendix A: Executive Orders Defining the Reservation

EXECUTIVE MANSION, December 21, 1882.
It is hereby ordered that the following-described country in the Territory of Dakota, viz: Beginning at a point on the international boundary where the tenth guide meridian west of the fifth principal meridian (being the range line between ranges 73 and 74 west of the fifth principal meridian) will, when extended, intersect said international boundary; thence south on the tenth guide meridian to the southeast corner of township 161 north, range 74 west; thence east on the fifteenth standard parallel north, to the northeast corner of township 160 north, range 74 west; thence south on the tenth guide meridian west to the southeast corner of township 159 north, range 74 west; thence east on the line between townships 158 and 159 north to the southeast corner of township 159 north, range 70 west; thence north with the line between ranges 69 and 70 west to the northeast corner of township 160 north, range 70 west, thence west on the fifteenth standard parallel north to the southeast corner of township 161 north, range 70 west, thence north on the line between ranges 69 and 70 west to the international boundary; thence west on the international boundary to the place of beginning, be, and the same is hereby, withdrawn from sale and settlement and set apart for the use and occupancy of the Turtle Mountain Band of Chippewas and such other Indians of the Chippewa tribe as the Secretary of the Interior may see fit to settle thereon.
Chester A. Arthur.

EXECUTIVE MANSION, March 29, 1884.
It is hereby ordered that the tract of country in the Territory of Dakota withdrawn from sale and settlement and set apart for the use and occupancy of the Turtle Mountain Band of Chippewa Indians by Executive Order dated December 21, 1882, except townships 162 and 163 north, range 71 west, be, and the same is hereby, restored to the mass of the public domain.
Chester A. Arthur.

EXECUTIVE MANSION, June 3, 1884.
The Executive order dated March 29, 1884, whereby certain lands in the Territory of Dakota previously set apart for the use and occupancy of the Turtle Mountain Band of Chippewa Indians were, with the exception of townships 162 and 163 north, range 71 west, restored to the mass of the public domain, is hereby amended so as to substitute township 162 north, range 70 west, for township 163 north, range 71 west, the purpose and effect of such amendment being to withdraw from the sale and settlement and set apart for the use and occupancy of said Indians said township 162 north, range 70 west, in lieu of township 163 north, range 71 west, which last-mentioned township is thereby restored to the mass of the public domain.
Chester A. Arthur.

## Appendix B-1: From Murray, page 41
## Table II[413]
## Public School Enrollment and Attendance, May 1923

| School | Enrollment | Average Attendance | Percent |
|---|---|---|---|
| Couture #1, Room 1 | 27 | 25 | 93 |
| Room 2 | 25 | 19 | 77 |
| Room 3 | 36 | 24 | 78 |
| Couture #2 | 30 | 26 | 88 |
| Couture #3 | 21 | 19 | 90 |
| Ingrebretson #1, 2, 3, 4 | 175 | 136.4 | 79.8 |
| St. John | 18 | 11.1 | 64 |
| Hillside #4 | 10 | 8.2 | 82 |
| Dunseith | 5 | 4.8 | 97 |
| Hillside #2 | 11 | 8.5 | 85 |
| Shell Valley | 17 | 16.1 | 91 |

---

[413] Turtle Mountain Agency, Day School Inspector Official Report, May 1923.

## Appendix B-2: From Murray, page 128
## Table IX[414]
## Enrollment and Personnel in Federal Schools
## Turtle Mountain Reservation

| Year | Enrollment | ADA | No. of Teachers | No. of other employees |
|---|---|---|---|---|
| **Turtle Mountain Community school, grades 1-12** | | | | |
| 1949–50 | 445 | 355.5 | 16 | 14 |
| 1950–51 | 489 | 391.3 | 16 | 14 |
| 1951–52 | 513 | 386.2 | 17 | 14 |
| 1952–53 | 530 | 414.6 | 18 | 15 |
| **Dunseith School, grades 1-8** | | | | |
| 1949–50 | 149 | 101.8 | 4 | 4 |
| 1950–51 | 143 | 110.01 | 4 | 4 |
| 1951–52 | 134 | 114.5 | 4 | 4 |
| 1952–53 | 137 | 123 | 5 | 4 |
| **Great Walker School, grades 1-6** | | | | |
| 1949–50 | 53 | 42.43 | 2 | 2 |
| 1950–51 | 54 | 47.1 | 2 | 2 |
| 1951–52 | 59 | 44.7 | 2 | 2 |
| 1952–53 | 58 | 49 | 2 | 2 |
| **Houle School, grades 1-6** | | | | |
| 1949–50 | 47 | 43.57 | 2 | 2 |
| 1950–51 | 52 | 56.6 | 2 | 2 |
| 1951–52 | 47 | 42.54 | 2 | 2 |
| 1952–53 | 58 | 54.2 | 2 | 2 |
| **Roussin School, grades 1-8** | | | | |
| 1949–50 | 52 | 45.81 | 2 | 2 |
| 1950–51 | 49 | 44.3 | 2 | 2 |
| 1951–52 | 47 | 44.8 | 2 | 2 |
| 1952–53 | 47 | 40.8 | 2 | 2 |

---

[414] U.S. Dept. of Interior, Statistics Concerning Indian Education, Haskell Press, Lawrence, Kansas, 1953.

[ADA = average daily attendance]

# Appendices B-3: ENR, ADM and ADA History for TMCS

| | 1959 1960 | 1960 1961 | 1961 1962 | 1962 1963 | 1963 1964 | 1964 1965 | 1965 1966 |
|---|---|---|---|---|---|---|---|
| **ENROLLMENT:** | | | | | | | |
| K | 0 | 0 | 0 | 0 | 0 | 0 | 0 |
| 1 | 61 | 67 | 73 | 79 | 96 | 100 | 133 |
| 2 | 36 | 49 | 42 | 49 | 50 | 60 | 74 |
| 3 | 42 | 38 | 52 | 46 | 48 | 31 | 62 |
| 4 | 44 | 49 | 40 | 55 | 47 | 51 | 60 |
| 5 | 40 | 48 | 51 | 35 | 62 | 44 | 65 |
| 6 | 32 | 40 | 51 | 46 | 40 | 54 | 66 |
| *1-6 Sbttl:* | *255* | *291* | *309* | *310* | *343* | *340* | *460* |
| 7 | 70 | 61 | 70 | 76 | 94 | 95 | 118 |
| 8 | 62 | 79 | 66 | 79 | 63 | 75 | 78 |
| *7-8 Sbttl:* | *132* | *140* | *136* | *155* | *157* | *170* | *196* |
| 9 | 87 | 96 | 110 | 81 | 110 | 122 | 128 |
| 10 | 64 | 68 | 70 | 80 | 63 | 52 | 80 |
| 11 | 54 | 42 | 52 | 58 | 68 | 54 | 35 |
| 12 | 22 | 46 | 37 | 41 | 47 | 52 | 38 |
| *9-12 Sbttl:* | *227* | *252* | *269* | *260* | *288* | *280* | *281* |
| *Oth Enr* | | | | | | | |
| **ENR GRAND TOTALS:** | **614** | **683** | **714** | **725** | **788** | **790** | **937** |
| **ADM:** | | | | | | | |
| K | 0.00 | 0.00 | 0.00 | 0.00 | 0.00 | 0.00 | 0.00 |
| 1-6 | 235.58 | 251.71 | 295.84 | 273.41 | 306.22 | 323.55 | 419.42 |
| 7-8 | 120.81 | 132.30 | 133.59 | 139.62 | 151.35 | 151.74 | 164.83 |
| 9-12 | 190.38 | 216.54 | 248.41 | 236.18 | 257.61 | 260.11 | 241.13 |
| *Oth ADM* | | | | | | | |
| **TOTAL ADM:** | 546.77 | 600.55 | 677.84 | 649.21 | 715.18 | 735.40 | 825.38 |
| **ADA:** | | | | | | | |
| K | 0.00 | 0.00 | 0.00 | 0.00 | 0.00 | 0.00 | 0.00 |
| 1-6 | 219.44 | 238.25 | 266.61 | 248.45 | 282.03 | 301.13 | 388.72 |
| 7-8 | 105.67 | 119.33 | 122.01 | 119.71 | 130.47 | 131.53 | 144.48 |
| 9-12 | 164.55 | 192.60 | 218.37 | 200.12 | 216.76 | 211.83 | 216.30 |
| *Oth ADA* | | | | | | | |
| **TOTAL ADA:** | 489.66 | 550.18 | 606.99 | 568.28 | 629.26 | 644.49 | 749.50 |
| **ATT %:** | | | | | | | |
| K | 0.0% | 0.0% | 0.0% | 0.0% | 0.0% | 0.0% | 0.0% |
| 1-6 | 93.1% | 94.7% | 90.1% | 90.9% | 92.1% | 93.1% | 92.7% |
| 7-8 | 87.5% | 90.2% | 91.3% | 85.7% | 86.2% | 86.7% | 87.7% |
| 9-12 | 86.4% | 88.9% | 87.9% | 84.7% | 84.1% | 81.4% | 89.7% |
| *Oth ADM* | | | | | | | |
| **TTL ATT %:** | 89.6% | 91.6% | 89.5% | 87.5% | 88.0% | 87.6% | 90.8% |

[ADM = average daily membership]
[ATT % = attendance percentage]

# The Trail of Misgivings

| | 1966 1967 | 1967 1968 | 1968 1969 | 1969 1970 | 1970 1971 | 1971 1972 | 1972 1973 |
|---|---|---|---|---|---|---|---|
| **ENROLLMENT:** | | | | | | | |
| **K** | 0 | 0 | 0 | 0 | 145 | 137 | 146 |
| **1** | 140 | 167 | 151 | 160 | 179 | 167 | 149 |
| **2** | 114 | 136 | 112 | 121 | 136 | 149 | 157 |
| **3** | 85 | 102 | 109 | 130 | 139 | 117 | 169 |
| **4** | 91 | 93 | 96 | 118 | 146 | 133 | 139 |
| **5** | 70 | 106 | 97 | 104 | 166 | 143 | 161 |
| **6** | 77 | 102 | 100 | 114 | 141 | 135 | 164 |
| *1-6 Sbttl:* | *577* | *706* | *665* | *747* | *907* | *844* | *939* |
| **7** | 110 | 107 | 104 | 106 | 142 | 115 | 160 |
| **8** | 112 | 114 | 101 | 104 | 141 | 127 | 136 |
| *7-8 Sbttl:* | *222* | *221* | *205* | *210* | *283* | *242* | *296* |
| **9** | 97 | 115 | 108 | 115 | 107 | 147 | 153 |
| **10** | 94 | 73 | 101 | 88 | 105 | 96 | 117 |
| **11** | 63 | 67 | 57 | 85 | 82 | 96 | 84 |
| **12** | 49 | 50 | 58 | 54 | 69 | 65 | 89 |
| *9-12 Sbttl:* | *303* | *305* | *324* | *342* | *363* | *404* | *443* |
| *Oth Enr* | | 12 | 25 | 24 | 34 | 52 | 7 |
| **ENR GRAND TOTALS:** | **1102** | **1244** | **1219** | **1323** | **1732** | **1679** | **1831** |
| **ADM:** | | | | | | | |
| **K** | 0.00 | 0.00 | 0.00 | 0.00 | 120.65 | 122.78 | 133.81 |
| **1-6** | 507.38 | 642.26 | 614.81 | 688.32 | 832.53 | 786.54 | 864.34 |
| **7-8** | 194.71 | 187.97 | 184.93 | 183.16 | 260.34 | 217.32 | 263.62 |
| **9-12** | 252.07 | 266.89 | 281.10 | 285.47 | 313.13 | 349.27 | 377.44 |
| *Oth ADM* | | 10.68 | 22.57 | 23.76 | 29.12 | 51.64 | 7.00 |
| **TOTAL ADM:** | 954.16 | 1107.80 | 1103.41 | 1180.71 | 1555.77 | 1527.55 | 1646.21 |
| **ADA:** | | | | | | | |
| **K** | 0.00 | 0.00 | 0.00 | 0.00 | 107.53 | 107.46 | 119.58 |
| **1-6** | 468.39 | 586.79 | 572.17 | 640.02 | 788.89 | 738.44 | 804.87 |
| **7-8** | 167.49 | 166.17 | 169.93 | 165.70 | 241.19 | 203.06 | 240.36 |
| **9-12** | 226.70 | 245.20 | 256.26 | 253.55 | 284.58 | 319.52 | 346.85 |
| *Oth ADA* | | 9.47 | 21.21 | 22.43 | 27.53 | 48.41 | 6.67 |
| **TOTAL ADA:** | 862.58 | 1007.63 | 1019.57 | 1081.70 | 1449.72 | 1416.89 | 1518.33 |
| **ATT %:** | | | | | | | |
| **K** | 0.0% | 0.0% | 0.0% | 0.0% | 89.1% | 87.5% | 89.4% |
| **1-6** | 92.3% | 91.4% | 93.1% | 93.0% | 94.8% | 93.9% | 93.1% |
| **7-8** | 86.0% | 88.4% | 91.9% | 90.5% | 92.6% | 93.4% | 91.2% |
| **9-12** | 89.9% | 91.9% | 91.2% | 88.8% | 90.9% | 91.5% | 91.9% |
| *Oth ADM* | | 88.7% | 94.0% | 94.4% | 94.5% | 93.7% | 95.3% |
| **TTL ATT %:** | 90.4% | 91.0% | 92.4% | 91.6% | 93.2% | 92.8% | 92.2% |

| | 1973 1974 | 1974 1975 | 1975 1976 | 1976 1977 | 1977 1978 | 1978 1979 | 1979 1980 |
|---|---|---|---|---|---|---|---|
| **ENROLLMENT:** | | | | | | | |
| K | 120 | 112 | 134 | 141 | 125 | 130 | 115 |
| | | | | | | | |
| 1 | 143 | 134 | 102 | 132 | 131 | 143 | 135 |
| 2 | 126 | 121 | 123 | 113 | 121 | 120 | 119 |
| 3 | 144 | 128 | 108 | 118 | 91 | 128 | 115 |
| 4 | 162 | 133 | 125 | 111 | 121 | 93 | 125 |
| 5 | 132 | 159 | 133 | 116 | 110 | 121 | 91 |
| 6 | 145 | 133 | 159 | 141 | 124 | 107 | 107 |
| *1-6 Sbttl:* | *852* | *808* | *750* | *731* | *698* | *712* | *692* |
| 7 | 162 | 164 | 143 | 183 | 153 | 139 | 120 |
| 8 | 153 | 161 | 151 | 148 | 169 | 150 | 134 |
| *7-8 Sbttl:* | *315* | *325* | *294* | *331* | *322* | *289* | *254* |
| 9 | 151 | 190 | 190 | 173 | 158 | 196 | 240 |
| 10 | 129 | 134 | 163 | 181 | 155 | 151 | 150 |
| 11 | 94 | 107 | 95 | 144 | 147 | 167 | 114 |
| 12 | 70 | 81 | 81 | 104 | 124 | 105 | 106 |
| *9-12 Sbttl:* | *444* | *512* | *529* | *602* | *584* | *619* | *610* |
| *Oth Enr* | 6 | 6 | 25 | | 6 | 6 | |
| **ENR GRAND TOTALS:** | 1737 | 1763 | 1732 | 1805 | 1735 | 1756 | 1671 |
| | | | | | | | |
| **ADM:** | | | | | | | |
| K | 108.36 | 100.41 | 118.67 | 125.60 | 112.79 | 117.37 | 103.75 |
| 1-6 | 767.73 | 742.60 | 691.30 | 663.71 | 634.75 | 647.27 | 635.69 |
| 7-8 | 279.73 | 289.12 | 262.29 | 289.09 | 284.77 | 202.96 | 224.05 |
| 9-12 | 375.54 | 441.44 | 454.17 | 508.32 | 565.02 | 521.37 | 513.51 |
| *Oth ADM* | 5.37 | 5.06 | 22.44 | | 5.00 | 5.70 | |
| **TOTAL ADM:** | 1536.73 | 1578.63 | 1548.87 | 1586.72 | 1602.33 | 1494.67 | 1477.00 |
| | | | | | | | |
| **ADA:** | | | | | | | |
| K | 95.78 | 89.60 | 106.96 | 114.47 | 101.28 | 105.33 | 95.01 |
| 1-6 | 719.74 | 694.43 | 653.26 | 625.34 | 595.46 | 603.68 | 594.89 |
| 7-8 | 256.58 | 262.60 | 235.74 | 262.55 | 257.64 | 181.98 | 203.43 |
| 9-12 | 344.48 | 422.86 | 423.20 | 456.32 | 492.40 | 449.44 | 458.73 |
| *Oth ADA* | 4.88 | 4.74 | 21.10 | | 4.87 | 5.62 | |
| **TOTAL ADA:** | 1421.46 | 1474.23 | 1440.26 | 1458.68 | 1451.65 | 1346.05 | 1352.06 |
| | | | | | | | |
| **ATT %:** | | | | | | | |
| K | 88.4% | 89.2% | 90.1% | 91.1% | 89.8% | 89.7% | 91.6% |
| 1-6 | 93.7% | 93.5% | 94.5% | 94.2% | 93.8% | 93.3% | 93.6% |
| 7-8 | 91.7% | 90.8% | 89.9% | 90.8% | 90.5% | 89.7% | 90.8% |
| 9-12 | 91.7% | 95.8% | 93.2% | 89.8% | 87.1% | 86.2% | 89.3% |
| *Oth ADM* | 90.9% | 93.7% | 94.0% | | 97.4% | 98.6% | |
| **TTL ATT %:** | 92.5% | 93.4% | 93.0% | 91.9% | 90.6% | 90.1% | 91.5% |

# The Trail of Misgivings

| | 1980 1981 | 1981 1982 | 1982 1983 | 1983 1984 | 1984 1985 | 1985 1986 | 1986 1987 |
|---|---|---|---|---|---|---|---|
| **ENROLLMENT:** | | | | | | | |
| K | 128 | 132 | 154 | 139 | 130 | 155 | 139 |
| | | | | | | | |
| 1 | 119 | 119 | 141 | 146 | 118 | 126 | 148 |
| 2 | 118 | 112 | 109 | 133 | 138 | 109 | 122 |
| 3 | 104 | 125 | 112 | 101 | 130 | 131 | 118 |
| 4 | 106 | 103 | 110 | 94 | 88 | 112 | 127 |
| 5 | 119 | 116 | 101 | 104 | 97 | 93 | 106 |
| 6 | 88 | 112 | 98 | 101 | 108 | 96 | 96 |
| *1-6 Sbttl:* | *654* | *687* | *671* | *679* | *679* | *667* | *717* |
| 7 | 128 | 96 | 127 | 127 | 106 | 115 | 101 |
| 8 | 123 | 119 | 91 | 119 | 96 | 98 | 110 |
| *7-8 Sbttl:* | *251* | *215* | *218* | *246* | *202* | *213* | *211* |
| 9 | 213 | 148 | 144 | 106 | 147 | 138 | 138 |
| 10 | 136 | 154 | 141 | 133 | 105 | 130 | 124 |
| 11 | 103 | 142 | 129 | 117 | 115 | 93 | 113 |
| 12 | 136 | 109 | 133 | 124 | 114 | 112 | 92 |
| *9-12 Sbttl:* | *588* | *553* | *547* | *480* | *481* | *473* | *467* |
| *Oth Enr* | | | | | | | |
| **ENR GRAND TOTALS:** | **1621** | **1587** | **1590** | **1544** | **1492** | **1508** | **1534** |
| | | | | | | | |
| **ADM:** | | | | | | | |
| K | 113.83 | 121.44 | 142.14 | 125.23 | 115.68 | 134.67 | 123.42 |
| 1-6 | 602.73 | 631.62 | 632.62 | 622.85 | 620.78 | 622.52 | 665.52 |
| 7-8 | 217.33 | 187.13 | 197.31 | 215.73 | 183.49 | 193.16 | 184.34 |
| 9-12 | 494.97 | 466.27 | 467.36 | 398.94 | 402.27 | 396.21 | 395.06 |
| *Oth ADM* | | | | | | | |
| **TOTAL ADM:** | 1428.86 | 1406.46 | 1439.43 | 1362.75 | 1322.22 | 1346.56 | 1368.34 |
| | | | | | | | |
| **ADA:** | | | | | | | |
| K | 107.19 | 114.57 | 133.96 | 117.70 | 107.18 | 127.44 | 115.92 |
| 1-6 | 573.31 | 605.92 | 609.62 | 596.88 | 593.44 | 595.58 | 640.56 |
| 7-8 | 198.12 | 173.26 | 181.87 | 198.38 | 170.65 | 178.84 | 170.59 |
| 9-12 | 454.95 | 420.25 | 426.13 | 364.08 | 366.16 | 354.84 | 360.05 |
| *Oth ADA* | | | | | | | |
| **TOTAL ADA:** | 1333.57 | 1314.00 | 1351.58 | 1277.04 | 1237.43 | 1256.70 | 1287.12 |
| | | | | | | | |
| **ATT %:** | | | | | | | |
| K | 94.2% | 94.3% | 94.2% | 94.0% | 92.7% | 94.6% | 93.9% |
| 1-6 | 95.1% | 95.9% | 96.4% | 95.8% | 95.6% | 95.7% | 96.2% |
| 7-8 | 91.2% | 92.6% | 92.2% | 92.0% | 93.0% | 92.6% | 92.5% |
| 9-12 | 91.9% | 90.1% | 91.2% | 91.3% | 91.0% | 89.6% | 91.1% |
| *Oth ADM* | | | | | | | |
| **TTL ATT %:** | 93.3% | 93.4% | 93.9% | 93.7% | 93.6% | 93.3% | 94.1% |

# Appendices

| | 1987 1988 | 1988 1989 | 1989 1990 | 1990 1991 | 1991 1992 | 1992 1993 | 1993 1994 |
|---|---|---|---|---|---|---|---|
| **ENROLLMENT:** | | | | | | | |
| K | 145 | 110 | 140 | 134 | 137 | 138 | 154 |
| | | | | | | | |
| 1 | 129 | 137 | 112 | 138 | 146 | 143 | 153 |
| 2 | 152 | 141 | 139 | 113 | 134 | 135 | 143 |
| 3 | 117 | 132 | 136 | 134 | 115 | 136 | 141 |
| 4 | 111 | 122 | 135 | 138 | 144 | 114 | 133 |
| 5 | 124 | 108 | 118 | 135 | 140 | 148 | 121 |
| 6 | 105 | 130 | 110 | 125 | 135 | 137 | 145 |
| *1-6 Sbttl:* | *738* | *770* | *750* | *783* | *814* | *813* | *836* |
| 7 | 98 | 116 | 131 | 118 | 144 | 139 | 140 |
| 8 | 97 | 102 | 114 | 135 | 124 | 131 | 145 |
| *7-8 Sbttl:* | *195* | *218* | *245* | *253* | *268* | *270* | *285* |
| 9 | 146 | 134 | 135 | 157 | 183 | 163 | 181 |
| 10 | 133 | 141 | 128 | 126 | 139 | 172 | 146 |
| 11 | 113 | 113 | 123 | 119 | 108 | 117 | 160 |
| 12 | 110 | 115 | 108 | 110 | 104 | 96 | 116 |
| *9-12 Sbttl:* | *502* | *503* | *494* | *512* | *534* | *548* | *603* |
| *Oth Enr* | | | | | | | |
| **ENR GRAND TOTALS:** | **1580** | **1601** | **1629** | **1682** | **1753** | **1769** | **1878** |
| | | | | | | | |
| **ADM:** | | | | | | | |
| K | 125.88 | 97.69 | 129.81 | 118.33 | 125.26 | 125.84 | 142.99 |
| 1-6 | 680.25 | 705.60 | 695.00 | 717.27 | 752.85 | 748.60 | 761.67 |
| 7-8 | 178.14 | 190.74 | 223.32 | 230.66 | 240.99 | 237.09 | 255.40 |
| 9-12 | 423.48 | 430.13 | 419.82 | 439.20 | 461.12 | 480.63 | 522.71 |
| *Oth ADM* | | | | | | | |
| **TOTAL ADM:** | 1407.75 | 1424.16 | 1467.95 | 1505.46 | 1580.22 | 1592.16 | 1682.77 |
| | | | | | | | |
| **ADA:** | | | | | | | |
| K | 119.21 | 90.74 | 122.06 | 110.56 | 116.45 | 118.06 | 132.49 |
| 1-6 | 653.74 | 670.40 | 664.01 | 687.38 | 722.68 | 717.24 | 728.61 |
| 7-8 | 166.25 | 173.07 | 205.04 | 215.58 | 226.11 | 222.92 | 239.26 |
| 9-12 | 380.39 | 381.73 | 378.35 | 399.58 | 413.69 | 442.21 | 475.59 |
| *Oth ADA* | | | | | | | |
| **TOTAL ADA:** | 1319.59 | 1315.94 | 1369.46 | 1413.10 | 1478.93 | 1500.43 | 1575.95 |
| | | | | | | | |
| **ATT %:** | | | | | | | |
| K | 94.7% | 92.9% | 94.0% | 93.4% | 93.0% | 93.8% | 92.7% |
| 1-6 | 96.1% | 95.0% | 95.5% | 95.8% | 96.0% | 95.8% | 95.7% |
| 7-8 | 93.3% | 90.7% | 91.8% | 93.5% | 93.8% | 94.0% | 93.7% |
| 9-12 | 89.8% | 88.7% | 90.1% | 91.0% | 89.7% | 92.0% | 91.0% |
| *Oth ADM* | | | | | | | |
| **TTL ATT %:** | 93.7% | 92.4% | 93.3% | 93.9% | 93.6% | 94.2% | 93.7% |

# The Trail of Misgivings

| | 1994 1995 | 1995 1996 | 1996 1997 | 1997 1998 | 1998 1999 | 1999 2000 |
|---|---|---|---|---|---|---|
| **ENROLLMENT:** | | | | | | |
| K | 141 | 156 | 186 | 171 | 163 | 139 |
| 1 | 168 | 136 | 155 | 179 | 156 | 156 |
| 2 | 139 | 164 | 135 | 150 | 170 | 153 |
| 3 | 142 | 135 | 166 | 140 | 139 | 159 |
| 4 | 149 | 136 | 133 | 169 | 155 | 140 |
| 5 | 133 | 146 | 149 | 144 | 168 | 139 |
| 6 | 123 | 134 | 147 | 151 | 161 | 170 |
| *1-6 Sbttl:* | *854* | *851* | *885* | *933* | *949* | *917* |
| 7 | 164 | 116 | 142 | 155 | 173 | 149 |
| 8 | 148 | 146 | 126 | 148 | 171 | 163 |
| *7-8 Sbttl:* | *312* | *262* | *268* | *303* | *344* | *312* |
| 9 | 185 | 169 | 221 | 163 | 192 | 180 |
| 10 | 174 | 178 | 181 | 210 | 158 | 180 |
| 11 | 131 | 141 | 152 | 147 | 172 | 142 |
| 12 | 131 | 116 | 127 | 136 | 126 | 165 |
| *9-12 Sbttl:* | *621* | *604* | *681* | *656* | *648* | *667* |
| *Oth Enr* | | | | | | |
| **ENR GRAND TOTALS:** | **1928** | **1873** | **2,020** | **2063** | **2104** | **2035** |
| **ADM:** | | | | | | |
| K | 124.87 | 141.62 | 169.90 | 77.50 | 73.00 | 60.90 |
| 1-6 | 804.00 | 793.71 | 829.90 | 871.40 | 870.40 | 841.30 |
| 7-8 | 270.04 | 241.18 | 244.70 | 270.00 | 277.80 | 277.40 |
| 9-12 | 548.99 | 521.53 | 577.80 | 567.10 | 568.90 | 569.90 |
| *Oth ADM* | | | | | | |
| **TOTAL ADM:** | 1747.90 | 1698.04 | 1,822.30 | 1786.00 | 1790.10 | 1749.50 |
| **ADA:** | | | | | | |
| K | 117.21 | 129.68 | 154 | 73.00 | 67.66 | 56.70 |
| 1-6 | 766.61 | 750.59 | 785 | 827.00 | 823.20 | 804.80 |
| 7-8 | 249.64 | 224.22 | 227 | 249.00 | 257.60 | 254.10 |
| 9-12 | 491.94 | 458.61 | 515 | 506.50 | 507.70 | 513.30 |
| *Oth ADA* | | | | | | |
| **TOTAL ADA:** | 1625.40 | 1563.10 | 1,680 | 1655.50 | 1656.16 | 1628.90 |
| **ATT %:** | | | | | | |
| K | 93.9% | 91.6% | 90.6% | 94.2% | 92.7% | 93.1% |
| 1-6 | 95.3% | 94.6% | 94.6% | 94.9% | 94.6% | 95.7% |
| 7-8 | 92.4% | 93.0% | 92.8% | 92.2% | 92.7% | 91.6% |
| 9-12 | 89.6% | 87.9% | 89.0% | 89.3% | 89.2% | 90.1% |
| *Oth ADM* | | | | | | |
| **TTL ATT %:** | 93.0% | 92.1% | 92.2% | 92.7% | 92.5% | 93.1% |

| | 2000 2001 | 2001 2002 | 2002 2003 | 2003 2004 | 2004 2005 | 2005 2006 |
|---|---|---|---|---|---|---|
| **ENROLLMENT:** | | | | | | |
| K | 126 | 126 | 137 | 129 | 114 | |
| 1 | 145 | 120 | 128 | 143 | 111 | |
| 2 | 152 | 131 | 117 | 123 | 127 | |
| 3 | 156 | 148 | 137 | 130 | 117 | |
| 4 | 153 | 143 | 152 | 137 | 123 | |
| 5 | 139 | 142 | 136 | 152 | 128 | |
| 6 | 148 | 139 | 150 | 147 | 145 | |
| *1-6 Sbttl:* | *893* | *823* | *820* | *832* | *751* | |
| 7 | 151 | 134 | 135 | 154 | 144 | |
| 8 | 148 | 159 | 125 | 132 | 167 | |
| *7-8 Sbttl:* | *299* | *293* | *260* | *286* | *311* | |
| 9 | 207 | 199 | 269 | 228 | 252 | |
| 10 | 171 | 194 | 184 | 166 | 157 | |
| 11 | 154 | 152 | 130 | 121 | 128 | |
| 12 | 129 | 147 | 113 | 131 | 108 | |
| *9-12 Sbttl:* | *661* | *692* | *696* | *646* | *645* | |
| Oth Enr | | | | | | |
| **ENR GRAND TOTALS:** | **1979** | **1934** | **1913** | **1893** | **1821** | |
| **ADM:** | | | | | | |
| K | 112.10 | 112.14 | 121.11 | 125.33 | 106.60 | |
| 1-6 | 820.80 | 759.73 | 738.81 | 748.24 | 708.00 | |
| 7-8 | 257.90 | 258.33 | 232.70 | 259.12 | 274.05 | |
| 9-12 | 567.50 | 596.73 | 589.62 | 567.21 | 559.04 | |
| Oth ADM | | | | | | |
| **TOTAL ADM:** | 1758.30 | 1726.93 | 1682.24 | 1699.90 | 1647.69 | |
| **ADA:** | | | | | | |
| K | 102.90 | 104.24 | 114.99 | 124.50 | 97.87 | |
| 1-6 | 779.70 | 721.95 | 704.01 | 712.34 | 673.94 | |
| 7-8 | 240.70 | 237.65 | 218.65 | 243.60 | 256.44 | |
| 9-12 | 506.70 | 533.51 | 517.33 | 498.06 | 489.15 | |
| Oth ADA | | | | | | |
| **TOTAL ADA:** | 1630.00 | 1597.35 | 1554.98 | 1578.50 | 1517.40 | |
| **ATT %:** | | | | | | |
| K | 91.8% | 93.0% | 94.9% | 99.3% | 91.8% | |
| 1-6 | 95.0% | 95.0% | 95.3% | 95.2% | 95.2% | |
| 7-8 | 93.3% | 92.0% | 94.0% | 94.0% | 93.6% | |
| 9-12 | 89.3% | 89.4% | 87.7% | 87.8% | 87.5% | |
| Oth ADM | | | | | | |
| **TTL ATT %:** | 92.7% | 92.5% | 92.4% | 92.9% | 92.1% | |

## Appendix C: Teacher Salary Schedule for 2005-2006

| Base: | $30,600 | | | | | | | |
|---|---|---|---|---|---|---|---|---|
| *Exp Incr:* | | | | | | | | |
| *Stps 1-3* | $850 | | BA+15 | BA+30 | BA+45 | MA | MA+15 | MA+30 |
| *Stps 4-6* | $950 | *Educ Incr:* | $1,300 | $1,300 | $800 | $800 | $1,450 | $1,450 |
| *Stps 7-13* | $1,150 | | | | | | | |
| Years Exp | Step | BA | BA+15 | BA+30 | BA+45 | MA | MA+15 | MA+30 |
| 0 | 1 | 30,600 | 31,900 | 33,200 | 34,000 | 34,800 | 36,250 | 37,700 |
| 1 | 2 | 31,450 | 32,750 | 34,050 | 34,850 | 35,650 | 37,100 | 38,550 |
| 2 | 3 | 32,300 | 33,600 | 34,900 | 35,700 | 36,500 | 37,950 | 39,400 |
| 3 | 4 | 33,250 | 34,550 | 35,850 | 36,650 | 37,450 | 38,900 | 40,350 |
| 4 | 5 | 34,200 | 35,500 | 36,800 | 37,600 | 38,400 | 39,850 | 41,300 |
| 5 | 6 | 35,150 | 36,450 | 37,750 | 38,550 | 39,350 | 40,800 | 42,250 |
| 6 | 7 | 35,300 | 37,600 | 38,900 | 39,700 | 40,500 | 41,950 | 43,400 |
| 7 | 8 | 37,450 | 38,750 | 40,500 | 40,850 | 41,650 | 43,100 | 44,550 |
| 8 | 9 | 38,600 | 39,900 | 41,200 | 42,000 | 42,800 | 44,250 | 45,700 |
| 9 | 10 | | 41,050 | 42,350 | 43,150 | 43,950 | 45,400 | 46,850 |
| 10 | 11 | | 42,200 | 43,500 | 44,300 | 45,100 | 46,550 | 48,000 |
| 11 | 12 | | | | | 46,250 | 47,700 | 49,150 |
| 12 | 13 | | | | | | 48,850 | 50,300 |
| 13 | 14 | | | | | | 50,000 | 51,450 |

The School District also agrees to pay 7.75% of each teacher's retirement salary toward member assessments for North Dakota Teachers Fund for Retirement. (For the 2005-2006 and 2006-2007 school years only.) This amounts to 100% of each teacher's share.

## Appendix D: AGRICULTURE PROJECTS REPORT
## TURTLE MOUNTAIN COMMUNITY SCHOOLS
## 1942[415]

| Produce measured in pounds | Turtle Mountain Community School | Great Walker School | Roussin School | Dunseith School | Houle School | TOTALS |
|---|---|---|---|---|---|---|
| Beans | 928 | 276 | | 300 | 200 | 1704 |
| Beets | 1037 | 1800 | 900 | 160 | 400 | 4297 |
| Cabbage | | 400 | 1950 | 64 | 1200 | 3614 |
| Carrots | 718 | 1550 | 2400 | 2416 | 800 | 7882 |
| Corn | 780 | 1010 | 980 | | 200 | 2970 |
| Cucumber | 300 | 200 | 120 | 426 | 500 | 1546 |
| Lettuce | 200 | 300 | | | | 500 |
| Onions | 288 | 796 | 360 | 520 | 100 | 2064 |
| Potatoes | 2700 | 320 | 162 | 106 | 600 | 3888 |
| Peas | 948 | 1800 | 450 | 750 | 200 | 4148 |
| Pumpkin | | 700 | 600 | 110 | 500 | 1910 |
| Radishes | | 200 | 120 | | 75 | 395 |
| Raspberries | | | 300 | | | 300 |
| Rhubarb | 220 | | 360 | | | 580 |
| Rutabagas | 1750 | 2100 | 2400 | 1654 | | 7904 |
| Spinach-Swiss Chard | | 380 | 300 | 88 | 100 | 868 |
| Squash | | 850 | 270 | 75 | | 1175 |
| Tomatoes | | 2500 | 600 | 20 | 200 | 3320 |
| Turnips | 175 | 2875 | | | 300 | 3350 |
| Kohlrabi | | 600 | | | | 600 |
| Kale | | 200 | | | | 200 |
| Strawberries | | 10 | | | | 10 |
| Total in Pounds | | | | | | 282,617 |
| Total in Tons | | | | | | 141.3 |

---

[415] Courtesy of the 1943 Chipaway Yearbook.

## Appendix E: The School Board Through the Years

| | | Couture | Ingebretson |
|---|---|---|---|
| 1 9 1 7 | Director at Large<br>Clerk<br>Treasurer<br>Directors | S. J. Ladoucer<br>Edward C. Roy<br>Ernest A. Choinere<br>Joseph L. Ladoucer, John R. Wilkie | |
| 1 9 1 8 | Director at Large<br>Clerk<br>Treasurer<br>Directors | John R. Wilkie<br>Mrs. John R. Wilkie<br>Ernest Choiniere<br>Joseph L. Ladoucer, S. J. Ladoucer | George A. Courteau<br>Mrs. George Courteau<br>~<br>David Dauphinais, John Reueau |
| 1 9 1 9 | Director at Large<br>Clerk<br>Treasurer<br>Directors | John R. Wilkie<br>Mrs. John R. Wilkie<br>S. J. Ladoucer<br>Joseph Ladoucer, T. T. Disrud | George A. Courteau<br>Mrs. George Courteau<br>County Treasurer, Rolla<br>David Dauphinais, Alex Nicholas |
| 1 9 2 0 | Director at Large<br>Clerk<br>Treasurer<br>Directors | J. J. Jollie<br>J. J. Green<br>S. J. Ladoucer<br>T. T. Disrud, Joseph Ladoucer | George A. Courteau<br>Mrs. George Courteau<br>County Treasurer, Rolla<br>Joe Levie, Alex Nicholas |
| 1 9 2 1 | Director at Large<br>Clerk<br>Treasurer<br>Directors | Everett Euneau<br>James J. Green<br>M. J. McQuigg<br>Joseph Ladoucer, J. J. Jollie | George A. Courteau<br>Mrs. George Courteau<br>County Treasurer, Rolla<br>Alex Nicholas, Louis Gourneau |
| 1 9 2 2 | Director at Large<br>Clerk<br>Treasurer<br>Directors | Everett Euneau<br>James J. Green<br>M. J. McQuigg<br>John B. Dionne, J. J. Jollie | George A. Courteau<br>Mrs. George Courteau<br>J. O. Stadheim<br>Louis Gourneau, Alex Nicholas |
| 1 9 2 3 | Director at Large<br>Clerk<br>Treasurer<br>Directors | John B. Dionne<br>James J. Green<br>Virgile Logue<br>J. J. Jollie, Claud Azure | George A. Courteau<br>Mrs. George Courteau<br>J. O. Stadheim<br>Frank Delorme, Louis Gourneau |
| 1 9 2 4 | Director at Large<br>Clerk<br>Treasurer<br>Directors | H. T. Senical<br>Eugene L. Warren<br>Virgile Logue<br>J. J. Jollie, Claud Azure | Walter Tooke<br>Mrs. George Courteau<br>Martin Evenstad<br>Joe F. Wilkie, Frank Davis |
| 1 9 2 5 | President<br>Clerk<br>Treasurer<br>Directors | Virgile Logue<br>Leopold Marchand<br>Esdras Roberge<br>H. T. Senical, Leonard Hamley | Joe F. Wilkie<br>Mrs. George Courteau<br>Martin Evenstad<br>Frank Davis, Walter Tooke |
| 1 9 2 6 | President<br>Clerk<br>Treasurer<br>Directors | George Courteau<br>Edward C. Roy<br>Esdras Roberge<br>Leonard Hamley, Joe Primeau | George Courteau<br>Joe Monette<br>Martin Evenstad<br>Alex Gourneau, Frank Davis |
| 1 9 2 7 | President<br>Clerk<br>Treasurer<br>Directors | J. J. Jollie<br>Edward C. Roy<br>Esdras Roberge<br>Joe Primeau, P. B. Brunelle | Alex Nicholas<br>Joe Monette<br>Oliver Charbonneau<br>Alex Gourneau, John B. Wilkie |
| 1 9 2 8 | | | |

| | | | |
|---|---|---|---|
| 1 | President | J. J. Jollie | Alex Nicholas |
| 9 | Clerk | E. C. Roy | Joe Monette |
| 2 | Treasurer | Esdras Roberge | O. J. Charbonneau |
| 9 | Directors | Claud Azure, P. B. Brunelle | Leander Gourneau, Alex Gourneau |
| 1 | President | J. J. Jollie | Alex Nicholas |
| 9 | Clerk | E. C. Roy | Joe Monette |
| 3 | Treasurer | Esdras Roberge | O. J. Charbonneau |
| 0 | Directors | Claud Azure, P. B. Brunelle | Leander Gourneau, Alex Gourneau |
| 1 | President | Claud Azure | John B. Wilkie |
| 9 | Clerk | E. C. Roy | Robert Davis |
| 3 | Treasurer | Esdras Roberge | Allister McKay |
| 1 | Directors | P. V. Brunelle, Peter Turcotte | Alex Nicholas, Leander Gourneau |
| 1 | President | Claud Azure | John B. Wilkie |
| 9 | Clerk | Edward C. Roy | Robert Davis |
| 3 | Treasurer | Esdras Roberge | Allister McKay |
| 2 | Directors | P. V. Brunelle, Peter Turcotte | Alex Nicholas, Leander Gourneau |
| 1 | President | Claud Azure | Alex Nicholas |
| 9 | Clerk | Edward C. Roy | Robert Davis |
| 3 | Treasurer | J. E. Roberge | Allister McKay |
| 3 | Directors | Peter Turcotte, Peter B. Brunelle | John B. Wilkie, Joe Poitra |
| 1 | President | Claud Azure | Alex Nicholas |
| 9 | Clerk | Edward C. Roy | Robert Davis |
| 3 | Treasurer | Esdras Roberge | Allister McKay |
| 4 | Directors | Peter Brunelle, J. J. Jollie | Joe Poitra, John B. Wilkie |
| 1 | President | J. J. Jollie | Alex Nicholas |
| 9 | Clerk | Edward C. Roy | Robert Davis |
| 3 | Treasurer | Fred T. LeBrun | E. M. Anderson |
| 5 | Directors | Peter Brunelle, Robert O. Jollie | John B. Wilkie, Joe Poitra |
| 1 | President | J. J. Jollie | John B. Wilkie |
| 9 | Clerk | Edward C. Roy | Robert Davis |
| 3 | Treasurer | Fred T. LeBrun | E. M. Anderson |
| 6 | Directors | Robert O. Jollie, Peter B. Brunelle | Alex Nicholas, Toby Morin |
| 1 | President | J. J. Jollie | John B. Wilkie |
| 9 | Clerk | Edward C. Roy | Robert Davis |
| 3 | Treasurer | Fred T. LeBrun | E. M. Anderson |
| 7 | Directors | Peter B. Brunelle, Robert Jollie | Toby Morin, Alex Nicholas |
| 1 | President | Peter B. Brunelle | John B. Wilkie |
| 9 | Clerk | Edward C. Roy | Mrs. Alex Nicholas |
| 3 | Treasurer | Fred T. LeBrun | E. M. Anderson |
| 8 | Directors | Stanislaus Tetrault, Robert Jollie | Alex Nicholas, Tobie Morin |
| 1 | President | Robert O. Jollie | John B. Wilkie |
| 9 | Clerk | Edward C. Roy | Mrs. Alex Nicholas |
| 3 | Treasurer | Fred T. LeBrun | W. A. Lawston |
| 9 | Directors | Stanislaus Tetrault, Peter Turcotte | Alex Nicholas, Tobie Morin |
| 1 | President | Robert O. Jollie | John B. Wilkie |
| 9 | Clerk | Edward C. Roy | Mrs. Alex Nicholas |
| 4 | Treasurer | Fred T. LeBrun | W. A. Lawston |
| 0 | Directors | Stanislaus Tetrault, Peter Turcotte | Toby Morin, Alex Nicholas |
| 1 | President | Robert O. Jollie | John B. Wilkie |
| 9 | Clerk | Edward C. Roy | Mrs. Alex Nicholas |
| 4 | Treasurer | Fred T. LeBrun | W. A. Lawston |
| 1 | Directors | Stanislaus Tetrault, Peter Turcotte | Toby Morin, Alex Nicholas |

# The Trail of Misgivings

| | | | |
|---|---|---|---|
| 1 9 4 2 | President<br>Clerk<br>Treasurer<br>Directors | Robert O. Jollie<br>Edward C. Roy<br>Fred T. LeBrun<br>Stanislaus Tetrault, Peter Turcotte | John B. Wilkie<br>Mrs. Alex Nicholas<br>W. A. Lawston<br>Toby Morin, Alex Nicholas |
| 1 9 4 3 | President<br>Clerk<br>Treasurer<br>Directors | Peter Turcotte<br>Eli J. Marion<br>Fred T. LeBrun<br>John Lattergrass, Jr., Napoleon<br>Masse | Alex Nicholas<br>Rosalie Nicholas<br>Mrs. Beatrice M. Azure<br>Toby Morin, John B. Wilkie |
| 1 9 4 4 | President<br>Clerk<br>Treasurer<br>Directors | Peter Turcotte<br>Eli J. Marion<br>Fred T. LeBrun<br>John Lattergrass, Jr., Napoleon<br>Masse | Alex Nicholas<br>Rosalie Nicholas<br>Mrs. Beatrice M. Azure<br>Toby Morin, John B. Wilkie |
| 1 9 4 5 | President<br>Clerk<br>Treasurer<br>Directors | John Lattergrass, Jr.<br>Eli J. Marion<br>Fred T. LeBrun<br>Napoleon Masse, Henry Martin | Israel Azure<br>Rosalie Nicholas<br>Beatrice M. Azure<br>Toby Morin, John B. Wilkie |
| 1 9 4 6 | President<br>Clerk<br>Treasurer<br>Directors | John B. Lattergrass<br>Eli J. Marion<br>Fred T. LeBrun<br>Napoleon Masse, Henry Martin | Israel Azure<br>Dora Morin<br>Beatrice M. Azure<br>Toby Morin, John B. Wilkie |
| 1 9 4 7 | President<br>Clerk<br>Treasurer<br>Directors | Clifford LaFromboise<br>Eli J. Marion<br>Max Marion<br>Henry Martin, John Lattergrass,<br>Jr. | Israel Azure<br>Dora Morin<br>Beatrice M. Azure<br>Toby Morin, John B. Wilkie |
| 1 9 4 8 | President<br>Clerk<br>Treasurer<br>Directors | Clifford LaFromboise<br>Eli J. Marion<br>Max Marion<br>Henry Martin, John Lattergrass,<br>Jr. | Israel Azure<br>Dora Morin<br>Beatrice M. Azure<br>Toby Morin, John B. Wilkie |
| 1 9 4 9 | President<br>Clerk<br>Treasurer<br>Directors | Art Azure<br>Eli J. Marion<br>Fred T. LeBrun<br>Henry Martin, Clifford<br>LaFromboise | Israel Azure<br>Sara Morin<br>Beatrice M. Azure<br>Toby Morin, John B. Wilkie |
| 1 9 5 0 | President<br>Clerk<br>Treasurer<br>Directors | Clifford LaFromboise<br>Eli J. Marion<br>Fred T. LeBrun<br>Art Azure, Henry Martin | Israel Azure<br>Sara Morin<br>Beatrice M. Azure<br>Toby Morin, John B. Wilkie |
| 1 9 5 1 | President<br>Clerk<br>Treasurer<br>Directors | Clifford LaFromboise<br>Eli J. Marion<br>Fred T. LeBrun<br>Art Azure, Henry Martin | Israel Azure<br>Sara Morin<br>Beatrice M. Azure<br>Toby Morin, John B. Wilkie |
| 1 9 5 2 | President<br>Clerk<br>Treasurer<br>Directors | Henry Croteau<br>Eli J. Marion<br>Fred T. LeBrun<br>Henry Martin, Art Azure | Israel Azure<br>Sara Morin<br>Beatrice M. Azure<br>Toby Morin, John B. Wilkie |
| 1 9 5 3 | President<br>Clerk<br>Treasurer<br>Directors | Henry Croteau<br>Eli J. Marion<br>Fred T. LeBrun<br>Henry Martin, Art Azure | Gregory R. Davis<br>Collin Davis<br>Francis Poitra<br>Andrew Grant, Pascal Roussin |

| | | | |
|---|---|---|---|
| 1 | President | Henry Croteau | Gregory R. Davis |
| 9 | Clerk | Eli J. Marion | Collin Davis |
| 5 | Treasurer | Fred T. LeBrun | Francis Poitra |
| 4 | Directors | Henry Martin, Art Azure | Andrew Grant, Pascal Roussin |
| 1 | President | Art Azure | Gregory R. Davis |
| 9 | Clerk | Eli J. Marion | Collin Davis |
| 5 | Treasurer | Fred T. LeBrun | Francis Poitra |
| 5 | Directors | Henry Croteau, Henry Martin | Edward Davis, Joe Monette |
| 1 | President | Art Azure | Gregory R. Davis |
| 9 | Clerk | Eli J. Marion | Joe Monette |
| 5 | Treasurer | Fred T. LeBrun | Francis Poitra |
| 6 | Directors | Henry Croteau, Henry Azure | Edward Davis, Collin Davis |
| 1 | President | Art Azure | Gregory R. Davis |
| 9 | Clerk | Eli J. Marion | Joe Monette |
| 5 | Treasurer | Fred T. LeBrun | Francis Poitra |
| 7 | Directors | Henry Croteau, Henry Martin | Edward Davis, Collin Davis |
| 1 | President | Kade Albert | Gregory R. Davis |
| 9 | Clerk | Eli J. Marion | Joe Monette |
| 5 | Treasurer | Fred T. LeBrun | Francis Poitra |
| 8 | Directors | Henry Croteau, Henry Martin | Edward Davis, Frank C. Davis |
| 1 | President | Kade Albert | Gregory R. Davis |
| 9 | Clerk | Eli J. Marion | Joe Monette |
| 5 | Treasurer | Fred T. LeBrun | Francis Davis |
| 9 | Directors | Roy Ferris, Henry Martin | Edward Davis, Frank C. Davis |
| 1 | President | Kade Albert | Gregory R. Davis |
| 9 | Clerk | Philomene Jollie | Joe Monette |
| 6 | Treasurer | Fred T. LeBrun | Francis S. Poitra |
| 0 | Directors | Roy Ferris, Henry Martin | Edward Davis, Frank C. Davis |
| 1 | President | Kade Albert | Gregory R. Davis |
| 9 | Clerk | Philomene Jollie | Joe Monette |
| 6 | Treasurer | Fred T. LeBrun | Francis S. Poitra |
| 1 | Directors | Roy Ferris, Richard Drapeaux | Edward Davis, Frank C. Davis |
| 1 | President | Kade Albert | Gregory R. Davis |
| 9 | Clerk | Albert Wilkie | Joe Monette |
| 6 | Treasurer | Fred T. LeBrun | Francis S. Poitra |
| 2 | Directors | Roy Ferris, Henry Martin | Edward Davis, Frank C. Davis |
| 1 | President | Fayes Albert | Gregory R. Davis |
| 9 | Clerk | John Frederick | Joe Monette |
| 6 | Treasurer | Albert Wilkie | Francis S. Poitra |
| 3 | Directors | Roy Ferris, Kade Albert | Edward Davis, Frank C. Davis |
| 1 | President | Fayes Albert | Gregory R. Davis |
| 9 | Clerk | Betty Laverdure | Joe Monette |
| 6 | Treasurer | Albert Wilkie | Francis S. Poitra |
| 4 | Directors | Kade Albert, Roy Ferris | Frank C. Davis, Edward Davis |
| 1 | President | Fayes Albert | Gregory R. Davis |
| 9 | Clerk | Betty Laverdure | Joe Monette |
| 6 | Treasurer | Albert Wilkie | Francis Poitra |
| 5 | Directors | Roy Ferris, Charles McCloud, Jr. | Frank C. Davis, Edward Davis |
| 1 | President | Fayes Albert | Gregory R. Davis |
| 9 | Clerk | Betty Laverdure | Joe Monette |
| 6 | Treasurer | Albert Wilkie | Francis Poitra |
| 6 | Directors | Reginald Brien, Charles McCloud, Jr. | Frank Davis, Edward Davis |

# The Trail of Misgivings

| Year | Office | | |
|---|---|---|---|
| 1967 | President | Fayes Albert | Gregory R. Davis |
| | Clerk | Betty Laverdure | Joe Monette |
| | Treasurer | Albert Wilkie | Joseph E. Marcellais |
| | Directors | Reginald Brien, Charles McCloud, Jr. | Edward Davis, Alex Lafountain (F. Davis) |
| 1968 | President | Fayes Albert | Gregory R. Davis |
| | Clerk | Dorothy Laverdure | Joe Monette |
| | Treasurer | Betty Laverdure | Joseph E. Marcellais |
| | Directors | Reginald Brien, Charles McCloud, Jr. | Edward Davis, Alex C. LaFountain |
| 1969 | President | Fayes Albert | Gregory R. Davis |
| | Clerk | Dorothy Laverdure | Joe Monette |
| | Treasurer | Betty Laverdure | Joseph E. Marcellais |
| | Directors | Reginald Brien, Charles McCloud, Jr. | Edward Davis, Alex C. LaFountain |
| 1970 | President | Fayes Albert | Gregory Davis |
| | Clerk | Dorothy Laverdure | Jeanette Parisien |
| | Treasurer | Betty Laverdure | Joseph Marcellais |
| | Directors | Reginald Brien, Charles McCloud, Jr. | Verna C. LaFountain, Alex C. LaFountain |
| 1971 | President | Fayes Albert | Gregory Davis |
| | Clerk | Dorothy Laverdure | Jeanette Parisien |
| | Treasurer | Sandra K. Thomas | Alex C. LaFountain |
| | Directors | Theresa M. Davis, Reginald Brien | Joseph Marcellais, Verna LaFountain |
| 1972 | President | Fayes Albert | Joseph Marcellais |
| | Clerk | Dorothy Laverdure | Jeanette Parisien |
| | Treasurer | Sandra K. Thomas | Gregory Davis |
| | Directors | Theresa M. Davis, Reginald Brien | Edward LaFountain, Verna LaFountain |
| 1973 | President | Fayes Albert | Joseph Marcellais |
| | Clerk | Dorothy Laverdure | Jeanette Parisien |
| | Treasurer | Sandra K. Thomas | Gregory Davis |
| | Directors | Theresa Davis, Reginald Brien | Edward LaFountain, Verna LaFountain |
| 1974 | President | Fayes Albert | Verna LaFountain |
| | Clerk | Dorothy Laverdure | Jeanette Parisien |
| | Treasurer | Sandra K. Thomas | Gregory Davis |
| | Directors | Theresa Davis, Reginald Brien | Joseph E. Marcellais, Edward LaFountain |
| 1975 | President | Fayes Albert | Joseph Marcellais |
| | Clerk | Howard Frederick | Jeanette Parisien |
| | Directors | Reginald Brien, Theresa Davis | Edward LaFountain, Verna LaFountain |
| 1976 | President | Reginald J. Brien | Joseph Marcellais |
| | Clerk | Howard Frederick | Jeanette Parisien |
| | Directors | Theresa M. Davis, Jerilyn Decoteau, Edward Herman, Sr., Roy J. LaFontaine | Ed LaFountain, Verna LaFountain |
| 1977 | President | Reginald Brien | Wayne Keplin |
| | Clerk | Howard Frederick | Rochelle Gourneau |
| | Directors | Theresa Davis, Jerilyn Decoteau, Edward Herman, Sr., Roy J. LaFoutaine | Edward LaFountain, Verna LaFountain |

| | | | |
|---|---|---|---|
| 1 9 7 8 | President<br>Clerk<br>Directors | Reginald J. Brien<br>Howard Frederick<br>Ed Herman, Richard Frederick,<br>Raphael Trottier, Susan M. Wilkie | Ed LaFountain<br>Rochelle Gourneau<br>Wayne Keplin, Verna LaFountain |
| 1 9 7 9 | President<br>Clerk<br>Directors | Raphael Trottier<br>Howard Frederick<br>Ed Herman, Richard Frederick,<br>Susan Wilkie, Reginald Brien | Judy Delonais<br>Rochelle Gourneau<br>Ken Davis, Ed LaFountain |
| 1 9 8 0 | President<br>Clerk<br>Directors | Raphael Trottier<br>Howard Frederick<br>Richard Frederick, Susie Wilkie,<br>Ed Herman, Reginald Brien | Judy Delonais<br>Rochelle Gourneau<br>Ken Davis (resigned), Maureen<br>Frederick (assigned), Gene Bruce |
| 1 9 8 1 | President<br>Clerk<br>Directors | Richard Frederick<br>Howard Frederick<br>Raphael Trottier, Lynn Davis, Ed<br>Herman, Susie Wilkie | Judy Delonais<br>Rochelle Gourneau<br>Stanley Gourneau, Gene Bruce |
| 1 9 8 2 | President<br>Clerk<br>Directors | Raphael Trottier<br>Howard Frederick<br>Ed Herman, Lynn Davis, Susie<br>Wilkie, Richard Trottier | Judy Delonais<br>Rochelle Gourneau<br>Stanley Gourneau, Gene Bruce |
| 1 9 8 3 | President<br>Clerk<br>Directors | Raphael Trottier<br>Howard Frederick<br>Reginald Brien, Ed Herman, Lynn<br>Davis, Susie Wilkie | Judy Delonais<br>Rochelle Gourneau<br>Stanley Gourneau, Yvonne St.<br>Claire |

## Belcourt School District #7

| | | | | |
|---|---|---|---|---|
| 1 9 8 4 | President<br>Clerk<br>Directors | Raphael Trottier<br>Howard Frederick<br>Reginald Brien, Stanley<br>Gourneau, Lynn Davis, Mike<br>Nelson, Yvonne St. Claire, Ed<br>Herman | Ed Herman<br>Howard Frederick<br>Lynn Davis, Stanley Gourneau,<br>Mike Nelson, Reginald Brien,<br>Raphael Trottier, Louise<br>Dauphinais | 1 9 8 5 |
| 1 9 8 6 | President<br>Clerk<br>Directors | Edward Herman<br>Howard Frederick<br>Reginald Brien, Mike Nelson,<br>Louise Dauphinais, Patty<br>Allery, Lynn Davis, Ray<br>Trottier | Ed Herman<br>~<br>Reginald Brien, Phyllis Jollie,<br>Patty Allery, Ray Trottier, Lynn<br>Davis, Louise Dauphinais | 1 9 8 7 |
| 1 9 8 8 | President<br>Directors | Lynn Davis<br>Ray Trottier, Reginald Brien,<br>Allan Malaterre, Lynn Davis,<br>Phyllis Jollie, Tony Davis | Lynn Davis<br>Richard Frederick, Tony Davis,<br>Allan Malaterre, Patty Allery,<br>Phyllis Jollie, Reginald Brien | 1 9 8 9 |
| 1 9 9 0 | President<br>Business Manager<br>Directors | Richard Frederick<br>Howard Frederick<br>Patty Allery, Lynn Davis,<br>Reginald Brien, Phyllis Jollie,<br>John Anthony Davis, Allan<br>Malaterre | Richard Frederick<br>Duane Poitra<br>Lynn Davis, Patty Allery,<br>Phyllis Jollie, Charles LaFloe,<br>Allan Malaterre, James Parisien | 1 9 9 1 |
| 1 9 9 2 | President<br>Business Manager<br>Directors | Allan Malaterre<br>Howard Frederick<br>Dallas Morin, Lynn Davis,<br>Phyllis Jollie, Charles LaFloe,<br>Dalbert Brien, James Parisien | Allan Malaterre<br>Howard Frederick<br>Lynn Davis, Dallas Morin,<br>Phyllis Jollie, Charles LaFloe,<br>Dalbert Brien, James Parisien | 1 9 9 3 |

# The Trail of Misgivings

|  |  | | |  |
|---|---|---|---|---|
| 1994 | President<br>Business Manager<br>Directors | Allan Malaterre<br>Howard Frederick<br>Lynn Davis, Dallas Morin,<br>Phyllis Jollie, Jeff Desjarlais,<br>Dalbert Brien, James Parisien | Lynn Davis<br>Howard Frederick<br>Allan Malaterre, Jeff Desjarlais,<br>Phyllis Jollie, Dallas Morin,<br>James Parisien, Richard<br>McCloud | 1995 |
| 1996 | President<br>Business Manager<br>Directors | Allan Malaterre<br>Howard Frederick<br>Jeff Desjarlais, Dallas Morin,<br>James Parisien, Richard<br>McCloud, Patty Allery, Richard<br>Schroeder | Jeff Desjarlais<br>Duane Poitra<br>Allan Malaterre, Dallas Morin,<br>James Parisien, Richard<br>McCloud, Patty Allery, Richard<br>Schroeder | 1997 |
| 1998 | President<br>Business Manager<br>Directors | Allan Malaterre<br>Duane Poitra<br>James Parisien, Patty Allery,<br>Richard Schroeder, Richard<br>McCloud, Jeff Desjarlais,<br>Richard Marcellais | Richard McCloud<br>Duane Poitra<br>James Parisien, Richard<br>Schroeder, Jeff Desjarlais,<br>Richard Marcellais, Allan<br>Malaterre, Kurt Peltier | 1999 |
| 2000 | President<br>Business Manager<br>Directors | Richard McCloud<br>Duane Poitra<br>James Parisien, Richard<br>Schroeder, Richard Trottier,<br>Richard Marcellais, Allan<br>Malaterre, Kurt Peltier | Richard McCloud<br>Duane Poitra<br>Doug Delorme, Richard<br>Schroeder, Richard Trottier,<br>Richard Marcellais, Allan<br>Malaterre, Kurt Peltier | 2001 |
| 2002 | President<br>Business Manager<br>Directors | Allan Malaterre<br>Duane Poitra<br>Doug Delorme, Richard<br>Schroeder, Richard Trottier<br>(resigned), Wanda Laducer<br>(assigned), Richard Marcellais,<br>Allan Malaterre, Kurt Peltier | Richard McCloud<br>Duane Poitra<br>Wanda Laducer, Richard<br>Schroeder, Doug Delorme<br>(ressigned), Will Grant<br>(assigned), Richard Marcellais,<br>Allan Malaterre, Kurt Peltier | 2003 |
| 2004 | President<br>Business Manager<br>Directors | Allan Malaterre<br>Duane Poitra<br>Richard Schroeder, Wanda<br>Laducer, Richard Marcellais,<br>Allan Malaterre, Kurt Peltier | Richard McCloud<br>Duane Poitra<br>Wanda Laducer, Richard<br>Schroeder, Will Grant, Richard<br>Marcellais, Allan Malaterre,<br>Kurt Peltier | 2005 |
| 2006 | President<br>Business Manager<br>Directors | Allan Malaterre<br>Duane Poitra<br>Richard Schroeder, Wanda<br>Laducer, Richard Marcellais,<br>Allan Malaterre, Kurt Peltier | | 2007 |

# Appendices F: Time Line
## 1654 – 2006

1654 Half-breeds in Sault St. Marie descendants of Huron and Algonquin women and men

1700 (late) Cherokee Treaty

1775 Continental Congress (deal with Indian affairs)

1780 Plain Objiwa in Dakota Territory (separated from mother tribe)

1796 US Gov't Trading Houses set up

1802 Act of Congress annual appropriation to civilized tribes

1803 George Anthony Belcourt born Louisiana Purchase

1806 Office of Indian Trade est. (superintendent)

1809 Depletion of furred game

1818 US/Canadian border est. (49th parallel)

1819 Second Act of Congress permanent appropriation sum to civilize aborigines

1820 Organized buffalo hunt

1822 US Gov't Trading Houses and Office discontinued

1824 BIA created within War Department (civilization funds used to educate Indian students)

1825 Treaty of Prairie du Chien (Chippewa/Sioux)

1827 Father Belcourt ordained

1830 Father Belcourt in area
Indian Removal Act (Trail of Tears)

1832 Cherokee won case (recognized as a State)
Commissioner of Indian Affairs (War Dept.)

1834 Organic Act of the Indian Service (Reorganized Field Forces)

1838 "For every dead Indian" statement

1840 Summer and fall buffalo hunts

1848 Father Belcourt's first school for TM people at Pembina, ND

1849 BIA placed under Dept. of Interior

1850 Father Belcourt moved to St. Joseph
Father Belcourt dug in at Butte St. Paul

1854 Father Belcourt went to Washington, DC ("brief") on behalf of Indian people

1858 Sweet Corn Treaty (between Chippewa/Lakota)

1860 White settlers begin to arrive

1863 Old Crossing Treaty (Pembina , Red Lake Chippewa and US Gov't)

1864 Old Crossing Treaty signed

1867 Fort Totten Military Post est.

1870 Métis settling in Manitoba (parent's standards for education choices honored)
Indian Wars cost Gov't $1,000,000 (per dead)
Congress authorize federal industrial schools for Indians

1871 Treaties ended with tribes – Agreements continued

1873 US purchased White Earth land to induce Pembina Band to move

1877 Federal policy sends kids or go without rations

1879 Carlisle Indian School opened

1880 Foreigners flowed in filling the Chippewa land

1881 Helen Hunt Jackson's account *A Century of Dishonor* – historical account of Gov't Injustice

1882 Turtle Mountain Reservation est. – first Executive Order carved 20 townships, December 21
Perhaps last organized buffalo hunt
Father Malo's school (St. Claude at St. John, ND)

1884 Second Executive Order – reduction of reservation to two townships, March 29
Third Executive Order – est. present reservation boundary, May 3
Sisters of Mercy build school in Belcourt

1885 Dunseith School District est.
Reil Rebellion – attempt to protect Métis rights - Reil hanged

1886 Stephan, SD, Mission School est.

# The Trail of Misgivings

1887 Starvation on TM Reservation
Dawes Act – allotment period

1888 Father Genin's Report of severe
conditions
Rev. Wellington Salt arrived in
Belcourt (Mission Day School)
*TM Star* mentions Teachers' Salaries

1889 Federal policy no longer contracted
with sectarian schools
North Dakota Statehood

1890 Rev. Salt took position with Gov't
school on TM Reservation
Fort Totten decommissioned and
turned over for school
BIA enrolled students in Public
School (policy)

1892 McCumber Agreement (Ten Cent
Treaty)

1893 Gov't statues to withhold rations vs
poor attendance

1895 Federal Gov't built four log schools
on TM Reservation (Rev Salt taught
in one these)

1897 Congress no longer funded sectarian
schools
Fort Totten Boarding School est.

1899 Louis Marion and two others went to
St. Joseph's School in Rensselaer,
Indiana

1900 TM seasonal work
North of Dunseith people in limbo
(neither federal nor state would
educate students)

1904 Ten Cent Treaty Ratified

1905 Picture of Jerome brothers
Four new schools – Belcourt, Wilkie,
Roussin, and Gourneau schools
Rev Salt moves to new school in
Belcourt

1906 Congress abolished the Oklahoma
Cherokee school system

1907 Sisters of Mercy School burned

1908 Bismarck Indian School est.

1909 Estelle Reels, Director of Indian
School, Course of Study handed
down

1912 Federal Gov't built the Dunseith Day
School (one – room)

1916 Federal Gov't transferred
responsibility to state jurisdiction
Couture and Ingebretson School
Districts est.

1917 Couture elected school board
members and assumed
responsibility for one of the schools
Bismarck Indian School closed

1918 Ingebretson elected school board
members and assumed
responsibility for two of the four
schools
BIA Day school inspector appointed
to report on district schools
Carlisle Indian School closed

1919 Ingebretson took charge of two
schools and built a third
Couture took charge of second
federal school
Bismarck Indian School reopened
Kanick School constructed in
Couture

1920 Rev Salt died
Emily Lafromboise sixth grade photo
at Fort Totten

1921 Snyder Act for general support and
civilization including education

1923 Federal Boarding Schools extend to
grade eight
One classroom added at Belcourt and
two schools built in Ingebretson

1924 Both Couture and Ingebretson built
schools
Committee of One Hundred Report
(in part a study on Indian
Education)
Haskell Institute was the only school
beyond eighth grade
Indians granted US citizenship

1925 Ingebretson built a school

1926 Plans for a new education program to
remedy the Districts' neglects

1928 The Meriam Report (harshly judges
boarding schools; recommended
state course of study)

1929 Gov't Day Inspector's unsatisfactory
report
ND State Tuition to US Gov't

# Appendices

Six federal schools offering high school courses

The Great Depression Era began

1930 Butte St. Paul donated to State

1931 US Gov't completed TM Consolidated school

Natl Advisory Council on Educ. deemed Indian Educ. a tragic failure

Three schools in Couture and four schools in Ingebretson abandoned

1932 TM Constitution and By-Laws

Bus garage built

1933 Roosevelt's work program

Father Hildebrand and Sisters arrived in Belcourt

Gov't. reopens Roussin School

Another room added at Dunseith Day School

Early snowstorm closed school for the year

1934 Johnson O'Malley Act, P.L. 74–815

Indian Reorganization Act (IRA)

St Ann's Church and School being built

Gov't school went to spring to summer schedule

Bureau emphasized local needs instead of standard policy

TMCS operated on summer schedule

1935 Shop and Home Ec complex added

1936 St. Ann's Indian Mission School opens

Another room added at Dunseith Day

1937 Eleven eighth grade students graduated from St. Ann's

Bismarck Indian School permanently closed

1938 BIA teacher standards were raised

Ninth grade added TMCS

1939 Great Walker School built

St. Ann's Parish Hall built

TMCS returned to fall schedule

1940 Houle School built

Tenth grade added (TMCHS fully state accredited)

TM Tribe land purchased

TM Tribal rolls est.

1941 Eleventh grade added

Paintings on old gym walls by John Brien (grade 5)

1942 Twelfth grade added

Brave *looking to the future* painting on old gym wall by Sunbeam Necklace

Highway #5 paved and redirected

1943 First TMCHS graduates

TM Tribal rolls approved

1944 Most all of TMCHS males served in WWII

1948 St. Ann's Madonna Hall built

1950 TMCS needed more space

Congress amended PL 81–874 impact aid

Bureau allowed requirements for college prep

1952 Relocation programs implemented

1953 TM Tribe slated for termination

1956 Set up voting districts

1961 New TMCS built

1962 St. Ann's switches to winter schedule

Six Tribal Amendments Adopted

Couture paid for Band and other teachers

TMC High School completed

1963 The State permits payments to District that educate children in federal schools

1964 Old Crossing Treaty Settlement

Couture hired first social worker

Congress passed Economic Opportunity Act (Head Start, etc.)

1965 Congress passed Elementary and Secondary Educ Act

Head Start pilot program at St. Mary's

Couture Board challenges Rolla tuition payments (and loses)

1966 St. Ann's gym built

Couture Board re-challenged Rolla tuition payments (and wins)

Couture hired first principal

Head Start began at Belcourt and St. John and sponsored first special program

1967 Economic Opportunity Act

Roussin Day School fully state accredited

# The Trail of Misgivings

Senate Resolution 165–
Subcommittee on Indian Education
Someone challenged foundation
payments to Ingebretson

1968 Roussin Day School closed
Couture purchased Jollie land and
built four teacher houses

1969 Tribal Resolution to use Roussin Day
School as Community Center
Houle School received a provisional
accreditation
Great Walker School grades five and
six moved to TMCS
Couture hired first School
Superintendent
Couture built four-stall garage for
staff housing
A National Tragedy (Indian Educ
Report)
Future Indian Teacher Program
implemented at TMCS

1970 Teacher negotiations begin, early
1970's
Blue Cloud notice to withdraw from
all Dakota missions
St. Ann's Transitional School Board
appointed
Contract between Couture District
and St. Ann's to educate St. Ann's
students, grades 1 through 4
TMCES first grade students housed
at St. Ann's
Bureau added kindergarten to TMCS
Teacher Corps venture at TMCS
Title programs began
Belcourt School used Houle School
for special education until 1972

1971 TMCS 7th and 8th grades moved to
Armco buildings
St. Ann's/Couture contract renewed
with sixth grade moving to St.
Ann's instead of first grade
Great Walker School closed –
Special Ed used building
Follow Through implemented at
TMCS
Federal Gov't erected five steel
building and moved in two trailers
for grades seven and eight

ND law changed to full amount of
foundation payments
TMCHS won state wrestling
tournament

1972 TM Community College est.
Dunseith Day added kindergarten
Special Ed discontinued at Great
Walker School
Great Walker School burned
Two additional units added to TMCS
kindergarten area
Four-stalled bus garage built
Middle School program began
Indian Education Act (Office of
Indian Education)

1973 St. Ann's Indian Mission School
closed
Indian Self Determination Act
Fifteen-stall bus garage built
Tribal Resolution Regarding St.
Ann's School
TMCC first classes
A metal building added to Middle
School for reading and math
NCA for TMCHS

1974 Objiwa Indian School Named and
incorporated with ND State (K–8)
Couture erected an elementary
reading lab

1975 Couture built MS multi-purpose
building
KEYA on air
TMCES received NCA
PL 94–142 passed

1976 Couture built School Admin building
Couture completed two steel
structures at the MS (Admin and
Lunch bldg.)
Couture built vocational bldg. at MS

1977 Houle School turned over to tribe
and was razed
Couture membership increased to
five
NDIEA advocated Indian Studies

1978 PL 95–561
PL 94–638 TMCHS Contract
Teachers Suit against BIA, Dist, *et
al.* (teachers lost)

# Appendices

Tribal Controlled College Assistance Act

Congress passed Indian Educ Amendment (BIA educational Standards)

1979 Couture added Two additional sections to Admin Bldg.
MS Admin Bldg. Addition

1980 $47.3 m for Ten Cent Treaty
Eight more bus stalls built

1981 $4.9 m additional treaty settlement
OIS Admin bldg. built
TMCES began walling open classrooms

1982 Ten Cent Treaty settlement
ND Century Code 67–02–03–04 requires Indian Studies
NDOIEP est.

1983 Albert Lee Ferris restored and changed Necklace's Brave painting in the old gym
District Reorganization passed by vote of constituents

1984 New TM Community High School built
TMCHS conditional accreditation
TMC Middle School burned (classes continued on split shifts)
TM Community College fully accredited
Belcourt Learning Center tried
Belcourt School District reorganization went into effect
Title VII bilingual program

1985 TMCS resumed regular schedule
Shell Valley annexed
Federal Gov't took closer look at 874 funding to Cooperative Schools

1986 TMCES fire
Belcourt School District sold houses to Jollie

1987 TMCMS fire
Belcourt School District cuts funding to KEYA

1988 PL 100–297 called White House conference on Indian Education

TMCMS received NCA

1989 TMC Middle School rebuilt
SB 1232 foundation funding passed

1991 Mission School reopened as St. Ann's Native American School (SOLT)

1992 TM Times est.
Tribal Separation of Powers
New Dunseith Day School Completed
Dunseith Day School added grades 7 & 8
Natl Advisory Council on Indian Education (114 recommendations)

1993 Natl Advisory Council on Indian Education federal (entitlement programs)

1994 Dunseith Day School bus garage built
Land grant status is given to TMCC
Sought Attn. Gen. opinion re: OIS eligibility for funding

1995 OIS Kindergarten building built
Follow-up request for a second opinion re: OIS to no avail

1996 Dunseith Day School began receiving state foundation payments

1997 New TMCC building began

1998 *Turtle Mountain Morning News* est.
Canadian Govt. notice of reconciliation to Metis people

1999 TMCC completed
St. Ann's Native American School opens (SOLT)

2001 NCLB Act
TMCHS vocational building completed

2006 Construction of Objiwa Indian School restarted
Breaking ground for new TMCHS
CAU (Cooperative Agreement Unit) added
BIA realignment of ELO (move to Minot)

# The Trail of Misgivings

Andringa, Robert C, Antell, Lee and Williams George. *Indian Education Involvement of Federal, State and Tribal Government,* Sept. 1980.

Bailey, Thomas A. *The American Pageant, A History of the Republic.* D.C. Boston. Heath and Company. 1956.

Belgarde, Larry W., *Indian Control and Interdependency: A Study of the Relationship Between the Holders of Critical Resources and The Structure of American Indian Community Colleges.* A Dissertation Submitted to the School of Education and the Committee on Graduate Studies of Stanford University in Partial Fulfillment of the Requirements for the Degree of Doctor of Philosophy. January 1992.

Camp, Gregory. *North Dakota History, The Dispossessed: The Ojibwa and Metis of Northwest North Dakota.* Journal of the Northern Plains, Vol. 69 Nos. 1, 2, and 4. 2002.

Camp, Gregory. *The Turtle Mountain Chippewa and Metis, 1797-1935.* Albuquerque. The University of NM. 1987.

Code of Federal Regulation, Title 25, April 1, 2004.

Cohen, Felix S. *Handbook of Federal Indian Law with Reference Table and Index.* United States Government Printing Office, Washington, 4th 1945.

Delorme, David P. *History of the Turtle Mountain Band of Chippewa Indians.* Collections of the State Historical Society, Bismarck, ND. July 1955.

Fey, Harold E. and McNickle, D'Arcy. *Indians and Other Americans. Two ways of Life Meet.* New York. Harper and Brothers Publishers. 1959.

Gourneau, Patrick. *History of the Turtle Band of Chippewa Indians,* Ninth Edition.

Gray, David P. and Newborg, Gerald G. *North Dakota a Pictorial History.* Norfolk/Virginai Beach. 1988. The Donning Company/Publishers.

Hesketh, John. *History of the Turtle Mountain Chippewa.* Collection of the State Historical Society, Bismarck, ND. July 1955.

Hesketh, John,. *History of the Turtle Mountain Chippewa.* North Historical Collections, Vol. V.

Hesketh, John. *Prairie Past and Mountain Memories a History of Dunseith, ND 1882-1982.* . Collection of the State Historical Society, Bismarck, ND.

Howard, James H., *The Plains-Ojibwa or Bungi: Hunters and Warriors of the Northern Prairies with special reference to the Turtle Mountain Band.* Museum Volume 24, Nos. 11 & 12, November, December, 1963.

# Bibliography

Howard, Joseph Kinsey. *Strange Empire*, New York: William Morrow and Company. 1952.

Indian Education Involvement of Federal, State and Tribal Governments, Education Commission of the States, Denver, Colorado, Peport135, 9/80.

The Jerusalem Bible. Doubleday and Company, Inc. Garden City, NY. 1961.

Josephy, Jr., Alvin M., *The Indian Heritage of America*. New York: Alfred A. Knopf. New York. 1969.

Kulas, Cheryl Rosc Marion. *The Impact of Indian Education Course on the Instruction of Teachers in North Dakota*. A Thesis Submitted to the committee on American Indian Studies in Partial Fulfillment of the Requirements for the Degree of Master of Arts in The Graduate College, The University of Arizona, 1989.

Murray, Robert J., *History of the Education in the Turtle Mountain Reservation of North Dakota*. UND, August, 1953.

Murray, Stanley N., *The Turtle Mountain Chippewa, 1882 - 1905, North Dakota History, Journal of the Northern Plains*, Vol. 51 Winter 1984, No. 1.

*North Dakota Blue Book – 1919*, Legislative Manual, Published under the Direction of Thomas Hall, Secretary of State, Bismarck Tribune Co. Printing and Binding, Bismarck, ND.

North Dakota Century Code.

Pelletier, Joanne. *The Buffalo Hunt*. Regina: Gabriel Dumont Institute of Native Studies and Applied Research. 1985.

Reardon, James Michael, P.A. *George Anthony Belcourt: Pioneer Catholic Missionary of the Northwest*. St. Paul: North Central Publishing Company. 1955.

*St. Ann's Centennial. One Hundred Years of Faith 1885 – 1985*. Belcourt, ND.

*St Ann's Parish 1985 Centennial Cook Book*

Sealey, Bruce D. *The Other Natives the-les Metis One plus One Equals One*. Vol. One – Tome Premier. 1700 – 1885. Winnipeg: Manitoba Metis Federation Press and Editions Bois-Brules. 1978.

Sisters of Mercy of the Americas, Omaha Regional Community, *Our History: North Dakota*. (http://www.mercyoma.org/north_dakota.htm.)

Slaughter, Linda W., *Leaves from Northwestern History*, Collections of the State Historical Society of North Dakota. 1906, Vol I.

# The Trail of Misgivings

Stanley, G. F. G. *Confederation 1870 – A Metis Achievement* One – Vol. One Tome Premier, 1700 – 1884. Winnipeg: Manitoba Metis Federation Press and Editions Bois-Burles. 1978.

Stanley, G. F. G. *The Other Native the-les Metis, Louis Riel: Patriot or Rebel?* Vol. One – Tome Premier, 1700 – 1884. Winnipeg: Manitoba Metis Federation Press and Editions Bois-Burles. 1978.

Stein, Wayne J. *Tribally Controlled Colleges, Making Good Medicine.* Peters Lang Publishing, Inc. NY 1992.

*Turtle Mountain Band of Chippewa Indians, Historical Overview and Tribal Government* Falls Church, VA and Albuquerque, NM. Management Concepts Incorporated. April 1980.

U.S. Department of Interior, BIA, TM Agency, Belcourt, ND, 58316

**OTHER SOURCES**

Belcourt School District # 7 School Superintendent's Files.

Belgarde, Gaylene. Notes 1/2006

Career Opportunity Program FIT Proposal, 1969

Department of Public Instruction, Bismarck, ND

District School Superintendent Files

Genealogy.com. Rev. Wellington Salt (April 2006) http://henforum.genealogy.com/salt/messages/12.html.

History of Stephan, South Dakota/Highmore.org.

Indian and Northern Affairs, Canada. (www.Ainc-inac. Ge.ca)

Insights, New School, Behavioral Studies in Education, UND, Grand Forks

Introduction and Summary Planning for Middle School Construction, 1985.

Jerome, Dan, *Early Education Paper of Superintendent*, December/1984

Jerome, Daniel. *History of the School Districts on the TM Reservation*, Summer of 1984.

Jerome, Daniel F. Lilley-Dionne American Legion Post 262 History, 1980

Jerome, Daniel. Statement in Support of a Request for an Additional Appropriation for the BIA FY 1976 Construction of a High School Complex at Belcourt, ND.

Middle School Staff Paper, *Mandate for Change*, 1971-72.

Nelson, Thomas O. Atlas Rolette County, ND. Fergus Falls, MN. 1959.

# Bibliography

*No Child left Behind, A Parent Guide*, US Dept of Educ. 2003.

Office of Indian Education, CAU, 2006.

Ojibwa Indian School Board Handbook, SY 2005-2006.

Ojibwa Indian School Employee Handbook, SY 2005-2006.

Ojibwa School Files.

Poitra, Ronald. Informational Paper on Head Start, Belcourt, ND. 4/18/06.

Rolette County Court House Minutes: Shell Valley Annexation 1985.

Rolette County Records, Clerk's Annual Reports. 1919 – 1924

Rolette County Records, Teacher's Report, 1919 – 1931

Rolette County Reorganization Board Meeting Minutes, 1978.

Sisters of Mercy of the Americas. Omaha Regional Community, *Our History: North Dakota*

Thomas, Sandy, Transition Paper, 2003

Title 5, *Turtle Mountain Children's Code*

TM Agency Records

TMCC Records

*TMCHS Student Handbook* 2005-06.

TMCS Records

TMCS Superintendent's End of Year Report, 1984–85 to 1990.

TMCS Superintendent Files.

*Turtle Mountain Exceptional Education LEA Cooperative Agreement*, TM Schools, Belcourt, ND 1/20/06.

## PERIODICALS

*Grand Forks Herald*. Grand Forks, ND, 1/18/68.

*New Earth*, Catholic Diocese of Fargo, November 2006.

*The Sunday Forum*. Fargo-Moorhead. 10/23/77.

*Turtle Mountain Star*. Rolla , ND. June 23, 1938 Edition, Reprint 1988.

*Turtle Mountain Star*. Rolla, ND, October 29, 1984

*Turtle Mountain Times*. Belcourt, ND.

Seven – B Class, First Row: Joseph Jerome, William Jollie, Raymond Montriel, Ernest Decoteau, Eugene Brunnelle, Lloyd Boyer, Clarence Purdy; Second Row: Stella Allard, Madeline Parisien, Daniel Jerome, Marian Henry, Nora Jeannotte, Emil Bradford, Claude Grant; Third Row: Doris Allery, Ernest Poitra, William Frederick, Charles Gourneau, Betty Wilkie, Rose Dionne, Miss Zoldoske. Courtesy of 1944 Chipaway Yearbook.

KEYA 88.5 FM began broadcasting in 1975 and Mr. Dallas Brien was their General Manager. Courtesy of the 1976 Agawase Yearbook.

High School Class 2006.

Margaret Leonard's high school business class, 2006.

The 1970-71 State Chanpionship Wrestling Team: Duane Falcon, Logan Davis, Micky DeCoteau, George Falcon, Steve Peltier, Howard Azure, Larry Azure, Gerald Davis, Pat Delorme, Victor Baker, Alex Albert, Coach George Schlager, Fred Schindler. Courtesy of the 1971 Agawase Yearbook.

First Graduating class of TMCS
Hazel "Haze" Demontigny
Mabel "Mab" Grant
Marion Morin
Leona "Lee" Poitra
May Thomas
Courtesy of the 1943 Chipaway Yearbook

Bus Drivers Row 1: Llyod Martin, Fred LaFountaine, LeRoy Martin. Row 2: Charlie Lillie, Bill Keplin, Fred Schindler, Earl Houle. Row 3: Gary Thomas, Gene Thomas, John Peltier. Row 4: Sonny Brunelle, Pete Peltier, Dave Keplin. Row 5: Roy Malterre, Walter Davie, Melvin Laducer, Alvin LaFountain, John Chrissler. Courtesy of the 1973 Agawase Yearbook.